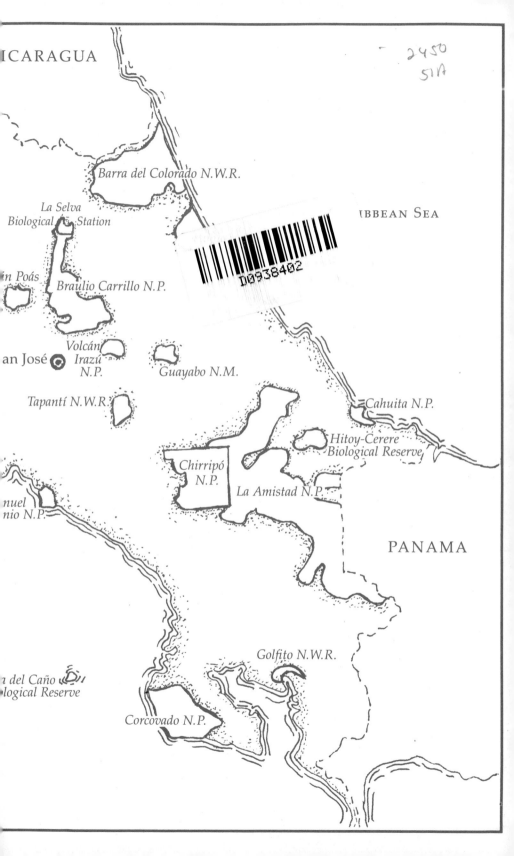

ICARAGUA

Barra del Colorado N.W.R.

La Selva
Biological Station

ᴵBBEAN Sᴇᴀ

n Poás

Braulio Carrillo N.P.

Volcán
an José ◉ Irazú
N.P.   Guayabo N.M.

Tapantí N.W.R.

Cahuita N.P.

Hitoy-Cerere
Biological Reserve

Chirripó
N.P.
                    La Amistad N.P.

nuel
nio N.P.

PANAMA

Golfito N.W.R.

a del Caño
logical Reserve

Corcovado N.P.

The Quetzal and the Macaw

The Quetzal
and
the Macaw

The Story of Costa Rica's National Parks

by

DAVID RAINS WALLACE

Sierra Club Books · *San Francisco*

The Sierra Club, founded in 1892 by John Muir, has devoted itself to the study and protection of the earth's scenic and ecological resources—mountains, wetlands, woodlands, wild shores and rivers, deserts and plains. The publishing program of the Sierra Club offers books to the public as a nonprofit educational service in the hope that they may enlarge the public's understanding of the Club's basic concerns. The point of view expressed in each book, however, does not necessarily represent that of the Club. The Sierra Club has some sixty chapters coast to coast, in Canada, Hawaii, and Alaska. For information about how you may participate in its programs to preserve wilderness and the quality of life, please address inquiries to Sierra Club, 730 Polk Street, San Francisco, CA 94109.

LIBRARY OF CONGRESS CATALOGING-IN-PUBLICATION DATA
Wallace, David Rains, 1945–
The Quetzal and the Macaw: the story of Costa Rica's national parks / David Rains Wallace.
p.   cm.
Includes bibliographical references and indexes.
ISBN 0-87156-585-4
1. National parks and reserves—Costa Rica—History.
2. Costa Rica. Servicio de Parques Nacionales—History.
3. Nature conservation—Costa Rica—History.   I. Title.
SB484.C8W35   1992
333.78'097286—dc20   91-30500
                                                                    CIP

Production by Janet Vail
Jacket design by Amy Evans
Book design by Amy Evans
Printed in the United States of America

10   9   8   7   6   5   4   3   2   1

Printed on acid-free paper containing a minimum of 50% recovered waste paper, of which at least 10% of the fiber content is post-consumer waste.

To the Memory of
Olof Wessberg & Antonio Zuñiga,
who died defending
Costa Rica's Natural Heritage

Contents

Acknowledgments

Many people contributed to this book. Pedro León and Alvaro Ugalde had the idea of a book about the Wessbergs and the parks, and David Wake and Harry Greene helped them suggest it to me. Pedro, Alvaro, and Harry also helped me to get a Fulbright Fellowship to research the book, as did Jon Beckmann and Harry Kendall. I'm grateful to the Fulbright Program; to Leslie Hunter of the Council for International Exchange of Scholars for expediting my grant; and to Louise Crane, Anna Luisa de Salas, Robert Hallauer, and Patrick Duddy of the U.S. Embassy in San José for helping to make my stay in Costa Rica enjoyable.

Alvaro Ugalde and Pedro León provided essential guidance through Costa Rica's conservation community as well as generous hospitality and counsel. George Gorman, Harry Greene, Juan Carlos Crespo, Michael Kaye, and Karen Wessberg helped me get into the field, and provided hospitality as well. Daniel Janzen and Winnie Hallwachs provided hospitality and field guidance on a 1988 trip as well as a 1990 one. David Carr let me raid his extensive files on the park system in Gainesville, Florida, an unexpected windfall. My wife Betsy served as a language assistant and travelling companion.

Finally, I'm grateful to the most essential contributors, those who took the time to tell me about the parks: Juan Diego Alfaro, Jim Barborak, Victor Manuel Begacampo, Mario Boza, Gerardo Budowski, Eduardo Carillo, David Clark, Juan Carlos Crespo, Vernon Cruz, Gladys de Marco, David Dudenhoefer, Gilberto Fallas, Luis A. Fournier, Gordon Frankie, Joaquin Gamboa, Rodrigo Gámez, Feynner Godinez, Wilford Guindon, Carlos Hernandez, Chip Isenhart, Jill Isenhart, Daniel Janzen, Michael Kaye, Pedro León, Sergio León, Sigifredo Marín, John McPhaul, Roger Morales, Susan Pierce, Fabio Quiros, José Maria Rodriguez, Eduardo Rojas, Mario Rojas, Marvin Santamaria, Ronald Suarez, Anna Maria Tato, Joseph Tosi, Alvaro Ugalde, Vera Varela, Sergio Volio, and Karen Wessberg.

"The more we accelerate, the more we populate,
and the more we jostle for vital space . . .
I just don't know. Maybe that's why I
became an agnostic."
José "Don Pepe" Figueres Ferrer
Tico Times interview, July 25, 1986

Introduction

The Rockefeller Treasure

While on a trip to Tortuguero National Park in northeast Costa Rica in 1987, I got in a conversation with a young man sitting next to me on a bus. He was Honduran, an architect going to Tortuguero to inspect construction on a client's hotel. During the conversation, which mainly was about his dislike of neighboring Nicaragua's Sandinista government, I mentioned that I'd just been to Corcovado National Park, at the other end of Costa Rica from Tortuguero.

"Oh yes," he said. "You know, the Rockefellers got that park established because they have big deposits of gold and precious stones there. It's their own personal treasure chest."

I was surprised by this story, but not incredulous. I knew the Rockefellers had been active in establishing national parks in the United States, including Virgin Islands National Park in the Caribbean, and I knew there was gold in Corcovado. I hadn't heard that the Rockefellers got parks established as a way of hoarding mineral riches, and it didn't sound very sensible offhand. It seemed at least possible, especially since I knew little about Costa Rica from one visit there.

I expressed polite interest in the story, and the conversation returned to the architect's main interest. He asked if I thought the U.S. would invade Nicaragua. I said I doubted it, because most North Americans (I'd caught on that Central Americans think of themselves as generic Americans just as people in the U.S. do) were reluctant to invade small tropical countries with big, Soviet-equipped armies after the Vietnam experience. The architect evidently didn't like this answer. He barely spoke to me for the rest of the trip.

When I visited Costa Rica again, I asked people familiar with the national parks about the architect's Corcovado story. I thought the story would have at least some basis in fact. The Rockefellers might have owned land in the vicinity or something. Nobody knew what I was talking about. Apparently the story had no factual basis at all. "You can't believe any of the stories you hear," one source told me. "There's an enormous amount of fictitious tiger tales floating around."

Despite television, Costa Rica still has a flourishing folkloric tradition. To find a street address, one uses a traditional description—so many meters past such and such a landmark—instead of street numbers. Fabulous stories easily take root in this oral milieu. "Here, everything depends on talking," someone told me.

Yet the Latin American vernacular isn't the only place one encounters fictions about national parks. A recent North American book about the destruction of the Amazonian rainforest written by a well-known journalist and a college professor maintained that native Miwok Indians had been driven out of California's Yosemite Valley so that a national park could be established there. The authors either were unaware of or indifferent to the facts that miners and settlers expelled the Miwoks from Yosemite in 1851, fifty-five years before the valley became part of a national park, and that national parks didn't exist until 1876.

Perhaps one reason why it seems easy to tell "tiger tales" about national parks is that society doesn't quite perceive them as part of history yet. Although the United States established the first national parks, many U.S. citizens have extremely vague ideas about what they are and how they came to be. People seem to take national parks for granted rather as they take the natural ecosystems in them for granted, as though parks don't arise from complicated social, cultural, and political factors just as factories or churches do, but simply "grow." Mass media occasionally run stories about the establishment of parks, or threats to parks, but they seldom report on the arduous process of creating and maintaining parks, the years of research, discussion, lobbying, and political maneuvering that go into making them.

In the past four decades, global mass media have reported almost daily on Central American wars. These wars obviously have been very important to the people suffering through them, yet their significance for human history as a whole is probably small. Until the past few years, global mass media largely ignored another Central American story that is likely to have major significance for human history as a whole.

Humanity's immediate ancestors evolved in tropical forest, and many of the foods, fibers, medicines, and other goods that have made history possible came from tropical forest. A large proportion of tropical forest has disappeared in the past forty years, a disappearance that closes countless unknown avenues of future evolution and cultural development. This disappearance was particularly rapid in Central America, which has a great diversity of life forms, but a relatively small land mass and a rapidly growing human population. It was fastest in Costa Rica, which had the highest deforestation rate in Latin America. Costa Rica lost almost half its forest cover from 1950 to 1990. Much of this wasn't even used as timber, but was burned for pasturage to produce low-grade beef for export.

Yet during the last two decades, millions of acres of Costa Rican forest weren't destroyed, although they were subject to the same pressures as the rest. Most of this forest survived because, beginning in the 1960s, it was protected in one of the most remarkable national park systems in the world. Almost from the beginning, this system has set out not simply to preserve remnant wildlife and scenery for sentiment and recreation—as park systems have traditionally done—but to perpetuate all of Costa Rica's biological resources—habitats and ecosystems as well as scenery and wildlife. It is not a "paper" system of well-meaning laws erected flimsily against inexorable destructive forces, but a strong social and political network that has fought loggers, miners, ranchers, government development bureaucracies, and other interests to a standstill many times. It generally has the respect of the Costa Rican people, and has enjoyed considerable support from the Costa Rican government.

The Costa Rican park system's development has great implications for other tropical and developing nations, since it shows that forest can be preserved in the face of both rapid economic and population growth, and serious economic problems. The system's broad ecological orientation stands as an example to the older park systems of temperate zone and developed nations, many of which protect only parts of their nation's biotic resources. The Costa Rican system is exemplary also in that it has served as a focus of efforts to integrate Costa Rican society as a whole with new ideas of environmental protection and sustainable development.

In 1989, Alvaro Umaña, the Minister of Natural Resources, Mines, and Energy, the minister responsible for parks, said that because of its conservation achievements, Costa Rica was "biologically a superpower." The claim may seem exaggerated: could a nation the size of New Jersey be a superpower of any kind? Yet, if history continues, power will reside with societies that have conserved their resources, not with those that have spent them. Costa Rica has limited resources, but if it manages to conserve 25 percent of its forest in parks and ecological reserves, and another 25 percent in commercial timberlands and extractive reserves—as its leading conservationists propose to do—it may well become a "superpower" of a new kind. Biologist Peter Raven described the park system as "one of the great accomplishments of the human race over the last thirty years."

If history continues, the growth of park systems will be more important than wars. Although the Costa Rican system has caught relatively little attention from global media, it is a dramatic story of constant struggle against relentless destructive forces. The fact that the struggle has largely been carried out with words and ideas (including some clever political maneuvering and public relations) instead of weapons doesn't make it less significant. The story may lack the magic-realist panache of the Rockefeller treasure, but it has the advantage of being true to the extent I've been able to tell in a society where "talking is everything."

The Quetzal and the Macaw

one

The Nicoya Peninsula

When Karen and Olof Wessberg came to Costa Rica's Nicoya Peninsula in 1955, it was a kind of microcosm of what would happen in the rest of the country in the next thirty-five years. Located in the northwest, the peninsula gets less rain than Costa Rica's Caribbean coast, or even than its Pacific coast farther south. Yet it had largely been covered with a mixture of evergreen and deciduous forest at the beginning of the twentieth century. (The Spanish conquistadors had drastically reduced the peninsula's sizable native population.) A man still living on the peninsula when the Wessbergs arrived had sailed along its coast around 1920 and had seen only forest.

"He went into every little beach," Karen Wessberg told me, "and never found anybody."

"Imagine to yourself the beauty of it," the old man, a Nicaraguan named Victor Bravo, had said to the Wessbergs. The eastern side of the Nicoya had been known as far north as Nicaragua as the waterfall coast because so many rivers emptied from it into the Gulf of Nicoya. Tapir, jaguar, puma, deer, three species of monkeys, and other game had been common.

The Wessbergs found a peninsula greatly changed from that of a few decades before. Costa Rica's population, largely confined to the cool, healthy Meseta Central during the four hundred years after the Spanish conquest, more than doubled from 1920 to 1955. Lying directly west of Puntarenas, the port from which Costa Rica exported its mainstay coffee crop, the Nicoya Peninsula was a convenient release valve for population pressure. The lush rainforests of the Caribbean and southern Pacific lowlands were still largely inaccessible, without roads, but Nicoya was a mere boat ride away.

Soon after Victor Bravo cruised its coast, a process began on the Nicoya that would be repeated throughout Costa Rica's other lowlands. First, loggers came and took out big, valuable hardwoods—espavels, panamas, pochotes, and mahoganies. Small farmers followed, burning logged-over valleys to plant rice, corn, and beans. The land yielded big harvests at first, and frontier families were large. Karen Wessberg knew of one woman who had twenty-seven children. Forest clearing expanded with population, and by 1955 original trees remained only on the steepest parts of the peninsula.

Although there were still no roads, the Nicoya was a fairly prosperous place while the farming boom lasted. When the Wessbergs arrived at Montezuma, the town near the peninsula's south end where they settled, they found "three grocery stores, a drugstore, a saddlemaker shop, a shoemaker shop, a big warehouse where they were selling hardware, and a big warehouse where they kept all the rice, corn, and beans that they grew," Karen told me. She added that "some women used to buy a dress every week.

"You used to meet so many people waiting for the launch to Puntarenas," Karen said. "You got to know so many in those days. Now, with the roads, you meet much fewer. Of course, many of those people left later, and that was sad. Ten years after we got here, they were leaving to San José to get work, because the soil was gone. They couldn't grow crops anymore."

The Nicoya settlers had discovered what farmers in other parts of the tropics would discover: that lush forest doesn't necessarily make lush farmland. Tropical forest soil fertility tends to be confined to a thin surface layer of tree roots and other organic matter. When cultivation removes forest cover, this surface layer comes under heavy pressure from tropical rains, an erosive force that must be experienced to be understood. The Nicoya Peninsula's rains come seven months of the year instead of twelve as in the Caribbean lowlands, but they are torrential when they come. It was only a matter of time before nutrients washed out of small valley fields on the hilly east side.

When settlers left the Nicoya, they usually sold their land to people who were consolidating small farms into large cattle ranches. The eroded land would still grow exotic African grasses, pasture for

Brahma cattle. Many ranches had absentee owners for whom live-stock was a sideline to more lucrative pursuits.

The Nicoya scenario played again in the rest of Costa Rica's low-lands as the population doubled again from 1955 to 1990. From the swampy plains of San Carlos in the northeast to the steaming valleys of El General and Coto Brus in the southwest, small farmers followed loggers, and were followed (or preceded) by more organized entre-preneurs who turned former forest, if not into cattle ranches, into pineapple fields or plantations for oil palm, bananas, or sugar cane. Ninety-percent forested in 1900, by 1990 Costa Rica had about twenty-five percent forest cover, much of it second growth.

Yet something else started on the Nicoya Peninsula that would make Costa Rica's deforestation less disastrous than it might have been. Karen and Olof Wessberg would help to start it, although they had no idea of this when they arrived in 1955. They came to be small farmers, although not of the corn-and-beans variety prevalent at the time; the Wessbergs wanted to grow fruit, a kind of farming still prac-ticed on a small scale on the Nicoya, where the launch back to Punta-renas may have to wait for a load of papayas to be loaded.

Olof Wessberg had been an officer in the Swedish Air Force when he met Karen, a Dane, in the late 1940s, but his real interest had been a fruit farm in central Sweden. He'd already owned it for seven years, and had planted apple and cherry trees. His father had been the for-ester on a large estate, so he had grown up close to trees. When he and Karen married, Olof resigned from the Air Force and they moved to the farm.

"It was a very beautiful place, with a lake . . . very perfect for being in Sweden," Karen told me. "But then the winter came, and it was *soooo* much colder than Denmark. The trees would get yellow in August."

Passing the long winter nights reading, Karen began to dip into books about tropical travel left lying about by Olof, an enthusiastic naturalist. "I wasn't interested in that to begin with," she said. "I liked philosophy. But then I read a little Thoreau, and I read in my hus-band's books that you could grow things all year in the tropics, and you didn't need money. I began to think: 'What am I doing in this cold climate?' But I didn't want to tell my husband because he'd spent so many years working on that place, and he was so proud of it.

"But he'd also started to dream of going to a warm place, but *he* didn't want to tell *me* because he didn't imagine I'd want to leave. But then finally, one spring morning he said to me: 'Look here, we never took a honeymoon. Shouldn't we take a trip to South America?' And I said: 'Yes!'"

The Wessbergs boarded a Norwegian cruise ship bound for Ecuador, where they planned to work for a Swedish banana planter. They'd heard that the man was a kind of Albert Schweitzer figure, building schools and a hospital for his employees. When they arrived, however, they discovered he was more like Simon Legree. The planter had completely alienated the local people with land grabs and ill treatment, and the Wessbergs found themselves threatened by resentment caused by his behavior.

"One day we were working on his plantation," said Karen, "when a man on a horse came swinging a machete. I think if I hadn't been there, something would have happened to my husband. A Swedish surveyor who worked for the planter had been cut all over his body with machetes. He showed us the scars. So we didn't stay there long."

They departed for Guatemala, flying over unbroken rainforest up the whole east coast of Central America. They had friends living at Lake Atitlan there, but when they arrived, they found foreigners fleeing the country because a leftist government had come to power. "We didn't have anything to do with politics," said Karen, "but when we were in the marketplace an Indian woman told us: 'Look, you shouldn't be here. It's very dangerous for you to be here,' because my husband was very tall and thin and blonde, obviously a capitalist."

Despite the danger, the Wessbergs stayed in Guatemala, caretaking the properties of more affluent but nervous Europeans who had fled. "They were very nice places," Karen said, "but little by little we discovered that we didn't have much chance to buy land the way the politics were then. And we were running out of money. So we went to work at a health resort in California near San Diego. We worked in return for room and board."

The Wessbergs were virtual slave laborers without work visas, however, so they left California for Mexico. They planned to reenter the U.S. with work visas in six months. "But then we got so used to Mexico that we didn't want to go back to California. We wanted to buy a piece of land in Mexico. We went to Mexico City to get residency papers so we could do this, but it was impossible. We thought it was because they didn't like foreigners. We were so innocent we never thought they might want us to pay a 'mordida.' One day, my husband came home and said: 'Look here, this official invited me to have coffee in a restaurant, and then he started showing me furs he wants to give his wife for Christmas in shop windows on the avenue. Isn't that odd?'"

"We didn't know what to do," Karen said. "We didn't want to go back to Europe or California, and we couldn't stay in Mexico. So I said—I'd never said anything like this before—'Let's see if we can have a dream of where to go.' Next morning, I asked my husband if he'd had a dream."

"No. Did you?"

"Yes! I dreamed I was in Costa Rica."

"In the dream," Karen told me, "there were two peninsulas on the west coast of Costa Rica. I was standing on one, and I could somehow see the other to the south. At that time, I didn't know there *were* two peninsulas on the west coast. I'd never been there, of course." (The Osa Peninsula juts out from Costa Rica's southwest coast about a hundred miles south of the Nicoya.)

"Also in the dream, when I turned around, I saw these huge trees like apple trees with pink, trumpet-shaped flowers. It's a species of tree they have here, that they call 'robles.' But I'd never seen those trees before I came to Costa Rica. And there was something else: I was standing, looking over the ocean from the northern peninsula. It was very steep and high. A girlfriend from Sweden was in the dream, and she said, 'Be careful, Karen,' so I wouldn't fall down.

"Anyway, after I told the dream, my husband said, 'Okay, we'll go to Costa Rica,' because that's the way he was about deciding things. Once he had a plan, he always carried it out. It was the military training."

The Wessbergs flew from Mexico to Costa Rica, with a brief stop in

Nicaragua when a piece of the plane's fuselage fell off. Within two months they had acquired residency papers at the cost of fifty colones, about six dollars then. They began looking for land, going first to the southwest, around the town of Golfito, where there was a lot of fruit-growing by big companies. It was too wet there for some of the fruits they wanted to grow, which needed a long dry season. They consulted a meteorologist and found that the northwest part of the country, Guanacaste and Nicoya, had the longest dry season.

"So we went down there," said Karen, "first to Puntarenas. The road from San José, the capital, was dirt then, very bumpy. Most of the people were barefoot. When we got to Puntarenas, across the Gulf of Nicoya from the peninsula, my husband asked a farmer where he was going. The farmer said he was going to Point Montezuma, so we got on the launch and went too. It took five hours. When we got there we rented a little house for five colones a day, and we stayed."

The Wessbergs bought a steep, rocky piece of land overlooking the gulf and spent most of the next ten years developing fruit orchards on it. They planted thirty-two kinds of fruit trees. They built their own house with lumber from dismantled buildings in Montezuma. They were successful enough to make a modest living, and to employ some local men to help in the orchards, but it wasn't a lotus-eater's dream. Olof caught malaria and nearly died. Karen told me he worked too hard in the sun. She still has a lump on her neck where a mildly poisonous snake bit her when she was working in the orchards.

They had enough leisure to enjoy the place: the beach, the forest that remained on the steep slopes, and the flocks of parrots and troops of monkeys and coatis that lived in the forest. They had a series of pet parrots and coatis that would stay with them until they found mates and returned to the forest. One coati brought her young back to visit.

"We began to get a feeling for the animals that way," Karen said. "They were so independent, strong. And they seemed so happy."

The Wessbergs also began to get a feeling for the last patch of wilderness in the vicinity, a mountainous tract at the southern tip of the peninsula called Cabo Blanco, white cape. Too steep for corn and beans, it still supported troops of howler and capuchin monkeys, and even a few spider monkeys, usually the first species to disappear from forest remnants because they are esteemed as game. "Olof went down there because he'd heard of a big zapote colorado tree," Karen told me. "He was interested in developing domestic strains of wild fruits like that. When he came home he exclaimed about how beautiful it was. He'd seen a troop of pisotes [the southern Latin American name for coatis] there, and a female had helped her young to cross a gap between two branches by standing across it while they used her as a bridge. Pisotes are so clever. The whole mountain was covered with big trees.

"But then he went there another time, in 1960, and got a shock. A little square of cleared land had appeared. And I said, 'Very soon they're going to cut down that forest, and the monkeys and pisotes are going to lose their ranges.' We'd seen troops of monkeys fighting for territory when they'd lost their patches of forest. So my husband came home and thought about that."

The Wessbergs suggested to some rich California friends that they buy Cabo Blanco to preserve the forest. The friends declined, but sent a list of conservation organizations that might help. "So one night, the twenty-sixth of December, 1960, my husband suddenly left his bed at 2 A.M. and went up and wrote an appeal." They sent the appeal to several organizations. In April 1961 the World League Against Vivisection and For the Protection of Animals published it in their magazine.

"Only in one spot," Olof wrote, "is there today some of the wildlife that was formerly everywhere in the northwest. . . . Here live the puma and manigordo [ocelot], deer, peccary, tepiscuintle, pizote, kinkajou, chulumuco [tayra], kongo [howler monkey], carablanca [capuchin monkey], and miriki [spider monkey]. The jaguar and tapir are already extinct. . . . When we settled here six years ago the mountain was always green. Today it has great brown patches, and in March and April it is shrouded in smoke, much of it on fire. . . . Two years more, and the mountain will be dead. Who is going to save it? It can be had at the ridiculously low price of $10 an acre. . . . But it has to be done immediately."

Olof's appeal came at a propitious time. Conscious of European conservation organizations' increasing activities in the African and Asian tropics, North American conservationists were getting more interested in the tropics of their own hemisphere. Very little was protected. Mexico and Chile had park systems, but the parks were largely in areas of temperate climate and vegetation. One of the organizations to receive the Wessbergs' appeal, the Philadelphia Conservation League, told them they'd been very happy to get it, because they'd wanted to do something in tropical America, but hadn't been able to make any contacts.

The Wessbergs must have been surprised by the response. Three other North American conservation organizations sent contributions for Cabo Blanco: the Sierra Club, The Nature Conservancy, and the Friends of Nature (although the British World League Against Vivisection gave fifty-one percent of the money). By the time Olof's appeal was published, biologists from San José were already at Cabo Blanco surveying its suitability as a nature preserve.

It took much longer to protect the area, however. Pleased though they were by Olof's appeal, the conservation organizations wanted to give their money to the Costa Rican government, not to some Swedish fruit farmer. The Costa Rican government was willing to acquire the land by expropriation from private owners, but it had no experience in establishing or managing nature preserves. The agency charged with acquiring Cabo Blanco was the Institute of Lands and Colonization (ITCO), which, Karen said, "was interested in helping farmers to get more land to clear—the opposite of what we wanted. And they never did understand what it was all about. The conservation groups didn't want to give money until there was at least a map of the area, and the government didn't want to map it unless they were sure they'd get the money. So Olof had to go to San José twenty-three times because the government never answered letters. It took three years to expropriate the land, and people moved in quick when they heard it was going to be expropriated, and they started cutting trees because the law says the land is worth more if there are improvements, which includes clearing of forest.

"A lot of people here really didn't understand what the land was being expropriated for. They thought Olof was doing it so he could take over the land. 'What does your husband want the land for?' they'd ask me. 'Is he going to start a ranch?' Then, when the government finally paid, it was in bonds instead of cash, and the bonds were only worth seventy-five percent of face value. People felt very bad about that here."

The Wessbergs discovered that the acquisition of Cabo Blanco was only the beginning of their problems. "They only hired one warden," said Karen, "and the first one they hired was a big drinker. He killed the last ten spider monkeys on the reserve for the oil in their fat. People use it for medicine. These monkeys were the last of an endemic subspecies, *Ateles geoffroyi frontalus,* that once lived all along the western side of the peninsula. They were a beautiful gray color . . . but he killed them. So Olof had to get him fired. The next warden spent most of his time working on the docks in Puntarenas. The government didn't pay them much. The next one started cutting trees in the reserve to put in crops.

"Then there was a warden who spent his time running a building contractor business. He really got mad at my husband, so he went to ITCO, I heard, and complained. I've been told that ITCO was really tired of all the trouble Olof was causing by that time, so they told this warden: 'Why don't you denounce him for some crime? Get him thrown out of the country.' So the warden went on the radio in Puntarenas, and said there was a dangerous foreigner in Montezuma who made people get off their horses and then shot the horses.

"That was a very serious charge in those days," Karen said, "because the only way to get around was on horseback. And Olof *had* been shooting horses. We got so sorry for the old horses, which people would abandon once they couldn't work anymore. It was supposed to be bad luck to kill a horse, so people would just let them starve to death. Olof would buy them for a little money, make the owners sign a certificate that he'd bought them, give the horses a good feed, then take them up the hill and shoot them with a big gun, so they'd feel nothing.

"But of course the warden didn't tell about these details. So the police heard about this horse-killing foreigner and sent messengers to San José. Very shortly a detachment of Civil Guards arrived in Puntarenas with submachine guns. My husband happened to be in Puntarenas waiting for the launch, and somebody came up to him and said, 'Nicolas, the police want to talk to you.'" (Costa Ricans called Olof Nicolas, one of his series of Swedish names, perhaps because it's easier to pronounce in Spanish than Olof.) "So my husband went to the police. They took him to the commander, who said: 'We heard you killed another horse.'

"Olof replied: 'Well, I've killed a hundred and eighty horses, actually.'" (At this point in the story, Karen mimicked horrified Civil Guards reaching for their guns.) "'But they were all my property.' Then he explained why he killed the horses, and that he was head of the local Society for the Prevention of Cruelty to Animals. The commander understood, and asked him to excuse the mistake.

"At about that time, Allston Jenkins of the Philadelphia Conservation League was in Costa Rica. Allston had been an enormous help when we were trying to get the land acquired. He was talking to the president, or some people in the government, and he told them: 'Look here, what you need is a national park service to manage the land for you.' And since they'd had so much trouble because of my husband, they said: 'Oh yes, let's have it!' They could let the national park service deal with him.

"But then they needed to get somebody to run it for them. So they found two students in San José to be the national park service, one of them twenty-seven years old and one twenty-four. That was Mario Boza and Alvaro Ugalde."

two

The Two Students

The idea of protecting nature wasn't as novel to Costa Rican official-dom as it seemed from the tip of the Nicoya Peninsula. Leaders had been worrying about it since before Costa Rica became a nation in 1822. In 1775 Spanish colonial governor Don Juan Fernandez de Boba-dilla issued a proclamation against burning fields and forests, "since the practice is followed by sterility of the soil." In 1828 the new Costa Rican government reserved a mile-wide strip of the coast for fisheries and called on municipalities to provide for conservation of communal forests and plantations. In 1833 the government mandated green belts of permanent farmland, pastures, and woodland around cities; in 1846 it set aside forested watersheds; and in 1859 it prohibited white-tailed deer hunting. In 1895 Costa Rica passed a law setting aside all uncultivated lands in a fifteen-kilometer zone on both sides of the main rivers draining the Meseta Central.

The twentieth century brought a virtual flood of legislation against wildlife destruction, water pollution, soil erosion, and "the unlim-ited, absurd, and devastating cutting of the forests and burning of the soils. . . disgraceful practices from which future generations will suf-fer greatly," as engineer Rafael A. Chavarría wrote in 1939. "Fire," wrote Secretary of State Enrique Jiménez Nuñez in 1913, "destroys humus, which gives land its most precious quality, takes from land its ability to retain water, completely eliminates nitrogen, principal ele-ment of fertility, eliminates soil nutrients much more rapidly than could crops. . . . Regions in which they burn every year are charac-terized by sterility of land and poverty of inhabitants."

Costa Ricans began trying to establish national parks in 1939, when Law No. 13 of February 10 established a two-kilometer preserve around Poás and Irazú volcanoes overlooking the Meseta Central and a preserve of equal extent on both sides of the Cordillera Central summit from Cerro Zurqui to Concordia. In 1945 another law established a park on both sides of the newly built Pan American Highway where it crossed the mountains south of San José. The park was meant to preserve the magnificent oak forests that had been discovered along the new road. In 1940 Costa Rica made a clear international statement of intent to protect nature by signing the Western Hemisphere Convention on Nature Resources in Washington, D.C., although the Costa Rican Legislative Assembly didn't get around to ratifying the convention until 1966.

The Wessbergs were by no means the first foreigners to admire and try to protect Costa Rican nature. Travelers had been marveling at its diverse splendors since at least as early as 1538 when the Italian adventurer Giralomo Benzoni raved of its "huge abundance of peccaries, jaguars, pumas . . . serpents of incredible size." "This province is very fine," wrote Juan Yanez de Castro in 1562, "fertile land and an abundance of good and sweet water and air, sky and soil, with a climate as much cool as warm, with different kinds of oaks and other trees like those of Spain."

In the nineteenth century, European scientists such as Henri Pittier found a fertile field for application of new geological and evolutionary theories in Costa Rica's extraordinarily varied topography, flora, and fauna. In the twentieth century, increasing numbers of North American naturalists found their way south in the wake of the big fruit companies (as the Europeans had followed the coffee trade). By the time the Wessbergs arrived, nature-loving gringos were all over the map. Ornithologist Alexander Skutch and botanist Leslie Holdridge bought lowland farms with the idea of preserving some rainforest. Herpetologist Archie Carr was studying sea turtle reproduction on the Tortuguero beaches and wondering how to protect the turtles from egg collectors and calipee hunters so he'd have something left to study. A group of Quaker dairy farmers had set aside a private reserve called the *bosque eterno* in the cloud forest of the Cordillera de Tilarán. Holdridge's land and the bosque eterno became the nuclei for two important private preserves, the La Selva Biological Station and the Monteverde Cloud Forest Reserve.

Yet there was something unprecedented in Cabo Blanco, justifying one Costa Rican conservationist (Alvaro Ugalde, in fact) calling the Wessbergs "messengers from the future." The Wessbergs were the first to link the Costa Rican leadership's old desire to protect nature with the developed world's new willingness to support such protection. The problem with the "paper parks" of the 1940s and 1950s (indeed, with virtually all Costa Rican conservation legislation) had been that the government either didn't have or didn't allocate the money to establish, enforce, and maintain the parks. Laws notwithstanding, the volcanoes had been cleared for cow pasture and the oak forests had been cut and shipped to Spain to make wine barrels. Cabo Blanco set a legal and financial precedent that encouraged the government to take action.

That action was of course more complicated than simply finding two students to run a park service. The very existence of two students capable of running even a one-unit park system was the result of several decades of major social and political development. Traditionally a liberal caretaker for large agricultural and commercial interests, the Costa Rican government had begun taking a more activist role in education and other social welfare issues after a series of extremely complicated upheavals in the 1930s and 1940s. The upheavals ended in abolishment of the armed forces in 1948, an astonishing development that freed a lot of government money for new, constructive uses. The two students were among the early graduates of the University of Costa Rica's College of Arts and Sciences, founded in the 1950s.

The growing educational system played a seminal role in establishing the park system. In 1964 Dr. Rafael L. Rodríguez Caballero, head of the Biology Department at UCR, published a list of natural areas that would serve as a kind of agenda for establishing parks. In 1966 the Inter-American Institute of Agricultural Sciences in Turrialba began offering a course in national parks and wildlife taught by Kenton Miller, a North American biologist. University of Costa Rica biology professor Luis Fournier participated in a commission that drafted a

Forestry Law, passed by the Legislative Assembly in 1969, which included a provision for establishing a national park system.

"In 1967," Fournier told me, "during the government of President Joaquín Trejos, the Ministry of Agriculture organized a committee to review all the information about conservation, forestry, and national parks. I was the representative of the University of Costa Rica. It also included people from the electrification agency, the water agency, and the agricultural colonization agency. After three years of work we developed a project which was sent to the Legislative Assembly, and one chapter in that was about the national parks."

The two students arrived at just the right time in these developments. Mario Boza got a degree in agronomy at UCR in the mid-1960s and went to Turrialba to study forestry in 1967. He wanted to work on teak, an Asian tree widely planted commercially, but his professor, Gerardo Budowski, didn't see "much fire" when he visited teak plantations with Boza. Budowski suspected he was more interested in biology, so he encouraged Boza to go and study wildlands with Kenton Miller.

While taking Miller's course in 1968, Boza had an experience that became somewhat legendary. "Our scholarships included a field trip," he told me in a 1990 interview, "and it usually went to Mexico, but this time Miller said we should go to the U.S. We were very happy with that. We took two cars in Miami and started visiting industries, forestry plantations, parks, and such things. I became particularly interested in parks after we visited the Great Smoky Mountains National Park in Tennessee."

I'd heard about Boza's Smoky Mountains visit from several sources, and it had come to seem like a revelation from which the entire Costa Rican park system had sprung. One North American conservationist told me the story with Alvaro Ugalde as the protagonist instead of Boza. I naturally wanted Boza to elaborate on all this in the interview, so I asked him what it was about the Smokies that attracted him. I asked him if it had been the fact that the Smokies are a forest park, projecting a 1990 concern with ancient forest back to 1968. Boza shook his head.

"The first time I saw a whole park working was in the Smokies," he said. "I saw the people going back and forth, using the facilities. And Gatlinburg, and all the things that had grown up around the park because it was there. And I thought Costa Rica was ready for that."

In May 1969 Boza wrote an editorial in a Costa Rican daily, *La República*, which may have reflected his thoughts in the Smokies: "Although from a commercial viewpoint parks might seem an unnecessary investment, they could become one of the major sources of revenues for the nation. East Africa, by having more vision than us in this field, increased its annual income from tourism by fifteen percent. What couldn't our country do, being closer to the main source of tourists in the world?" In another piece published that year in *La Prensa Libre*, Boza wrote that the doubling of Costa Rican population in the past three decades had caused major scientific, recreational, and economic problems, and that "the establishment and management of national parks is the best solution to these problems."

After the U.S. trip, Boza talked to Kenton Miller about writing a national park master plan as his M.A. thesis at Turrialba. Miller recommended that he do one for Poás Volcano, one of the paper parks of 1939, and Boza turned out a very professional plan complete with visitor center, nature trails, and other facilities for giving visitors access to an active volcano an hour's drive from downtown San José. The Agriculture Ministry hired him to work in its forestry directorate after he finished the plan. When the 1969 forestry bill mandated a park system under the Agriculture Ministry, Boza became its first director, and Poás one of its first two parks. (Cabo Blanco was established not as a park but as a "reserva biológica absoluta," with restricted public access.)

Alvaro Ugalde came into the park system because of the other initial park, Santa Rosa, located in Guanacaste Province five hours' drive northwest of San José. (Five hours, that is, on the paved roads of 1990. Gerardo Budowski told me it took three days to get there in the 1950s.) Santa Rosa was then a large, private hacienda, but it had been the site of Costa Rica's most famous historical event, the battle in which a volunteer army turned back William Walker's invading "filibusters" in

1856. The Battle of Santa Rosa is the Costa Rican equivalent of Lexington and Concord. When Nicaraguan dictator Anastasio Somoza *bought* Santa Rosa in the 1930s it was as though some British gangster had bought Lexington, and the issue had been a thorn in the side of the Legislative Assembly ever since. In 1966 the Assembly finally passed a law expropriating the hacienda with the idea of having the Costa Rican Institute of Tourism (ICT) manage it as a national monument.

The original plan was to buy just the three thousand acres of land around the Casona, the still-existing hacienda house where the battle took place. Santa Rosa is a very beautiful place, however, with volcanoes on the eastern horizon and remnants of dry deciduous forest, a tropical forest type that in Central America is much more threatened than rainforest because most of it has already been cleared for crops and pastures. Hired as a consultant by ICT, Kenton Miller suggested the government buy *thirty* thousand acres, and he developed a master plan for a national park. The government eventually paid Somoza the equivalent of about $500,000 for the hacienda from the Pan American Highway to the Pacific Ocean.

While a biology student at the University of Costa Rica, Alvaro Ugalde joined the mountaineering club. In 1968 the club sent him as its representative to a roundtable discussion on natural resources and the media. Mario Boza also attended, and the two got acquainted there and on a subsequent trip to the turtle beaches at Tortuguero. Also on that trip were José Figueres, his American wife Karen, and their children. Figueres, also known as Don Pepe, was arguably the major Costa Rican leader of the mid-twentieth century: He served an unprecedented three terms as president and instituted many of the major reforms, including the abolition of the armed forces. Figueres wasn't particularly interested in national parks but his wife was. Doña Karen became a key supporter of the park system, especially during her husband's last term, 1970 to 1974.

"It was quite a trip," Ugalde told me in a 1990 interview. "We went by bus, then we took a train for a while, then we got on mules, then we took a boat, then we walked. Mario and I talked a lot with Karen when we walked the trails. Then later, during the turtle season, Don Pepe's son José María and I spent a month in Tortuguero tagging turtles with Archie Carr and his wife, Marjorie, and son, David." David Carr, who now runs the Caribbean Conservation Corporation his father started in the 1950s, remembers that he and Ugalde argued a lot about whether rock music or salsa was better.

"A month or so after that," Ugalde told me, "Mario called me and asked if I wanted to go to a national parks training seminar in the States. I didn't want to go because I was still in school and I didn't want to lose a whole semester. So I asked Pedro León about it, and he said, 'Go, the hell with it.'" (León was another biology student at UCR, having gotten interested in the subject from taking a high school biology class taught by Marjorie Carr. "She was actually interested in it," León told me, "and didn't just drone it out.")

"Anyway," Ugalde continued, "I said, 'Yes. But how am I going to pay for it?' So Mario called Archie Carr, and he got the funds from the Caribbean Conservation Corporation, from the Phipps family, and I went, and wound up spending an extra two months at the Grand Canyon at another course. I didn't have *any* money for that one, but I figured I could do it. I paid ten dollars a month for rent, and I had just enough left for soup once a day. I remember getting dizzy from hunger, and I actually fainted once, but the course was fun, jogging up and down the canyon walls, and learning how to rappel, and how to search at night for lost people.

"I got back to Costa Rica in November 1969, the same time the forestry bill was being passed. I was a so-called expert on national parks because I'd spent three months running up and down the Grand Canyon. Mario had taken the one-month course before me, but when I got back, he left to take the rest of it. So, in effect, just after it had been established, the whole Park Service left the country, including the wife of the Park Service, because they'd only hired Mario to work for the parks. What was left here was Santa Rosa, pretty much abandoned by ICT because the Forestry Law said it was to be managed by the park system, and Cabo Blanco, still being managed by the Wessbergs, and that was it.

"School was over," Ugalde said, "and I was looking for something to do. The Park Service didn't have the money to hire me, even if

Mario Boza had been in the country. There was a Peace Corps volunteer named Tex Hawkins working for the Fish and Wildlife Office of the Agriculture Ministry, and he and I wrote some articles about wildlife and got them published in *La Nación* [Costa Rica's biggest daily newspaper]. We got interested in Santa Rosa, so we went down there.

"We realized immediately that they had serious problems. There were forty families of squatters down at Playa Naranjo [one of the park's Pacific beaches]. They'd already chopped down part of the evergreen gallery forest down there, and they were getting ready to chop down the rest. One of the rancher neighbors up on the dry forest area of the volcanic plateau had stolen sixty hectares—just moved his fences sixty hectares into the park. The historic building was falling down. And there was one workman to take care of all this. Actually, the park hadn't been declared yet, but it was government land, and it was supposed to be a park.

"So Tex and I dedicated to fight for Santa Rosa as volunteers. Mario had left the keys of his apartment in Santa Rosa with me, so Tex and I would meet and raise hell from there. *We* were the Park Service, and neither of us worked for it. It got very heated. We wrote a letter to Mario informing him of the situation, and Mario answered with a very strong letter. So the first big scandal of the national parks began, engineered by Tex and me. I told the forestry director we were going to make a scandal if things didn't get solved, and he was so naive, he said, 'Oh, I think it's a great idea!' And I said, 'Well, it's against *you!*' "

Boza's letter to Agriculture Minister Fernando Batalla Esquivel was published in *La Nación* on May 14, 1970. "The first national historic park in the country, Santa Rosa, is about to disappear," it said. "But this is not due to any great natural disaster nor to any supreme national necessity that obliges such sacrifice. It is due only to a few squatters who with fire, axes, and rifles are destroying the heritage of all Costa Ricans, of present and future generations. And what is the benefit to the country of this situation? Nothing, except to demonstrate that the country's laws are worthless, if that is any benefit."

In response to this letter and other pressures from the scientific and educational communities, the government issued bonds for Santa Rosa development and began planning to relocate the squatters. Ugalde had given up in despair in May, however. "I had all the responsibility," he told me. "I wasn't getting paid, I still hadn't gotten my degree. At that time, I was driving government cars, totally illegal, and pretty dangerous on those roads. One day I was driving and one of the balancing weights they add to the outside of the car's tires came off and hit the windshield of a big truck. The guy came out of the truck, bleeding, glass in his face, although luckily not in his eyes. . . . So I said, 'This is it, Mario, I'm finished.' I got a job with the university, to go around interviewing the main leaders in the country. Then, suddenly, there was a decree appointing me administrator of Santa Rosa National Park, and even assigning a salary for me. So the Park Service now had two people—or three, if you included Mario's secretary."

Many writers have called Boza and Ugalde the founders of the Costa Rican park system. In a sense, this is an exaggeration: It was the Costa Rican leadership that founded the parks, the politicians and civil servants who drafted and passed the park decrees, and the scientists and conservationists who helped and pushed them to do so. Yet in another sense, it is quite true, because both men have shown an extraordinary dedication to the system. They not only helped to start it, but kept working for it throughout their careers, sometimes at considerable personal cost. Everyone I talked to saw them as the essential nucleus of the system. "They keep coming back to the parks like moths to a candle," one longtime park employee told me.

Everyone I talked to was also fascinated that two such different personalities have been able to work together for so long toward a common goal. Boza and Ugalde even belonged to rival political parties—Ugalde to José Figueres's Liberación Party, Boza to the Social Christian Unity Party of Rafael Calderón, Figueres's main rival. The difference between the two men virtually leapt out at me during my introduction to the Costa Rican conservation community, at the International Union for the Conservation of Nature's 1988 General Assembly in San José. I attended a panel workshop on financing parks at which Boza was one of the scheduled panelists. He was inexplicably absent, but Ugalde, who wasn't a scheduled panelist, stood up in the audience and gave an inspiring speech on the need for innovative thinking to get the money to make parks work. "We've *got* to make them work," he said in a deep, resonant voice that might have been coming from a generalissimo in medals and sunglasses instead of a compact, amiable-looking individual in a purple-striped sport shirt and white Levis.

Alvaro Ugalde is possibly one of the most gregarious people in Costa Rica. "I had a reputation as a talkative child," he recalled, "sitting with relatives and visitors and speaking as though I was a grown-up." When I asked him, in the course of a March 1990 interview at his San José house, how he got interested in natural history and conservation, I found out a good deal about his family and childhood. His father, a former divinity student, participated in Figueres's 1948 coup against the Calderón faction. He took his wife and the two-year-old Alvaro into the forest with him at one point during the insurrection. Later, after getting a technical education at night school and leaving his native village, Ugalde's father took him on trips into the forest while he worked as a surveyor for the government road-building agency. Ugalde thought these experiences might have stimulated a love of nature in him. A high school biology teacher named Nidia Abarca also triggered his curiosity.

Ugalde has great generosity (I saw him walk a block out of his way to give an old man a hundred colones) and a wry, self-deprecating sense of humor. His charm is part of a very determined nature, however, and when he thinks something is wrong, his gray eyes turn steely. He is quick to disagree, and stubborn in argument, but his generosity and charm have made him popular with people who work with and for him, and his stubbornness and combativeness have kept his career as stormy as it was when he began "raising hell" from Boza's apartment in 1970.

I learned very little about Mario Boza's personal background from talking to him or others. I was only able to get a single interview with him during the three and a half months I was in Costa Rica in 1990. Boza was extremely busy at that time, having just been appointed to a position in the new administration. "Every day when I get home," he told me, holding his hand two feet above a table, "I have a stack of documents like this to read." Yet Boza was equally laconic in an interview with David Carr in 1982.

With thick glasses and conservative, if informal, clothes, Boza gave the impression of a good-humored but no-nonsense professional whose personal thoughts were beside the point. I'd learned from another source that he was the only son of a San José businessman. When I asked him how he'd gotten interested in natural history and conservation, Boza smiled, shook his head slightly, and said it had been from taking Kenton Miller's course in wildlands management.

It's possible that agronomist Boza never happened to get interested in nature until he took a graduate course in it, although in reading what Boza has written about nature one senses a deeper attraction. "Four enormous fig trees, a cedar and a yellow saman spread a delicious shade and peaceful quiet over the area," he wrote of the Santa Rosa historical site in his *The National Parks of Costa Rica* (1981), "only broken from time to time by the noisy outbursts of parrots and parakeets that pose in great flocks on the fig tree branches where they eat the fruit—sweet little figs. The raucous chattering of these birds can be heard for several hundred meters."

Such writings suggest a more imaginative temperament than Boza the official likes to acknowledge. There was an imaginative, even visionary quality about his perception of Smoky Mountains National Park. It wasn't a poet's vision, or even a naturalist's, strictly speaking. As he said, Boza saw the parks not as forest ecosystem but as facilities and people using them. It was a manager's vision, and in the end perhaps more valuable to maintaining the forest than less pragmatic points of view. There's certainly no doubt, anyway, about the expertise Boza has developed in the field. Someone told me, by the way, that Boza has the largest private library on conservation and natural history in Costa Rica.

It might seem surprising that reticent, scholarly Boza and outgoing, combative Ugalde should have even communicated, much less cooperated, for over two decades. The impression I got from talking to park people was that the association has worked as much because of their differences as in spite of them. The same person who said they were like moths to a candle said they worked like lock and key. "One very politic, one very aggressive—a good pair." "Mario's good at starting things," someone else said, "and Alvaro's good at building them up, keeping them going." One source thought that Boza restrained Ugalde when he got too combative; another source thought that Ugalde restrained Boza from becoming too intellectually grandiose.

Of course, Boza and Ugalde are real people and therefore unpredictable. In 1990 Boza showed up at a public event at which he was not a scheduled speaker and gave an even wittier speech than Ugalde, who was on the program. Ugalde, who also has a house full of books, wrote the following about the establishment of Santa Rosa National Park: "The wildlife suddenly realized that there was silence again after many, many decades of persecution. Soon after that, they also realized that they were free to move; the park was real, and it was for them, to live and evolve. Man had finally become their ally, at least in Santa Rosa. Twenty years later, their descendants are still there, even though they don't know this story."

Whatever the psychodynamics of Boza and Ugalde's working relationship, it was a good thing it came to be. They had a lot of work to do. Within the next decade, the park system would more than quintuple, from three units in 1970 to seventeen in 1978. Some units would present as many problems as Santa Rosa did when it drove unpaid Alvaro Ugalde to despair.

three

The Quetzal and the Macaw

Although nobody really planned to make Poás and Santa Rosa the first two national parks, there could hardly have been better choices. Few places in Costa Rica are more central to the nation's character, which is complex despite the country's small size. Santa Rosa was the site not only of the antifilibuster battle of 1856, but of lesser battles in 1919 and 1955 that also resulted from Nicaraguan invasions. The 1955 invasion, a Somoza-backed attempt to overthrow Don Pepe Figueres's second presidency, must have been a spectacle. "Several chase planes of the invaders constantly machine-gunned the government troops," Boza wrote in *The National Parks of Costa Rica*, "which in turn used grenades, mortars, and machine guns."

Poás Volcano has caused much greater spectacles, sending up towering eruptions of steam and ash visible throughout the heavily populated Meseta Central. In 1910 Poás expelled a 24,000-foot-high cloud that dropped an estimated 640,000 tons of ash on the area. Similar eruptions occurred in 1952, 1974, and 1978. In 1990, the farms around the volcano had just been declared a disaster area because renewed volcanic activity was causing acid rain and air pollution. Poás's eruptions may have been the motive, although nobody knows, for one of Costa Rica's main folk customs: a mass pilgrimage to its summit on the Saint's Day of San José, March 19.

Poás and the other active volcanoes that ring the Meseta Central have been a central fact of life since the Costa Rican colony was founded in the early sixteenth century. The fertile soils they deposited in Meseta valleys encouraged a dense farming population. Yet their eruptions and related earthquakes repeatedly destroyed cities and towns, and their ruggedness kept the colony isolated until the nineteenth century. Costa Rica was one of the poorest and most backward of Spain's imperial possessions. Landowners and clerics had to keep shops to make ends meet. One imperial governor complained that he would have starved if he hadn't grown food with his own hands.

Development of coffee and other lucrative export commodities in the mid to late nineteenth century transformed Costa Rica into one of the more cosmopolitan and prosperous Latin American nations. Costa Ricans benefited from an open attitude toward changing cultural influences from Europe and North America. Yet nationhood remained heavily centered on the original highland colonial areas, with their largely Spanish population and culture. A relatively small number of original colonial families retained most land ownership. Ethnic groups distinct from the colonial nucleus—Caribbean blacks and tribal Indians, for example—had to struggle to participate in nationhood. For all their pride in their recent contributions to peace in Central America, their self-characterization as "the garden of peace and democracy," Costa Ricans also are proud of the ferocity with which they have repelled invaders. At the Battle of Santa Rosa, according to The National Parks of Costa Rica, "our brave soldiers preferred to use their bayonets, there being cases of their lifting up one or even two filibusters in this way, tossing them off to one side, and continuing the attack."

One reason that Santa Rosa was the site of so many invasions is that it is located in the northwestern province, Guanacaste, which was originally part of Nicaragua. Costa Rica annexed Guanacaste peacefully, by vote, in the early nineteenth century, but it has a different history and culture than the Meseta Central. Guanacastan settlement centered around large ranching haciendas instead of the small farms and coffee fincas of the Meseta. Its population, like Nicaragua's, is more mestizo than the Meseta's. Guanacaste occupies a place in Costa Rican geography rather similar to that of Arizona and New Mexico in the U.S.—it's a place of dry heat and wide open spaces apart from the cooler, greener center of population.

Santa Rosa and Poás thus embody two sides of Costa Rica—a past of colonial, highland isolation that led to lowland national expansion. They also embody a basic division of the Costa Rican landscape. Enormously diverse as that is, ranging within a hundred miles east-to-west from soaking rainforest in Tortuguero to baking savanna in Guanacaste, the difference between highlands and lowlands is the most important one.

Although much of the country is visible from its summit on rare clear days, Poás is usually a place of fog and rain, of which it gets an average of 3,500 mm per year. Frost is not unusual at night, but the tropical sun has a searing power at the ten-thousand-foot elevation. The combination of extravagant moisture and climatic extremes has produced a vegetation of overwhelming vitality. Tough but succulent plants occupy every vacant niche, including the available surfaces of other plants. Not only vines and bromeliads but entire trees, such as the leathery-leaved *Clusias*, grow on other trees. Poás's dominant tree families—evergreen oaks, magnolias, laurels, and podocarps—are descended from great subtropical forests that covered the northern continents before the climate began to cool and dry from ten to twenty million years ago. Costa Rican mountain forests are a refuge for some very ancient plants, including *Drimys* or winterbark, a small tree that has the most primitive wood of any living angiosperm.

For all its lushness, the Poás forest is rather silent. One hears some beautiful bird songs, such as the hermit thrush–like song of the black-faced solitaire, but the sounds seem to fade into the matrix of mosses and epiphytes. One seldom sees the singer, and although hundreds of animal species are known to inhabit Poás, one seldom sees anything larger than the endemic, reddish Poás squirrel. Animals have more difficulty adapting to a world of continual chill and damp than plants do.

Santa Rosa seems the exact opposite of Poás during its November-to-May dry season. Vegetation seems burnt to a crisp by ninety-degree daytime temperatures and endlessly blustering trade winds. Except beside streams, trees are leafless, and the peeling, coppery branches of Indio desnudo trees or the spiky gray leaves of pochote and ceiba look more dead than alive. Only the cactuses that stand erect on rocks or creep as epiphytes on trees show much green. Santa Rosa's plants have more in common with Arizona's than with those at Poás.

Yet an early morning visit during the dry season to one of Santa Rosa's scattered water holes was like wandering into one of Henri Rousseau's jungle paintings, a tropical Eden lacking only green leaves. A big troop of white-faced capuchin monkeys appeared, running along the branches of smaller trees or on the ground. A family of black howler monkeys climbed placidly through the trees above the water, ragdoll babies clinging to their mothers' backs. Three rusty gray spider monkeys perched in a large tree. Just below them, a troop of coatis paraded along a low limb, tails erect, noses twitching. On the ground, big animals seemed to coalesce out of the gray underbrush—white-tailed deer, collared peccaries, flocks of turkey-sized great currasows. Lizards were everywhere, from tiny geckoes to three-foot ctenosaurs. Santa Rosa's warm, dry climate encourages animal life. Although it seems burnt out, the vegetation produces ample fruits, seeds, and insects in the dry season.

In its rainy season, the Santa Rosa forest becomes an overwhelming bright green maze like the lowland forests of Costa Rica's Caribbean and southwest. Wildlife tends to disappear into this maze: In places like Tortuguero and Corcovado, one can easily walk a day and see nothing but lizards and songbirds. Yet a sense of overwhelming animal vitality persists in a roar of cicadas and katydids and in frequent thumps and crashes as concealed creatures move away through the underbrush. In lowland rainforest, plant vitality equals or surpasses animal. There is a sense of impenetrability, not so much because underbrush is dense (although often it is) but because the sheer, interwoven biomass discourages notions of forward motion, progress.

Perhaps the most impressive sound of both wet and dry lowland forest, at least for sheer raucous volume, is the squawking of a flock of scarlet macaws. The conquistadors who first explored Costa Rica's Pacific coast are said to have complained about the racket, which went on almost ceaselessly because there were so many macaws. No bird embodies the noisy, teeming life of the lowlands more than the giant red, blue, and yellow parrots.

Similarly, no bird embodies the quiet, isolated life of the highlands more than Costa Rica's other most spectacular bird, the resplendent quetzal. Quetzals have a fairly loud, clucking call, and they are certainly showy with their iridescent green and scarlet plumage and three-foot tails. Yet instead of standing out from the forest as macaws do, they fade into it. Unlike the more cosmopolitan scarlet macaws, which live (or lived) from Mexico to Bolivia and Uruguay, resplendent quetzals are endemic to Mesoamerican mountain forests.

The most advertised birds in the Costa Rican parks, scarlet macaws and resplendent quetzals became their unofficial symbols, and it was appropriate that Santa Rosa and Poás were classic habitat for scarlet macaws and resplendent quetzals, respectively. Establishing protected parks in Santa Rosa and Poás was also appropriate in that both species were in trouble in both areas. By 1970, Poás's forested summit was so hemmed in by dairy farms, strawberry fields, and ornamental fern nurseries that quetzals were seldom seen. Santa Rosa encompassed a larger area of scarlet macaw habitat, but most of the macaws had already disappeared into cages and zoos, such was the popularity of the gregarious species. Sergio Volio, a Santa Rosa ranger in the late 1970s, told me that when he first started working there, "I'd see a pair flying down the Canyon de Tigre to roost in the mangroves near the shore. Or hear them: 'Scraaa! Scraaa!' Then, a little later, there was one. Then there were none."

Unfortunately, Santa Rosa's dwindling macaw population was one of the least of new park administrator Ugalde's problems in June 1970. For one thing, he had his own personal survival to worry about. Somoza had been persecuting the forty families of squatters at Playa Naranjo before he'd sold out, and they were armed and ill-disposed to owners, whoever they might be.

"It was very difficult at the beginning," Ugalde told me, "because even though I was supposed to be the authority, in reality *they* were. The park was divided into my authority and their authority, which started at the Canyon de Tigre, the drop from the savanna down to the beach where they had their homesteads. I had the historic buildings. They were very aggressive at first, with machetes and all that. But I went around the whole park by myself without a gun and started talking to them. Pretty soon we were having coffee and trying to negotiate.

"They said, 'Well, if that's official, then we need to get paid for our improvements, and we need land somewhere else, and we need transportation.' I told them I'd get them those things, and if I didn't get them, I'd resign. And they believed me, I guess. I would have resigned, but the government came through, and by July we were actually loading chickens and pigs in cars and taking them away. It was an adventure, the rainiest rainy season I'd seen in Santa Rosa, with those rivers in which you never see water practically dragging away our cars full of pigs and chickens and people.

"Then, on the day we removed the last squatter family, we found out that Daniel Oduber had presented a bill to Congress to take Santa Rosa away from the park system and give it back to the tourist board, to ICT. We were barely born, and already we were being eliminated."

Daniel Oduber was a powerful Guanacaste rancher and politician who also happened to be president of the Legislative Assembly under the incoming, third administration of Don Pepe Figueres. (Costa Rican presidents can't succeed themselves, but they can have multiple, nonconsecutive terms.) Oduber's position made him the second most powerful figure in the Liberación Party. ICT evidently had been disgruntled at having Santa Rosa taken away from them and had seen a chance to get it back. Oduber also happened to be a friend of the neighboring rancher who had moved his fence sixty hectares into Santa Rosa.

"Forget it, boys, you are going to lose Santa Rosa whether you like it or not," a source at the attorney general's office told Boza and Ugalde. "When Daniel Oduber decides something, he is likely to get it."

Boza and Ugalde didn't forget it, however. They began to work against Oduber with a combination of public relations and political maneuvering that would prove to be the park system's best defense in coming years. They found an obscure clause in Oduber's bill that would have taxed liquor, and they used this to lobby businessmen against the bill. They also incited the Colegio de Biólogos to write letters and lobby against the bill. Perhaps most important in this instance, they got First Lady Doña Karen to work against it.

According to Boza, Doña Karen talked with or wrote to every member of the assembly, asking them to vote against the bill. She also wrote a letter to Oduber asking him to withdraw it, and got Don Pepe to deliver it to Oduber without telling her husband what the letter was about. I also heard stories of Doña Karen pressuring President Figueres to support conservation, for example, by delaying his breakfast until he signed some piece of legislation. (I wasn't able to ask her about this because Don Pepe died just before I was supposed to interview her in 1990.) "Don't listen to my wife," José Figueres once reportedly told a group of Costa Rican conservationists. "She's a little crazy."

Oduber refused to withdraw the bill, but it was unanimously defeated when it came to a vote in the assembly. On March 20, 1971, Doña Karen acted for the president in cutting a ribbon formally opening Santa Rosa National Park, and Daniel Oduber gave a speech hailing the opening.

Boza and Ugalde had little leisure in which to enjoy this victory. On June 30, three months after the park's opening, *La Prensa Libre* carried a story headlined, "Santa Rosa National Park Is Being Destroyed." The story featured the text of a June 28 letter to the Legislative Assembly from the National Youth Movement complaining that the volunteer work they'd done on trails and picnic areas was being destroyed by cattle. The letter denounced Pedro Abreu, the rancher who'd moved his fence into the park, as the cattle's owner. Another daily paper, *La República,* printed a letter from the Colegio de Biólogos warning that "the national park has been transformed into a virtual ranch supporting several thousand head of livestock." *La República* also reported gossip that the minister of Agriculture actually had facilitated the cattle invasion and had blocked return of the stolen land to the park.

The July 2 *La Prensa Libre* carried an irate response to these attacks from Agriculture Minister Battala Esquivel. The minister complained of "organs of the press who have a special interest in sensational polemic" and maintained that controlled ranching was part of the park plan. He did promise that cattle would be watched more closely in the future. Boza and Ugalde weren't heard from publically in this "scandal," which wasn't surprising considering that the agriculture minister was their boss. Everybody, including the minister, probably knew what side they were on. (Eventually, the court ordered Abreu to return the land, and the cattle were removed, although the park service had to kill many and donate the meat to hospitals.)

Not all the news from Santa Rosa was scandalous. On January 31, 1971, *La Nación* reported on the first group of foreign tourists in the park. "Californians Surprised by Santa Rosa," read the article's optimistic headline. The tourists, travelling the Pan American Highway in two pickup trucks, said they hadn't expected to encounter a park right beside the highway. They'd seen nothing but fires and "destruction of what remaining vegetation there was" on the trip south from Mexico. They'd been particularly impressed, the article noted, at seeing a troop of howler monkeys. From the way they talked, the park ranger suspected that they'd never seen wild monkeys, and that this would be what pleased them most about arriving in Costa Rica.

Meanwhile, back in the Meseta Central, the Park Service acquired another employee as the Legislative Assembly decreed a 9,800-acre park at Poás Volcano. Vernon Cruz was an agriculture student at the University of Costa Rica in the 1960s. He'd wanted to work with ornamental plants, "but my teachers said 'we understand that you like them a lot, but what are you going to work at here in Costa Rica?' Then somebody told me that in the Ministry of Agriculture there was a new department called 'parques nacionales.' In that year, 1970–71, the only meaning of parks for me was city parks—and *parques nacionales* must be city parks for the nation, I thought. So I said, 'Well, that's where I have to go.'"

Vernon Cruz told me the story of his Park Service career at his house near San José, which was full of the ornamental plants he grows professionally. The plants included interesting tropical bonsais that he had cultivated, miniatures of tropical forest plants such as figs, *Burseras*, and *Scheffleras*, an idea so good I was surprised I hadn't

seen it before. Like many Costa Rican professionals, Cruz had studied in the U.S., and spoke good, sometimes innovative, English.

"So I went there [to the Ministry of Agriculture]," he told me, "and
asked for a job, and they gave me one. The day I was supposed to
start, I went to the main building, and they said, 'Okay, here you are,
you have to go to the Forestry Department.' I said, 'No. I'm not doing
forests. Parques nacionales.' They said, 'Yes, we know, but there's no
work there. And there's a lot of help we need in Forestry.'

"So what I had to do was go to Forestry and work for a year. Of
course, during that time, Mario Boza knew about me. I'd met him
when I was doing agriculture, and I'd met Alvaro Ugalde at a biology
course we both were taking at the university. They knew it when I finally quit the forestry job and went back to the university to work at a
laboratory for seed technology. So once I'd gotten that job and moved,
along came Mario and Alvaro. They told me they knew about my interest in parks, and promised they had a vacancy and they'd like to
have me. They knew I wasn't too interested in seed technology. I
really love nature. When I was growing up, my father would take me
out and teach me the names of plants. I had a photographic memory
for them, and that was the way he played with me. So I said, 'Okay, I'll
work with you at the national parks.'

"I went to the office for my first day, and I said, 'Well, Mario, what
should I do?' I realized by that time that national parks weren't in cities because of talks with Alvaro. But I still didn't know what they
were. Nobody in Costa Rica knew, unless they'd been in a country
that had them. So Mario said: 'Well, you don't have a job *here*. Here's
the key to a jeep. You know how to drive?'

" 'Yes, I know that.'

" 'You are appointed to work at Poás Volcano.'

" 'Is that right? Where is it? You have to show me.'

" 'No,' said Mario, shaking his head, 'there's only three of us in the
Park Service, and one secretary. And we need *you* in Poás. There are a
few workmen there. And there are some Peace Corps people that can
help you out there too.'

"Alvaro was in charge of Santa Rosa," Cruz explained, "and Poás
Volcano had recently been declared. There was a lot of trouble with

the owner because the government hadn't paid him. Well, I took this jeep and went to Volcán Poás with groceries and some papers, and that was it. I got there, and nobody knew me. There wasn't a radio to communicate with the main office, and the road was very bad. I had to introduce myself, and I remember that one of the Peace Corps volunteers who was in charge of personnel at the time was very . . . impressed that the main office had sent somebody with no experience in parks to be the administrator of the park.

"Well, I decided that I had to obey Mario, so I stayed there and tried to understand what they did every day. There were eleven people there, living in three rooms. There was also a shack where some people who had worked for the old owner lived. They were named Blanco, a man and his wife, with his brother, very old people. Mrs. Blanco cooked for the guardaparques while they tried to build trails and fix the house. The temperature was very near freezing every morning. That was in January 1972.

"We didn't have any money, so I went to the municipality of Poás, San Pedro de Poás, to tell them we needed electricity and to explain the importance of supporting national parks for conservation and tourism—that in the future it would be very important for the community. They were very helpful. They gave us an electric generator. We started work on a third house to prepare to display the new ideas about Poás for the nineteenth of March, when thousands of people would come to the crater for St. Joseph's Day. I had some friends at the university who helped me with learning about plants and things, and I showed the guardaparques what the common things were. And I had to supervise construction of the new building.

"One morning the old owner appeared and started building a fence. He said, 'You haven't paid me, and I'm bringing my cows back.' I had to stop this. Then he said he was going to put me in jail, and I said, 'Okay, put me in jail.' I was scared, of course, but I came down to San José and talked to Mario, and I didn't get put in jail. Another day, I heard a chain saw while I was out trying to get a little sun in my bathing suit. This was in spring 1972. I called two guards, and we went into the woods and found that Blanco had cut down two beautiful podocarpus trees, the only native gymnosperms we have, huge trees.

He'd been cutting trees and selling the lumber. So that was the end of the Blancos, because I fired them. I needed the help of a psychologist to do it, because I'd never fired anybody before.

"I was about a year at Poás, really working hard because it was going to be opened soon, and we needed to finish paving the road. When I was at my most enthusiastic, one afternoon about five, along came Mario Boza and Alvaro Ugalde, and they said, 'Hey, why don't we go to the crater? We need to talk.'

"So we went to the crater, and Mario told me, 'There's big trouble in Santa Rosa. There's a bad drought in Guanacaste, and the Agriculture minister has decided the park is going to be harvested for hay to feed cattle. The savanna that we've been protecting from fires and hunters for two years is going to be cut with machetes, everything. Alvaro decided to oppose the minister, and the minister decided that Alvaro had to be fired from Santa Rosa. We came to tell you you're going to work in Santa Rosa, and Alvaro in Poás.'

"I was furious," Cruz said. "Just a few days before the Poás opening, they were going to use an eraser and move me to Santa Rosa? I said, 'No, no, no, Mario,' and he said, 'Yes, yes, yes.'

" 'Well, when do I have to go?' I said.

" 'Tomorrow. We don't have much time. And you have to come with us now, because this problem is very serious, and the park system will be destroyed if we don't solve it.'

"I really didn't want to go. I thought I'd hate it because Santa Rosa was traditionally the place all the policemen used to run cattle and hunt deer, or fight with the Nicas [Nicaraguans]. But I agreed, because I think I understood better what was happening with the parks. But I said, 'I'm not going alone this time, because the minister's people are there.' And Alvaro accepted the danger to his life, and went with me.

"It was my first time in Guanacaste. I grew up in Cartago, in the Meseta, and I found Guanacaste magnificent in every sense. Ocean, trees, and savannas—everything about it fascinated me, even the old Casona. The park was more developed there than at Poás, with a little separate house for the administrator, and electricity, and I could always lock myself in the Casona if something happened. But somehow nothing did happen to me. There were at least a dozen Peace Corps people there, and they were furious at the government, but I couldn't hate it, because I was in it. [Cutting hay in the park wasn't a success anyway, and the government never tried it again.]

"At Poás, it had been quiet, really—basically just looking after plants and protecting visitors at the crater. At Santa Rosa it was more serious. We had to protect the animals from poachers, the tapirs, cats, deer, and peccaries, and the forest from fires, as well as do historical research and restoration. I was very quick to get rid of employees who were taking tips for bringing hunters into the park at night. Some nights I didn't sleep because of the need to patrol. We'd see deer hunters' lights in the darkness. And I can't tell you the terror you feel surrounded by fire. It runs and jumps ahead of you, fifty meters at a time. There were at least five months of terror during the dry season, when fires could start any time. All the houses could have burned along with the forest."

Vernon Cruz worked at Santa Rosa for a half year. By the end of that time, in late 1973, the park system was beginning to grow so fast that Boza moved him back to the office to take advantage of his experience. More government money was coming in, and a master plan team had been formed to develop Poás and Santa Rosa as model parks, places where Costa Ricans could experience all the recreational and interpretive services of national parks. Vernon Cruz was made a floating administrator, armed with a slide projector, and sent around to possible new park localities to introduce communities to the park idea and otherwise facilitate things.

"Of course, most of the time I was in the office," Vernon told me, "and I experienced very deeply the problems of bureaucracy. And the worm of gardens and plants started in my mind again. I hadn't had time to finish my university thesis. They'd promised I would, but I *never* had a chance. So in the middle of 1974 I decided to quit the parks and work with my hands in the soil and not behind a desk in San José. I didn't regret getting out of the office, but working for the parks was really good for me. It made me understand both the environment and society better.

"We never really stopped working, although we were supposed to get a week off every twenty-two days. Sometimes we'd work through the night at Boza's house. He was always working all the time with lots of projects. He kept us busy with all his ideas. It wasn't really working. We *liked* the problems, the feeling of responsibility for the nation's resources. The support of the workers was the strong base of the parks from the beginning. The conditions were very poor and hard, but all anybody thought about was how fantastic nature was, and how important it was to protect it for everybody. Now I guess the Park Service has grown so much that some people just work at it for the job. But it was survival conditions then, like camping, except we had to *stay* there."

four
___

Reefs, Rainforests, Caves, Ruins, and Rookeries

The Costa Rican park system grew so fast in the early 1970s that it seems there must have been some prearranged strategy, some master plan of conquest. A propark media blitz in that period strengthens the impression of deliberate promotion. Full-page ads in the dailies boosted Santa Rosa's opening celebration with Madison Avenue brashness. "Begin to enjoy the marvellous experience of visiting the national parks—*un mundo diferente, un mundo fascinante,*" they proclaimed, "and remember, bring your camera." Every week, newspapers carried articles about sea turtle slaughter, dwindling quetzal populations, deforestation, endangered species, and other problems, usually with some mention of national parks as a solution.

"Within ten years, there may not be either flora or fauna in the country," said a July 1972 article in *El Diario de Costa Rica*. The article consisted largely of Boza's testimony before a Legislative Assembly committee. He said that if parks, then under the Agriculture Ministry's Forestry Directorate, didn't get independent status as a park service, there would be no funds or personnel to develop new parks, and that if new parks weren't created, "within ten years, we'll be like other countries, like El Salvador, virtually without natural resources, with huge economic problems."

The swiftness of this attack seems to have caught potential park enemies off guard. As Boza told me, "There was the usual opposition to parks, but it wasn't strong." The only organized opposition that got media attention at that time was a group called the National Committee for Conservation of Renewable Resources. They got a letter published in *La Nación* in 1972 claiming that a park service would be too expensive and would conflict with existing government bodies. (It would take another five years to get an independent park service.)

The publicity blitz was one of a number of techniques Boza outlined in a little book entitled *A Decade of Development*, published in 1981. The book is a kind of handy, how-to guide on establishing and administering a national park system in a developing country. It explains concisely how to solve the successive problems of a system: how to select parks, staff them, fund them, and get the public to support them. How to "break the vicious cycle between the necessity to develop parks and the lack of means"? Establish parks, publicize them, and thus create a need for means. How to "avoid wasting the small means available"? Resist the temptation to establish as many parks as possible, and concentrate on areas one can develop and protect. How to get guides, guards, workmen, and cooks to staff parks with the small means available? Recruit Peace Corps volunteers from other government agencies, since parks are "popular with this kind of young person," and thus get a free, insured, Spanish-speaking labor supply. How to get highly qualified planning and research personnel? Borrow them from conservation agencies in developed countries, from international agencies like U.S. AID, or from private organizations like the World Wildlife Fund. How to get operating funds? Charge admission to the parks and get international bank loans. How to get public support? Continually publish short articles in the press (Boza had a Peace Corps volunteer writing articles full-time); escort businessmen, legislators, journalists, and other public figures to the parks; and have friends like Doña Karen Figueres in high places.

It appears that this shrewd strategy came after the fact, however. When I asked Boza in 1990 if he had planned it, he was so taken aback that he mentioned the question in a speech the next day. "*Nothing* was planned," he told me. "We had no experience, although the basic idea of what we wanted to do was clear. But we had to learn by doing it."

Every addition to the system brought with it a new set of problems to learn about. The next two areas on the agenda were Tortuguero,

Archie Carr's turtle beach, and Cahuita, a swampy spit of land on Costa Rica's southern Caribbean coast. Costa Rica's biggest coral reef, containing some thirty-five species of reef-building coral, lies offshore from Cahuita. Both areas contained lowland rainforest as well as marine resources, an obvious requirement for a park system within the second largest rainforest region of the Western Hemisphere.

Geographically, Tortuguero and Cahuita are about the same distance from San José as Santa Rosa is. Historically and culturally they were much farther away. Even in 1990 neither park had been integrated into the system to the extent that Poás and Santa Rosa had. Poás and Santa Rosa were about as fully developed as U.S. parks, with paved roads, campsites, visitor centers, and interpretive programs. Cahuita was accessible by dirt road in 1990, so it had a visitor center and camping area, but the government still hadn't gotten around to buying most of the land in it. The much larger Tortuguero was largely in government hands, but remained accessible only by plane, boat, or by hiking for hours through swampy forest, and it contained few public facilities.

Tortuguero and Cahuita were less a part of Costa Rica's colonial-national nucleus than Poás and Santa Rosa, or even than Cabo Blanco. For most of Costa Rica's existence, the Caribbean coast was largely uninhabited because of diseases, pirate raids, and other troubles. In the late nineteenth century, when big foreign companies began developing railroads and banana plantations on the coast, Jamaican blacks came and settled. At first they worked for the big companies; many then went on to develop small cacao and coconut plantations. They developed an English-speaking culture distinct from the rest of the nation. Laws prohibiting Caribbean blacks from immigrating to the Meseta Central helped keep the region distinct into the early twentieth century.

It wasn't surprising, then, that the prospect of the government expropriating land for such an obscure purpose as a national park should have met with even more suspicion on the Caribbean than in Guanacaste or Nicoya. "We are more concerned than anyone else about preserving the area, because it's our farms," said Alphaeus Buchanan, quoted in Paula Palmer's folk history of the Talamanca coast, *What Happen*. "That's what they don't realize, that these lovely coconut groves that they see along the beaches are our farms, something built by our people. They call it 'natural resources,' and it *is* natural resources, but it's our farms!"

It can be difficult for the outsider to distinguish between farms and natural landscape on the Caribbean. Traditional agriculture blends easily with the background of beaches and swampy forest. Farmers grow coconut palms in the sandy strip between beach and swamp, and cacao among the wild trees of inland rainforest. Even the gardens of fruit trees, herbs, and vegetables around towns and houses grade almost imperceptibly into forest. Walking Cahuita's beaches in 1990, I saw little suggestion that a road a few hundred yards inland was lined with farmhouses. The beach apparently belonged to thousands of red and blue land crabs that shuffled over the leaf litter or sat in swamp pools, to hundreds of lizards—geckoes, ameivas, and anoles—and to smaller numbers of howler and capuchin monkeys, three-toed sloths, and small red squirrels. A pair of white-necked puffbirds, a large uncommon rainforest species, seemed to be nesting in a tree above the trail. Similarly, swimming among the squirrel fish, parrot fish, butterfly fish, and wrasse of the reef, I saw little evidence aside from the odd dinghy that subsistence fishing went on.

Traditional farming does have its impacts. At Cahuita's Puerto Vargas visitor center, guardaparque Marvin Santamaría told me it has proved impossible to control poaching of iguanas and turtle eggs because of the farms' proximity. The park's nesting turtle population was thus negligible, and I saw no iguanas there. Crocodiles and manatees were no more than a memory. There is a Caribbean tradition that manatees contain every kind of meat—beef, pork, chicken, fish, even bacon—so they don't last long in settled areas. Santamaría also told me that there was some conflict between the park and subsistence fishermen. Spiny lobsters were rare from heavy exploitation. When the park tried to outlaw spearfishing in its waters, fishermen complained that they needed the guns for protection from sharks.

Yet such conflicts have had less impact on the park than such large-scale development as the banana plantations on the Estrella River north of Cahuita. A current carries silt from the plantations southward, and the silt has been smothering the reef since before the park was established. Santamaría told me that living corals remained abundant only at the tip of Cahuita point. The waters north of the point were a shallow, muddy expanse of dead reef where spiny sea urchins grazed on turtlegrass, and the blue plastic used to bag banana bunches littered the beach.

Vernon Cruz worked on the creation of Cahuita National Park when he was a floating administrator. He told me the streets of the little town of Cahuita north of the park "were grass then, just like a rug. A Chinese lady owned the only hotel, and the theater, dance hall, and grocery store. We had to be refugees with her in bad weather. Alvaro was in charge in the beginning, but he had some trouble with the local people because of his strong temper. I had to go there and tenderize the situation, because some of them said they'd kill Alvaro."

First created as a six-hundred-hectare marine national monument in 1970, later enlarged to include 1,067 hectares of swamp forest, Cahuita became a political football. In the 1970s it passed from park system administration to a local agency, the Junta de Administración Portuaria de la Vertiente Atlántica, then back to the parks. Residents and local officials complained that park administrators made arbitrary and unpredictable regulations, such as telling farmers with land in the park to clear brush under coconut plantations, then telling them not to clear it. Locals also complained that the park administration failed to tell them about legislation and plans to start expropriation hearings. Conflict came to a head in the mid-1970s when several hundred people, including the national Legislative Assembly deputy from Limón, gathered in Cahuita town to speak against the park.

The park staff and local people had something in common, however: a desire not to see mass commercial tourist development overwhelm the area. "I don't want to see our people sell it for any tourist complex in the future," Alphaeus Buchanan said, "because we know that if tourism takes over the area, that's the end of our boys and girls. Look at Acapulco. You know what that brings, venereal diseases, crime, prostitution, drugs . . ." Vernon Cruz told me that Alvaro Ugalde was able to turn around the antipark meeting in Cahuita by pointing out that the likely alternative to a national park would be a mass of hotels, marinas, and golf courses which nobody wanted except foreign companies waiting on the sidelines.

"I was the only speaker to defend the park," Ugalde recalled. "All the previous speakers had spoken in Spanish, and I saw a possibility open to me in support of the park. The majority of the audience were black men and women who communicated better in English. I started in Spanish, but after a few minutes my desperation forced me to turn to English. . . . I felt I had connected myself to a special communication system with the audience. I told them that in spite of the Park Service's mistakes and serious difficulties in communication between them and the young bureaucrats from San José, our intention was to continue the protection that they and their ancestors had bestowed on those beautiful forests and reefs. I asked them to give us time, and to work with us to solve the many problems.

"Somehow, as if guided by an unseen force, my voice became louder, and I soon was asking them questions, and they were responding en masse. I found myself asking them if they wanted the park to exist, and they said, 'Yes.' The only words I could find after that were 'thank you,' and I shut up. My speech happened to be the meeting's last, to the dismay of my enemies."

In contrast to settled Cahuita, Tortuguero remains one of the wildest regions of Costa Rica. Crocodiles and manatees still inhabit its swampy rivers. On my 1987 visit, I saw caimans, sunbitterns, and sungrebes along the rivers, increasingly uncommon creatures in the rest of Costa Rica. Beaches stretched empty as far as I could see, and an unforgettably large expanse of rainforest was visible from Cerro Tortuguero, an isolated mound just inland. White-lipped peccaries, usually the first mammals to disappear as forest dwindles, still inhabit Tortuguero.

Tortuguero may have been wilder in 1987 than it was when Archie Carr arrived to study green turtles in the 1950s. At that time riverside forests were being logged, and poachers and wild dogs routinely decimated turtle nests. In 1959 Carr and a group of other North American and Costa Rican scientists and conservationists founded the Caribbean Conservation Corporation (CCC) to protect the green turtles' nesting colony, one of only two major colonies in the Caribbean. It was Costa Rica's first nongovernmental conservation organization, or NGO. In addition to starting a hatchery program, the CCC began lobbying the government for official protection for the turtles.

A 1963 executive decree established a turtle nesting reserve under the Agriculture Ministry and also restricted turtle hunting and egg-gathering, but the actual protection it offered was limited. Archie Carr's son David told me that his mother, Marjorie, had to teach the guards assigned to patrol the beach how to camp out, since they were from San José. "I remember her telling them, 'Here's your pots and pans, here's your stove, and this is what you do with this and that,' like spending boys to camp."

When Tortuguero National Park was established by executive decree in 1970, Archie Carr wrote Mario Boza that "the decree has come none too soon. With the penetration of the region by a long-shore canal, the entire ecological organization of the zone will be threatened. . . . The potential of the park in saving threatened species is dramatically shown by the success of your program of sea turtle wardenship during the past two seasons. Three seasons ago illegal exploitation of the nesting colony of the green turtle was essentially out of control, the nesting female turtles were regularly killed for calipee, and there was an extensive open collaboration between turtle boats cruising just offshore and illegal hunters on the beach, who tied buoys to the fins of the nesting turtles so they could be picked up by the boats as they returned to the sea. These inroads, which were quite clearly wiping out the colony, were brought to a halt by the move of your office when it manned two shore warden stations at critical points along the nesting beach and arranged a schedule of coast guard surveillance and of shore patrols by armed guards."

In 1975 more legislation expanded Tortuguero to over eighteen thousand hectares of land, including fifteen miles of turtle nesting beach. Nesting turtles (over twenty thousand greens, three hundred leatherbacks, and lesser numbers of hawksbills and loggerheads) came under threat again in 1979, however, when the Legislative Assembly passed a law reducing offshore turtle hunting limits from twelve miles to three miles. Although the law maintained the twelve-mile limit in park waters, this meant turtles would have to swim through waters full of commercial hunters to reach the park. Archie Carr predicted that this would be the coup de grace for turtle populations on the brink of collapse. An international letter-writing campaign against the law convinced then-president Rodrigo Carazo to veto it in September 1979.

While Ugalde and Cruz sweated in the lowlands or shivered in the highlands, the Boza publicity mill continued to grind out articles on likely parks. A June 1969 *La Nación* piece boosted the attractions of a place called Barra Honda at the north end of the Nicoya Peninsula, and recommended it as a park. A flat-topped mass of grayish white rock looming over a hilly landscape, Barra Honda had been considered a volcano because sulfurous smells and strange roaring sounds came from holes in its top. A 1967 Mountaineering Club of Costa Rica expedition discovered that the holes were really the entrances to a system of spectacular limestone caves that drop vertically into the mountain to depths of over three hundred feet. Thousands of roosting bats caused the sulfurous smells and roaring sounds.

Apparently nobody had entered the caves before and lived to tell about it because they are sheer drops negotiable only with rapelling ropes. The explorers found blind salamanders and fish as well as rats, birds, crickets, beetles, and snails living in fantastic chambers of stalactites, stalagmites, terrazas, curtains, and other limestone cave formations. In 1970 explorers from the Group of Speleology found a number of pre-Columbian human skeletons in the cave, parts of which were covered with the same calcium carbonate forming the stalagmites.

Early accounts make Barra Honda sound like a bleak place. In *The Geography of Costa Rica*, Miguel Obregón described it as "a white park . . . cones and rocky slopes . . . adorned with shrubs." When I visited in 1990 I found it covered with dense second-growth evergreen forest mixed with occasional gigantic old ceiba, guanacaste, and saman trees. Eroded limestone along the path still resembled "the bones of fantastic animals." When I entered one small cave and looked at the ceiling, I thought a snake was crawling across it, then realized that it was a serpentine calcium carbonate formation. These formations covered the ceiling, twisting in every direction. The cave was close to the surface, and I wondered if the formations were tree roots that had gotten covered with calcium carbonate. At the yawning entrance to one of the deep caves, La Trampa ("the trap"), a tan, fluffy object struggled in an overhanging tree. It was a fledgling mottled owl, evidently just leaving a nest.

La Nación articles in 1971 and 1973 touted the national park potential of Rincón de la Vieja, the most active volcano in Guanacaste Province, located to the southeast of Santa Rosa. The articles dwelt on the value of the mountain's forests for protecting the watershed of the agriculturally vital Tempisque River, and on its scenic wonders, which are impressive. At a place called Las Pailas ("the kitchen stoves"), a belt of fumaroles and hot springs surfaces in mixed dry and evergreen forest at the volcano's western base, creating a landscape out of Arthur Conan Doyle's dinosaur novel, *The Lost World*. Boiling gray mud shoots clots eight feet in the air beside still-living Indio desnudo trees; steaming pits open under the roots of strangler figs; hidden waterfalls cascade into pools overhung with white frangipani flowers. Farther up the volcano, one stands on windswept, rocky ridges that resemble alpine tundra and looks up thousands of feet at other ridges covered with rainforest. Treeline begins at about 11,000 feet in Costa Rica.

Newspapers in the early 1970s also contained articles about the park potential of two places that both happened to be named Guayabo (guava tree). One was an island in the Gulf of Nicoya; the other was a tract of second-growth rainforest near the town of Turrialba southeast of San José. Guayabo Island, along with three nearby islands, provided safe nesting rookeries for the west coast's brown pelicans, magnificent frigate birds, and brown boobies. It also contained the only undisturbed dry forest in the country outside Santa Rosa. The other Guayabo was the main archaeological site in Costa Rica, the remains of a pre-Columbian city of stone mounds, causeways, aqueducts, and tombs. Very little is known about the culture that built it, except that they produced impressive stonework and occupied the site from about A.D. 800 to 1400.

Both Guayabos became part of the park system in 1973. Barra Honda and Rincón de la Vieja became national parks in 1974, although it took many more years to acquire all the land in them. Land acquisition problems would lead to a temporary squatter invasion at Rincón de la Vieja, yet what Alvaro Ugalde wrote about Santa Rosa would apply to the other rapidly acquired parks of the early 1970s as well. Twenty years later, in 1990, they were real parks, with rangers and visitor facilities, and the trees and wildlife they were created to protect were still there.

Within five years, the Costa Rican system had grown from paper hopes to actual landholdings that included not only some of the nation's most significant scenic and cultural sites, but also what was beginning to be a fair sample of its ecological diversity. It was beginning to catch up with much older systems like the United States' (which grew hardly at all from 1970 to 1975, its budget frozen by the Nixon administration), and it had begun to pass the U.S. in one respect.

The U.S. park system grew up mainly on the public domain lands of the West, which allowed creation of large parks, but resulted in lopsided representation of ecosystems. In 1990, only about half of U.S. ecosystems were represented in the park system. From its hasty beginnings, and despite the huge cost of acquiring land not in the public domain, the Costa Rican park system tried to acquire land throughout the country, in every type of landscape and ecosystem possible. It was evolving toward a new kind of park system that would be a repository of a nation's biodiversity, of its ecological capital, as well as a showcase of its scenery.

five

Capitalists and Communists

Not all the early parks were even on the agenda set by Costa Rica's biologists and conservationists. A park proposal for a place on the central Pacific coast called Manuel Antonio (named for a conquistador buried there) came from such an unexpected source, and became such an explosive political situation, that Mario Boza apparently wished that it would just go away at first. "Mario was in some ways furious at what was happening," Vernon Cruz told me, "because he had enough trouble with Poás, Santa Rosa, and Cahuita."

Cruz had visited Manuel Antonio when he was in college, and thought it was "best for beauty" in the whole country. "It's fantastic," he told me, "all the vegetation from the whole coast, the dry forest to the north and the wet forest to the south, is combined there. And the forest comes right down to the water, so you can watch monkeys in the trees while you're watching the sunrise. The ocean is the best too, and when you combine it with the fragrance of the forest it's just fantastic. It's a pearl."

The townspeople of the nearby community of Quepos were equally enthusiastic about Manuel Antonio. Cruz had heard about it from another student whose father worked building roads in Quepos. The student told Vernon that he took his girlfriend to Manuel Antonio on his motorcycle every time he was in Quepos, and that the place made them both so happy they never quarreled there. Although the roughly eight mile road from Quepos to Manuel Antonio was then very bad, going there to romance or swim at the crescent-shaped white beaches was an old tradition by the 1970s.

Manuel Antonio wasn't a public beach, however. In fact, in 1972 it was one of only three private beaches in the country. All beaches are public property according to Costa Rican law, but for political reasons the government had traded Manuel Antonio to United Fruit for another piece of land in 1939. United Fruit had (and still has, in present corporate reincarnations) huge landholdings in southern Costa Rica, which it cleared of forest to grow first bananas, then African oil palms. Not having any use for the country's most beautiful beach, or for the steep headlands above it, the company sold Manuel Antonio to a Costa Rican, who sold it in 1967 to a North American named Herbert Blackburn.

Blackburn evidently had ideas of developing a resort, and put up a gate to restrict public access. In 1971, however, two other developers forced him to sell to them (according to Blackburn in a January 1975 article in *The Tico Times*, a San José English-language weekly). These developers "calculated the immense value" of Manuel Antonio, as Vernon Cruz put it, and aggressively began to implement plans for a hotel, restaurant, and houses.

The Quepos townspeople of course didn't like being shut out of their beach, but the developers evidently thought property would prevail over sentiment. They failed to reckon with local politics, however, because many Queposians were not only beach-lovers, but militant Communists. First brought to Costa Rica by Italian bakers in the late nineteenth century, Communism (also called Syndicalism) had become a major political force during the 1930s Depression in the parts of southwest Costa Rica controlled by the big fruit companies. In the 1940s, Communists formed part of a ruling coalition with the Catholic Church under the presidency of Rafael Calderón, Don Pepe Figueres's rival. Figueres suppressed the Communists for a while after overthrowing the Calderón coalition in the 1948 insurrection, but let them back into the Legislative Assembly after they promised not to try to overthrow the government illegally. The party eventually declined (oddly enough) after the Sandinistas took over Nicaragua, when overconfident, hard-line leaders initiated disastrous strikes against the fruit companies, but in 1972 the party still had many adherents.

The developers' attempts to close the beach in preparation for building on it met with a response that seems more characteristic of the monkey-wrenching ecoradicals of the late 1980s than polite 1970s environmentalism. The developers put up a fence; it was cut with pliers. They put up another fence; it was knocked down. The developers responded like comic book capitalists: they went to a town meeting in Quepos and threatened to cut the forest, bulldoze the entire site, and sue the town for two million dollars if the protests continued.

"There was a family in Quepos," Vernon Cruz told me, "very educated and well-to-do, also leftists, the most important people in town. They ran the pharmacy, their name was Mora-Black. They'd heard about the national parks, and they called up Mario and told him about the beach, and wanted the Park Service to help them save it. So we began to take a look at that place. I went down there and talked to the people about the importance of national parks."

On May 25, 1972, *La Nación* ran an article headlined "They're Closing Manuel Antonio and Espadilla" (Espadilla is the next beach over) with photos of workmen building a gate across the entrance road. Journalist Miguel Salguero (who wrote a great many articles about potential parks) quoted one of the developers, a French-Canadian named Arthur Bergeron, as insisting that it was legal for him to close the road. The article suggested a national park as a solution to the problem, and described Manuel Antonio in lyrical terms. "I've said it before," Salguero wrote, "if there's any place where the earthly paradise could be realized, it's Manuel Antonio. Here Adam and Eve could have lived happily, while the serpent would never have started the trouble. The forest that shadows the ocean's edge, the yellow sands, the transparent waters, with colors ranging from intense blue to emerald green, these make up a whole that invites one to stay and forget about other things."

Unimpressed with such visions of harmony, the developers proceeded with their gate, which the Quepos monkey-wrenchers proceeded to bomb. "That was a real problem," Vernon Cruz told me. "We had to make a decision. Here's a bomb, and Communists, and a whole town asking for a park? With other parks, local people say 'no, we want the land for cattle or some other private purpose.' But here, it was different. Here was a community asking for a park.

"So Mario said, 'What are we going to do?' He was thinking of sending a plane with a Peace Corps volunteer to fly over it and evaluate the quality of the land. He'd never been there; he didn't have time. The only opinion he had was mine, which was, 'Yes! For sure!' But Mario couldn't take the chance of trying to make a park just on one person's advice.

"Then we got a call from the Moras in Quepos, saying that the developer was starting to cut trees to build rental houses on the beach. He was armed, and ready to fight the whole town by himself. He'd decided to cut the trees to force the situation and demonstrate he was the owner. So we made a flight with Chris Vaughn, a Peace Corps volunteer, over all the beaches on the Pacific side, and he and Mario decided that Manuel Antonio had the only good white beaches in the area. And Mario, with all his tools and promptness and everything, wrote a law declaring Manuel Antonio a national park."

Local Deputy Pedro Gaspar Zúñiga sponsored the park bill and presented it to the Legislative Assembly. In late August 1972 the Municipality of Quepos held a meeting to hear the local people's views on the proposal. According to *The National Parks of Costa Rica*, "The entire town, including the Association of Small Farming Enterprises, the Union of Progressive Councils, the Student Council of Quepos High School, and the Youth Movement of Quepos, all declared themselves, in the middle of a gigantic rally, enthusiastically in favor of the creation of the park."

The next month, Deputy Zúñiga led a group of seven legislators on a visit to Manuel Antonio to evaluate the situation. According to a September 25 *La Nación* article, developer Arthur Bergeron was "so disturbed that he didn't want to talk to them." The legislators observed that he'd cut trees and begun bringing in construction materials for a planned tourist complex of a twenty-room motel, twelve cabins, a restaurant, and a marina. Someone also had dumped herbicide into the mangrove swamp back of the beach, killing several mangroves.

Bergeron's behavior was a fatal error in Costa Rica, where negotiation is a kind of eleventh commandment. The legislators decided that, in view of his attitude, they would present a motion the same day asking authorities to stop the developer's activities. They also decided to ask the government to buy the land. In November 1972 the assembly passed Law Number 5100 establishing a Manuel Antonio National Recreation Park, later shortened to Manuel Antonio National Park.

For some time it seemed doubtful that the government would be able to come up with the roughly $700,000 needed to buy back the gem it had so blithely traded away four decades before. There were attempts to abolish the park bill on the grounds of expropriation's high cost. The two developers defaulted on their loan, and Herbert Blackburn told *The Tico Times* that he had to spend $35,000 in court costs and legal fees to foreclose on them. But in the end, according to *The National Parks of Costa Rica*, "The Committee for the Development of Manuel Antonio National Park, led by Mrs. Margarita Black de Mora, an enthusiastic local leader, together with the National Park Service, fought to maintain the park and obtain the necessary funds, which were raised in 1975, by means of a bond issued by the government."

In 1990, $700,000 seemed a very low price for several hundred acres of the most beautiful coastline in Central America. Any of the brand new hotels and resorts that lined the road from Quepos to the park probably cost as much to develop. The value of having a piece of undeveloped coast for the tourists staying at the hotels to visit (as well as the Quepos townspeople) had become evident. The park was so popular with tourists and Costa Ricans that it became necessary first to exclude motor vehicles, then to ban camping. Visitorship in 1990 was two hundred thousand a year, a lot of people for a four-hundred hectare park (it was enlarged in 1980 to include more forest).

Manuel Antonio's ecological value also has become increasingly evident. Despite its relatively tiny size, it was still bursting with biodiversity in 1990. I'd rarely seen so much wildlife in a rainforest area. On a short trail leading from the beaches into the hills, three-toed sloths were visible every few hundred feet, draped like soiled scatter-rugs over cecropia trees. Troops of squirrel monkeys fed busily on swarms of green and black grasshoppers, and on fat grubs which they extracted from branches. On the beach trail after a late afternoon storm, gray-necked wood rails and dinosaur-like basilisk lizards (also called JesuCristo lizards because they can walk on water) stalked through the dusk.

At Cathedral Point, a soaring ancient forest of guapinol, sura, royal palm, panama, and dozens of other tree species (Boza cites 138 in the park) covers a steep headland. Capuchin monkeys and endemic coal-black squirrels approached almost to arm's length as I stood on a cliff over the ocean. Although the west coast lacks coral reefs, the rocky waters around the point swarm with colorful fish. Waves pulled me back and forth through schools of black-and-white-striped sergeant majors, yellow-spotted wrasse, blowfish, and blue tang. Tiny golden fish hovered in the lee of boulders like swarms of underwater bees.

One of the last patches of undisturbed forest on Costa Rica's central Pacific coast, Manuel Antonio protects organisms that are disappearing or gone elsewhere. It is the northernmost extension of the squirrel monkey's range, and the local subspecies, *Saimiri oerstedi citrinellus*, has lost most of its habitat outside the park. Eduardo Carillo, a biologist working in the park, told me that cutting forest to plant bananas had recently increased in the vicinity, threatening not only squirrel monkeys but other dwindling species such as ocelots. As at Cabo Blanco, jaguar, tapir, and spider monkeys are gone. Park Sub-Director Eduardo Rojas pointed out a threatened species growing next to the trail, a dark-leaved tree called black guapinol that is found only in Manuel Antonio, except for a few individuals in more extensive forests to the south.

The potential for conflict between wildlife and tourists was obvious in 1990. Conservationist Pedro León called Manuel Antonio: "an example of the need to carry out private investment around a park in a planned way, a test of sustainable tourism." The park staff seemed to be making the best of the situation. Beach vegetation was recovering from the trampling it underwent when camping was allowed. With the park closed to visitors from 4 P.M. to 7 A.M., wildlife had a chance to resume normal feeding habits. Biologist Carillo was studying the park's two raccoon species (one South American and the other North American). He told me their populations had become so large from eating camp garbage that they'd become a threat to herons and hawks, with which they compete for crabs and other natural foods.

They'd gone back to eating crabs and fruit in the two years since camping had stopped. Eduardo Rojas told me that four sea turtles had been able to nest on the beach in the past year and that the mangrove swamps were less contaminated with soap and shampoo than in the days when camping was permitted.

There was hardly any litter in the park. A piece of conceptual art that the staff had contrived in the bushes between Manuel Antonio and Espadilla beaches may have contributed to this remarkable cleanliness on the part of visitors. A huge spider web of cotton string was festooned with litter the staff had collected from the park, every object imaginable—snorkels, shoes, broken appliances. A sign asked visitors to help the spider by not leaving more.

six

The Osa Peninsula

By the time Manuel Antonio was paid for, Mario Boza was no longer the national parks director. He quit in 1974 and went to the National University to start a forestry program at the Department of Environmental Sciences. In a 1982 interview Boza told David Carr that he'd left government service because the Agriculture minister had wanted to transfer him away from parks to another position in the ministry.

The park system may have been getting too successful for others within the bureaucracy. "That was a dangerous moment," Vernon Cruz told me. "There was a lot of jealousy." The parks were still under the Forestry Directorate, but they were getting a lot more media attention than forestry, more than fish and wildlife, and they were beginning to get international attention and support. "It's much easier to see the benefits coming from an area which has borders, and rangers inside, than of a system of hunting permits," Alvaro Ugalde told David Carr in 1981. "People say, 'Hey, I saw it. I went there, I saw a fence, and outside the fence is nothing and inside are trees and animals and rangers—not too good, but they're there.' For the other agencies, since they didn't have a reserve system, it was much harder. . . . I grant them the resentment, if it existed. And definitely, people and politicians were diving to help the Park Service, and kind of putting the others beside because of that."

When Boza resigned in September 1974, Ugalde had recently returned from one year studying at the University of Michigan's Natural Resources Department with an OAS scholarship. He hadn't resigned from the parks, however, and the Agriculture minister of the new administration that had come to power in spring 1974 appointed *him* the new national parks director. The ministry perhaps thought he'd be easier to handle than Boza (although it's hard to imagine why they would have thought this).

Things didn't look encouraging for the park system in late 1974. Not only was it getting squeezed within the Agriculture ministry, but Daniel Oduber, the Guanacaste rancher who tried to give Santa Rosa back to the tourist board in 1970, had been elected president to succeed Don Pepe. Although thousands of acres of land had been protected in parks, they were still a drop in the bucket compared to the hundreds of thousands being deforested every year.

Olof Wessberg was increasingly concerned about deforestation. He had brought the management of Cabo Blanco under control after Boza had allowed him to pick the wardens. Karen told me he advertised for young candidates on the radio, then questioned them at length about their interest in nature protection. "He also asked them, 'What are you going to say to a gringo if he comes and offers 100,000 colones for giving him permission to hunt a puma?' And, you know, in those conditions, many of them answered, 'Well, of course, one has to think about it.' But there were two of them that said, 'Of course not. That's the reason we're paid, so that will never happen.' My husband chose them, and one of them is still there. He's been there eighteen years now."

Wessberg was especially concerned about an Oduber administration proposal to spend $3.5 million to establish six parks of a few hundred acres each within twenty miles of San José by 1976. A June 17, 1975, *La Nación* article quoted Oduber as saying, "This is to prepare a great recreational reserve for when the metropolitan area reaches from Paraíso to Grecia in 1990." Most of the land proposed for the parks wasn't old-growth forest—very little remained in the Meseta Central—but farmland and second growth. Wessberg saw the need for urban parks, but felt President Oduber's plan proposed spending too much for too little at a time when $3.5 million would have paid for a lot of Costa Rica's fast-disappearing primary forest. "It would be interesting to know how many of the 3.5 million dollars have been paid by the World Wildlife Fund, International Union for the Conservation of Nature, FAO, UNEP, UNESCO," Wessberg wrote in a July 1975 letter.

Costa Rica's fastest-disappearing forests were those of the Osa Peninsula, the southern peninsula of which Karen Wessberg had dreamed in 1955. About half as large as the Nicoya Peninsula, the Osa protrudes from the Pacific coast just north of the Panamanian border. Unlike the Nicoya, it has a very wet climate, and it is the northern extension of many South American rainforest species.

"The lowlands of southern Costa Rica," wrote forest ecologist Gary Hartshorn in *Costa Rican Natural History* in 1983, "are the only wet forests still extant on the Pacific side of Central America. The abundant rainfall coupled with a short, three-month dry season seems ideal for tree growth, for these forests are by far the most exuberant in Central America. In fact, the Corcovado forests are just as impressive in height as the best forests I have seen in the Amazon basin or the dipterocarp forests of Malaysia and Indonesia." The area Hartshorn specifically referred to, Corcovado, was a tract of land in mid-peninsula extending from a central ridge across an expanse of swamp to the coast.

Hartshorn estimated there were at least five hundred tree species in Corcovado alone, about two-thirds as many as in the continental U.S. Another biologist, Daniel Janzen, said that the Osa Peninsula contained the complete tropical insect ecosystem from Mexico to Panama. Ornithologist Gary Stiles counted 365 bird species in southwest Costa Rica, including eight that occur nowhere else, as well as the last sizable scarlet macaw population in the country. Until the 1970s, at least, the Osa probably supported every species that had inhabited the area when the conquistadors arrived, from harpy eagles to squirrel monkeys.

Apparently, humans never occupied the Osa in significant numbers. Pre-Columbian remains indicate a scattered hunting and gathering population. A 1930s gold rush took place under primitive conditions and didn't bring permanent settlement to most of the peninsula. Fidel Castro planned to move his headquarters to the Osa if his Cuban guerrilla campaign failed to topple the Batista dictatorship, but the move was not necessary after all.

Development began to close in on the Osa's wilderness in the 1960s. Most of southwestern Costa Rica already had been logged and converted to agriculture. Timber companies and the land speculators and squatters who followed them were moving west. In 1957 Osa Productos Forestales, a Costa Rican company owned by North American timber interests, bought over 100,000 acres of the northern Osa, including about half the Corcovado area. They began logging and rice cultivation in the Rincón area northwest of the Golfo Dulce (the bay between Osa and the mainland), but the terrain's ruggedness prevented them from extending operations into the heart of the peninsula for the time being.

Scientists and conservationists also followed the loggers on the Osa. Leslie Holdridge and Joseph Tosi, forestry professors at the Instituto Interamericano de Ciencias Agricolas in Turrialba, worked as consultants for Osa Productos Forestales in the early 1960s, developing forest management plans. Gerardo Budowski remembered flying to the peninsula at that time and seeing "huge machinery, twenty Caterpillar tractors, huge winches." After leaving Turrialba and founding the Tropical Science Center, a nonprofit, Costa Rican research organization, Holdridge and Tosi opened a biological field station on the Osa in 1964 on land leased from Osa Productos. The Organization for Tropical Studies, a consortium of U.S. universities, began sending students to the station in 1965, and a generation of North American biologists such as Hartshorn and Janzen were introduced to the Osa forests.

In 1970 John Ewel, a doctoral candidate at the University of North Carolina, made the first biological survey of Corcovado, a highly enthusiastic one. In 1972 a party including Christopher Vaughn, the Peace Corps volunteer who flew Mario Boza over Manuel Antonio, hiked into Corcovado and recommended to the forestry director that the area be made a park or reserve. Alvaro Ugalde then flew over Corcovado with the director to promote a park, but the director thought a park wouldn't be feasible, because squatters had already invaded the area. A 1973 proposal for a three-hundred-square-kilometer park at Corcovado failed to get support from President Figueres or the Legislative Assembly.

Meanwhile, development pressures were increasing. A new Osa Productos Forestales manager abandoned attempts to control growing squatter incursions on company land and began promoting land sales to wealthy North Americans. He planned to extend a road across the peninsula, build retirement communities on the beaches, and dredge the wetlands in the heart of Corcovado to make a huge inland marina. Conservationists feared that even if Osa Productos was persuaded to sell its land for a park, the squatters would cut the forest anyway. Armed, aggressive, and supported by the Communist party of the nearby United Fruit towns of Golfito and Palmar, the squatters had only to occupy land for three years to get legal title. Local property disputes were accompanied by occasional shootings and murders. "It's rather a tragic situation about which little can be done," Joseph Tosi wrote in a letter to John Ewel. "One must not block 'progress,' especially when such progress brings dollars into the Costa Rican economy, and also makes a few more fortunes for American businessmen."

Olof Wessberg decided to visit Corcovado in the summer of 1975. "We'd been thinking about the area since '73 or '74," Karen told me. "People told us about how beautiful it was, and somebody said that there were very many tapirs down there. My husband really loved tapirs. I asked him why once, and he said, 'They look so peaceful and innocent, and they're so big, the biggest mammal in Latin America, you know.' And, of course, we never had any tapirs here. They'd all been killed before we arrived." Olof Wessberg's ostensible reason for the trip was to look for wild avocado trees to graft onto his orchard stock, but he probably also wanted to add his voice to the rising chorus of alarm about the situation. He evidently was something of an outsider in the conservation establishment that was growing up in San José (Gerardo Budowski said he found Wessberg "strange"), but he had influence with the Park Service and international organizations. Perhaps he thought of writing another appeal.

The Corcovado situation was approaching a crisis at that time. Many squatters had been there almost three years and would be able to file land claims and begin serious clearing and burning during the December 1975 to March 1976 dry season. Rumors about impending mass logging were flying: A Japanese company wanted to buy the Corcovado forest and grind it into chips to pack stereos; an American company wanted to develop huge citrus plantations on the logged areas.

Wessberg planned to go in June, but hurt his foot, so he suggested that Karen go first and get a look at the place. She went in mid-June, flying to a little settlement called Sirena on the Corcovado coast, then walking twenty-three miles north along the beach to a squatter's village at Punta Llorona ("point of the weeping woman"). Llorona is just south of Corcovado's finest forest.

There Karen asked Feynner Arias Godinez, a squatter's teenage son who made a living by hunting and guiding, if he would take her to find the wild avocado Olof wanted. Godinez told her, however, that the tree wasn't bearing fruit at that time of year. Karen hired him as a guide anyway, and he accompanied her back to Sirena and showed her around until she left the next day. Karen told me she also "talked with several people, farmers down there, and told them that we really wanted this to be a national park."

"The virgin forest there is the most beautiful you can imagine in this world," Karen wrote to an English biologist soon after her return from Corcovado. "It is completely incomprehensible that there still exists anything that marvelous. . . . One evening at sunset, many dozens of red loras [scarlet macaws] fluttered around a big tree. Their red wings looked like red flames in the red light of sunset. It looked as if the whole tree was on fire.

"After walking several hours through virgin forest near Llorona de Osa," the letter continued, "I suddenly entered the first clearing. Later I walked through several others. . . . When I told the new settlers how much I enjoyed the virgin forest, they assured me that it would be much more beautiful once the land was cleared! My guide told me that around Corcovado Lake are found many hundreds of peccaries, and hundreds of tapirs. He told me that people are killing them just for fun, because they are killing more than they can consume themselves or sell. He also told me that rich cattle raisers from the northern province of Guanacaste are getting title to huge parts of the forest and sending gangs of workmen to clear the land with chain saws and plant grass right away. . . . How I wish that we could get the government to declare the whole area a nature reserve! I feel sure that a little encouragement from you and other conservationists in Europe would help a lot to that end."

Excited by Karen's stories, Wessberg left for Corcovado when his foot was better at the end of July. He boarded a launch that ran down the coast from Puntarenas, planning to spend a few days in Corcovado, then return by bus via San José. He told Karen he wanted to buy a new backpack. Perhaps he also meant to lobby for a park.

"A day or so after he left," Karen told me in 1990, "I went to Montezuma to pick up the mail. But the mailman wasn't in his office, he was in his house, a place very high up. My husband had been there, and he'd said, 'You should go up, it's beautiful. You see ocean and all around you trees, so it's like you're in a big forest.' So I walked up there, and I went out to look, and the postman's wife said, 'Be careful, Karen.' And I thought, 'How strange. That was exactly as in my dream nineteen and a half years ago.' I looked south and wondered if Olof had arrived. He was due to arrive that day. Then I went home.

"I was very tired, and I stopped to eat something. Suddenly, I felt a terrible pain in my head, and I said, 'Am I having a stroke?' But then it disappeared. Then I went to the kitchen, and suddenly it was in my heart, the same.

"That night, I dreamt Olof had come home, dressed in just his green military overcoat. He was completely white in his face. I said, 'Wow, back so soon.'

" 'Oh, it's very cold down here,' he said.

"I'd been eating a lot of stuff," Karen told me. "Sometimes you get bad dreams when your stomach's upset. But then the next night I had the same dream, although he didn't say anything, just looked at me. And then, the third night, I was told there was a telephone for me— and at that time there was no telephone in Montezuma. I went to the telephone box, and it was Olof, and then I told him how much I loved him. I told him so many words that in reality you don't tell. I could feel he got so happy to hear that. And then suddenly in the dream he was there, present, and he had a branch. He doubled it, bent it over double, and he said, 'Now I'll give this to you.' "

A week passed, and Olof didn't return. Karen went to Puntarenas to ask the people who ran the launch about him. "I was walking down the street," she told me, "and a young girl came up and said, 'Hello, Karen, did you find your husband? The newspaper said he's been missing nine days.'

" 'No,' I told her. 'It's somebody else,' because in those days there were a lot of people being murdered down there.

" 'No, it's your husband's name. And your name was mentioned too.' "

On August 2, *La Nación* published a short article headlined "Search for Missing Man." It reported that "Robertson Wesberg, resident of Montezuma and husband of Karen Magnoen" had walked into the forest outside Punta Llorona on July 23 saying he would return to spend the night at the house of Ivo Salazar, Feynner Godinez's father, but had never returned.

"I ran to some friends," Karen told me, "and said, 'Show me the paper.' They told me not to worry, but I had to go down there and find out. So I got a plane down there. The pilot landed me on the beach, and the plane had to leave right away because it was high tide. When I came to the cottages at Llorona, some boys were standing on the beach with their arms folded. That's when I knew something was really wrong, because usually boys come running out when a plane lands. I asked them if my husband had left anything. They answered, 'Yes, he left everything.' They told me he'd arrived about three in the afternoon, talked until four, then said he was going for a walk, and never came back.

"I thought perhaps he was lying somewhere waiting for help. I had come with an old man who knew the area well. I asked the boys to ask people to please help look for my husband, and offered a reward of 20,000 colones. Then I went into the forest with the old man and two boys. There were no trails then, but the forest was very open. I felt an urge to go to the right, and in a half hour I saw my husband's scout knife leaning against a tree. It was on a ridge, and I and the old man stayed there while the boys looked on the slopes.

"He was very religious, the old man. He was praying to spirits. Suddenly, I looked up and there was a big, beautiful hawk going up to blue heaven. I thought of Olof's favorite poem, by Robinson Jeffers: 'To be part of that, those wings and beak, what an enskyment . . .'

"Then later, the boys came together, and called the old man. He came to me, and he said, 'Now, Karen, we have found your husband.' And I knew they hadn't found him alive, because they would have been happy. I almost fainted, because I knew all hope was gone. And the old man said, 'Don't sit down. Come with us.'

"I said, 'No, I don't want to.' Because you know, after fourteen days . . . But he said, 'Yes, of course, you have to see your husband.' And only the bones were left, spread all over, no two bones together, and completely clean . . . clean. And in a way it was better. His clothes and his identification were there, so there was no doubt.

"The next morning, the old man came to me and said, 'Look, Karen, I want to talk to you. It wasn't a branch that fell on your husband.' [Wessberg's skull had a large hole in the back.] 'It was murder.' "

The man at whose cabin Karen spent that night, a squatter named Heriberto Chavez Lopez, had been drinking heavily. He told the old man that his son had gone into the forest with Olof, but returned alone and left that same evening, walking south along the beach and chartering a plane to San José the next day. The son, whose name was Omar Morales, lived in San José, where he was married and had a job. He had arrived at Llorona on the launch with Wessberg; evidently they'd gotten acquainted on the trip from Puntarenas. Wessberg planned to hire Feynner Godinez as a guide, but Feynner was away on a gold-mining expedition, and Omar offered to guide him.

When Morales came out of the forest alone, Feynner Godinez's family asked him where Wessberg was. Morales calmly replied that Olof had decided to go looking for Feynner. He then bought a chicken from Feynner's brothers and played football with them while his step-mother cooked it. After eating, he left. Feynner's family was surprised when they heard he'd chartered a plane. They didn't know where he'd gotten the money. Morales had told them he'd come to Corcovado to sell a chain saw.

This probably is all that will ever be known for certain about Olof Wessberg's death. From here, the story dissolves into a tangle of inconsistent or conflicting press reports and apparently rather perfunctory police work. "I sent for detectives," Karen told me. "After about a week they came, but they didn't know anything about being a detective. They let everybody touch the knife."

On August 14, *La Nación* reported that Olof's bones had been examined by authorities in San José. They said death appeared to have been violent, but weren't sure if a crime had been committed. That same day, *La Prensa Libre* and *La República* reported the arrest and confession of Omar Morales in San José. Karen told me that when detectives arrived at his home, Morales asked them what had taken them so long. *La República* printed the following dialogue between Morales and two "procuradores penales."

"The foreigner was walking in front of me, and it occurred to me to kill him."

"Was there any reason? Did you have a motive?"

"No, I just felt like killing him, so I let him have it with a machete on the back of the neck, and then got him with a log so he stayed down."

"Were you drunk or under the effects of marijuana?"

"I don't use drugs."

"But then why kill him?"

"Because I felt like it, simply for that."

"The declaration given by the presumed killer satisfied none of those who heard it," the *La República* article went on. "Sources from the Procuraduria General of the Republic said yesterday they will ask for a detailed investigation into the case, suspecting that other persons could have been involved, and that Morales was withholding information."

Karen told me that her attempts to aid in the investigation weren't encouraged. "I went to the detective—he was a big man in a uniform—and told him my husband had been killed down there, and that I would like him to find out if the man had been paid for it, if he could send some detectives out to Morales's wife, and the people he worked with, and see if he had any special friends. But he said, 'No, Señora! There's no reason for that. It's so clear that the man just thought your husband had money, and he needed it because he had a girlfriend.' [Morales said he'd taken six or seven hundred colones (around $85) from the body.] 'He was married but he had a lover.

When a man has a girl he needs money. I myself almost committed murder twice in my life because I needed money for a woman.' "

On August 17 *La República* carried a story quoting Karen as saying, "Enemies of conservation of the great natural resources of Costa Rica killed my husband." Karen described the creation of Cabo Blanco, and concluded: "My husband also wanted that Llorona or at least the part of it that hasn't been destroyed be declared a nature reserve, and the day that he arrived there they killed him. . . . Costa Rica, such a marvellous country, shouldn't perish at the hands of those who care for nothing but cutting trees, fencing beaches and building destruction."

On August 22 *La República* reported that Omar Morales had withdrawn his confession and accused his father, Heriberto Chavez, of the murder. His father denied it, and the police decided to take them both back to Llorona to try to reconstruct the crime. The article said, "The police didn't wish to give details. Nevertheless this increased suspicions that the homicide of naturalist Wessberg could very well have been a 'contract' killing."

On August 25 *La Nación* broke a long silence on the case with an article headlined "Reconstruction of Crime Today on Osa Peninsula." It said father and son appeared to be the main suspects, but, from the interrogation, the police wouldn't rule out the possibility of others. The next day, *La Nación* carried a story headlined "No Clues to Trap Oloff Weisberg's Killers." It reported that the killing had not been solved, and that clues that had seemed certain had "faded." The article summed up the case to date, and quoted "Karen Moy de Weisberg" as saying that "her husband had come into conflict with certain organizations and people who, to start businesses of a certain kind, had dedicated themselves to destroying the natural resources her husband considered vital. The Señora implied that this could be a possible reason for the killing. She stressed that her husband was a peaceful person and well-liked. She emphasized that no one had a reason for killing him the way they did."

On August 28 *La República* carried an article headlined "Case Closed." "Presented with irrefutable proof," it said, "the youth Omar

Morales again admitted to being the sole author of the crime." Detectives had found presumed murder weapons, a machete and a branch, near where the body had been found. Shown the weapons, Morales had said "in a firm and decided voice: 'Good, let's leave it and stop lying. I was the one who did the homicide, and my father had nothing to do with it.' "

"Nevertheless," the article continued, "an uncertainty remained in the atmosphere. What was the true motive of the crime? It seemed Morales was hiding something very important that he didn't want to reveal. Perhaps with time, and when he's within the four private walls of his freedom, he'll be able to tell the truth. Morales will stay in the penitentiary and his sentence could be 25 years, only because he 'just felt' like killing another person who had the sole mission of turning the reserves of Punta Llorona into an 'absolute nature reserve' to rescue the few natural resources our country has."

An August 29 *La Nación* article headlined "Presumed Homicide of Señor Nicholas Weissberg" also reported Morales's renewed confession, "although the exact motive has not been established, because although Morales admitted he took 700 colones that the victim carried, he alleged he hadn't known he was carrying money." The press was silent on the case after that date, as far as I could determine.

"I saw the murderer in court," Karen told me. Newspaper photos showed a handsome, sad-looking youth with dark skin and curly hair. Morales looked like a typical Guanacasteco, which in fact was where he'd come from. "He had a very clever lawyer, a woman. She convinced the court it was an impulse killing, so he got the smallest sentence, eight years." An August 28, 1975, article in another paper, *Excelsior*, reported that "Morales affirmed that he'd been a communist for some years and that the communists would defend him."

"But very soon," Karen recalled, "the murderer got killed in prison. I knew his wife's brother, and one day I saw him in San José and he said, 'You know, your husband's murderer has been murdered himself. He was fighting with another prisoner, and the two of them killed each other.

"The murderer said my husband was looking up at some squirrel monkeys just before he hit him," Karen said. "I can imagine he was really happy to see the monkeys. A man who walked with him from San Pedrillo [near where the launch from Puntarenas had landed] to Llorona said that it usually took two hours for the walk, but that it took Olof six hours because he was so excited; he kept stopping to look at things."

I'd walked from San Pedrillo to Llorona in 1987, so I understood something of how Wessberg must have felt. Although I stubbed my toe so badly walking on the San Pedrillo rocks (the only access was still by boat) that it may have been fractured, I felt a surprising euphoria in the forest. We didn't see much animal life, just leafcutter ants, lizards, the odd antbird or quail dove. Yet one seldom gets a chance to walk for a morning through a forest of five-foot-diameter trees whose trunks don't branch until they're forty or fifty feet from the ground. Every few minutes, the guardaparque would nick a trunk with his machete and have a quizzical discussion with our Costa Rican guide about what species it might be. With leaves and fruit a hundred feet in the air, the color and taste of wood are among the more reliable ways of distinguishing among five hundred species.

I had never heard of Olof Wessberg then. When we got to Punta Llorona, which gets its name from a waterfall that drops over a cliff on the beach, I saw no evidence of the squatter village the Wessbergs had stayed in, no evidence that anyone had ever lived there. The only creatures on the beach were myriad delicate scarlet crabs that drifted over the sand like windblown dust, and a lone, motionless black hawk.

seven

Corcovado National Park

Whatever effect Wessberg's murder might have had on the Corcovado situation remains as obscure as the murder itself. Some accounts of Osa conservation issues ignore the murder, although it got some attention from Scandinavian media in the late 1980s. Most of the people I talked to in Costa Rica in 1990 thought Wessberg's killer was a lone madman, like Lee Harvey Oswald.

This was not so in 1975, however. On August 20 Actualidades Columbia Radio in San José broadcast the following editorial: "The saint's calendar of conservationists has one martyr more: Hugo [yet another of Olof's names] Wessberg. His blood has fallen on the land he loved so much and tried to set free from its voracious and pitiless enemies, and from this day it will continue to give support to his conservationist leadership, and to call for Justice from nature's Creator.

"Assassins! If they succeed in mocking the justice of men, they will not escape the justice of God. The blood of a righteous man has fallen on their consciences and will haunt them until the last day of their lives. The money they make from exploiting trees and human lives will burn their hands and lead only to their perdition. Costa Rica must save Punta Llorona from the destructive hands of these criminals, make it an absolute reserve as Hugo Wessberg wanted. This reserve should bear his name, and a monument should commemorate his martyrdom, as an example to future generations."

On August 21 *La República* carried an article headlined "Monument for Foreigner Who Died to Save Forests." The article quoted none other than Daniel Oduber, President of the Republic.

" 'The foreigner who died to defend natural resources deserves a monument,' declared President Daniel Oduber to a question from our reporter concerning government policy on defense of resources. 'Hugo Wessberg, a foreigner, dedicated most of his life to defending the forest reserve of Cabo Blanco from ranchers and loggers. He was assassinated by order of one of the big landowners of the region. . . . When one sees one of the films about the Middle East and compares it with our country we see that the situation is not much different. Here we kill people for defending a tree, an animal, a plant. This is very grave.'"

Yet if Wessberg's murder *was* a conspiracy, it was a very stupid conspiracy. The tide was already beginning to turn in favor of a park at Corcovado, as the rest of Oduber's August 21 remarks show. "The foreigner who protected the natural resources of Costa Rica will be vindicated. I am working to establish a reserve in the Corcovado region, one of the last natural areas in the country."

Oduber had undergone a change of attitude toward national parks since his attempt to remove Santa Rosa from the system. The change evidently grew at least partly from his fights with Boza and Ugalde. In a 1982 interview he told David Carr that he'd begun to favor parks because he wanted to promote tourism, and Boza and Ugalde had convinced him that tourism based on nature appreciation was more appropriate for Costa Rica than the casino and resort tourism of Mexico and the Caribbean. Oduber said he'd always been interested in natural history and archaeology, that he'd always known Costa Rica was a bridge between human cultures, and that Boza and Ugalde had convinced him that it was also an ecological bridge between continents. This seemed a good reason to set aside parks and reserves.

Apparently Alvaro Ugalde wasn't fully aware of Oduber's conversion to parks, because he told Robert Cahn in a 1979 *Smithsonian* article that he tried to keep out of the new president's way after the 1975 election. "But one day, I ran plunk into the President coming out of a building. 'Ah, Ugalde! Where are you now?' the President asked.

" 'In the parks department,' I replied.

" 'Come see me,' he said. My heart sank. But I was surprised. Instead of Oduber being revengeful, he became the greatest friend the national parks ever had."

"Daniel Oduber was a rancher, and a very smart person," Ugalde

told me in 1990. "He saw what happened in Guanacaste—the deforestation and overgrazing, then the droughts, streams drying up. He
also took part in the 1955 battle at Santa Rosa, so he liked it a lot. He
still visits there quite often, just shows up. All of a sudden, there was
a bunch of people fighting for it, and he had his ranching friends up
there pushing him to do evil, and there was us, pushing him to do
good things. He used to come to the park a lot when I was administrator. He'd come because Pedro Abreu, our enemy who moved his
fence into the park and ran his cattle on it, asked him to order me to do
something. But then, after we'd talked, he'd end up telling Abreu,
'Do what Alvaro says.' "

Sigifredo Marín, a park administrator in Guanacaste, told me another story about Oduber at Santa Rosa. Once, a guardaparque
named Felix found the president and his minister of security in the
park with guns in their car. When Felix told them it was illegal, the
minister pointed at Oduber and said, "You know, he's the president."
Felix took out his plastic guardaparque identification card, showed it
to them, and asked Oduber if he had a card identifying him as president. Oduber didn't, so Felix detained them and took them to the
park director. Oduber said it would be a better world if everybody did
their jobs as thoroughly as Felix.

"I think he liked us," Ugalde told me. "He saw that we were beginning to get Santa Rosa under control in spite of him and Abreu. And
he became aware that conservation could be a very good political issue. When I asked him to chair a commission to analyze Costa Rican
natural resources in 1975, everybody was very impressed with what
he said. He never said stupid things about conservation. You heard
other politicians say things that didn't make sense, but Oduber always made sense."

Nature tourism evidently was a major factor in Oduber's decision
to support protecting Corcovado. One of the many scientists who
had visited Corcovado and written Oduber about it was Dr. Paolo Capelli of the University of Bologna. Capelli's letter offered some sug-
gestions about how tourism revenue might help to pay for a park
there. Oduber gave Ugalde the letter and told him to look into the feasibility of a Corcovado National Park. Joseph Tosi had been writing a

report for the World Wildlife Fund on Corcovado's park potential, and Ugalde asked him to finish it. The report helped incline Oduber toward signing a decree establishing the park. (Costa Rican parks can be established either by presidential or legislative decree, unlike U.S. parks, which can only be created by Congress.)

The fall dry season was due to begin, and with it the expected mass invasion of squatters, but the government hesitated, waiting for tokens of support from the international conservation community. The international conservation community also hesitated, unsure whether the Costa Rican government was capable of supporting a park on Corcovado's wild frontier. Finally, Joseph Tosi took $10,000 which the Rare Animal Relief Effort had donated to the Tropical Science Center's Monteverde Cloud Forest Reserve and suggested that it be used for Corcovado immediately after it was decreed a park. The World Wildlife Fund then donated another $10,000 for Corcovado, and Oduber signed the park decree on October 31, 1975.

The decree was only a beginning, of course. Some of Oduber's ministers quickly began urging him to rescind it, but he held firm, supported by letters from scientists and conservationists. *La República* ran an article on one letter on December 18, 1975. Daniel Janzen had written Oduber that Corcovado was the first time anyone had shown the courage to establish a rainforest park in lowland Central America, a good precedent. Janzen reiterated that Corcovado was a complete ecosystem, with all the vertebrate and, even more important, all the invertebrate species native to the area. He added that, in the long run, Corcovado was too swampy for anything but a wildlife refuge. A few months later, *La Nación* carried an article headlined, "Creation of Corcovado Causes Admiration in 52 Countries."

Oduber eased concerns about the new park's future at a meeting on January 8, 1976. Ugalde and Tosi presented plans for developing and funding the park, and Oduber promised full political and financial support, including an initial grant of one and a half million colones in 1976 from the presidential office's discretionary fund. The Park Service was to get nine new guard positions as well as eleven members of the Rural Guard to man four posts and patrol property lines in the Osa. Although first hesitant at committing itself to the park, the Costa Rican government ultimately would pay most of its establishment costs (as it did for most parks).

Corcovado National Park had a definite advantage in that about half of it was already government land. The rest, about 16,000 hectares, had to be bought from Osa Productos Forestales. Fortunately, administrative changes had left the company more amenable to conservation. It had gotten rid of the land-promoter manager, whose antics had so enraged the Legislative Assembly that they'd begun debating expropriation of OPF lands in 1974. In 1976 the government acquired OPF's Corcovado property through a land trade.

The biggest problem facing the Park Service was relocation of the more than a hundred (possibly as many as three hundred) squatter families already living in the park. Most had entered within the past few years; conversion of banana plantations to less labor-intensive oil palm was causing unemployment in the area. About fifteen families had been there since 1950. The new arrivals had already cut about ten percent of the forest in the park (mainly in the southwest section) and had brought in hundreds of cows and pigs. As at Santa Rosa, Costa Rican law and public opinion demanded that squatters be compensated for improvements (including forest cleared) and moved away at government expense. At Corcovado, squatters would have to be relocated by boat or plane, since there were no roads.

Ugalde had seriously underestimated the numbers of squatters in his first park proposals. He went to Oduber with trepidation to break the news that it would cost almost ten times his original estimate to relocate them. "I was sure I'd be fired the day I had to tell the news to the president," he told Robert Cahn, "but he took it calmly, telling me, 'It may cost ten million colones now, but how much would it cost fifty years from now? We'll do it.'"

The Tropical Science Center lent the Park Service its Monteverde Reserve administrator, Roger Morales, as a special coordinator to deal with squatter relocation and other issues of starting the park. "My first problem," Morales told me in 1990, "was trying to identify the problems of the squatters, and how we could help them leave. And my first idea was to hire a man who lived there to get information, to find out who the leaders were." Morales hired Feynner Godinez, Karen Wessberg's former guide, to spend a month attending meetings of squatters' groups and talking to people. "He told me the first thing was that the Communist Party was very strong there. So after that, I made a date with the Communist deputies at the Legislative Assembly and asked them if they'd accept a national park. They said, 'Yes, but you must treat us well.' So we made a proposition: we'd treat them well, but we needed them out. And they accepted.

"The Communist Party gave us an adviser, a lawyer. Sometimes, when we were meeting with the squatters, he'd help to calm them. Sometimes, on the way in on the plane, he'd tell our representative what he was planning to do—warn him if he was going to give him a hard time. He'd say, 'The people are going to ask you this or that. What are you going to say?' But other times, he'd take advantage of the situation. It was difficult, because the non-Communist squatters didn't want to be treated the same as the Communists. Each group had its own committee, so we had to deal with that.

"From the first day," Morales told me, "we said the squatters couldn't do any more farming. They could harvest crops already planted, but nothing else. They said, 'Okay, but how are we going to feed our families?' So we did a census and decided to provide food staples for families every two weeks. But after three or four times of doing that, we saw it was impossible to control that and bring all the supplies in, so we changed to giving them money. Meanwhile, the Communists were saying we had to bring boats and planes in to take the people out.

"The amount they got from us was excellent. We probably spent ten percent more than we should have because of cheating. Many people took advantage of us. We had a lot of difficulties with over fifteen hundred people to be relocated on a very short schedule. Some people wanted to be paid twice the value of their property or improvements. People said they'd been there five years when they'd actually been there one year. Every family was different. Some took the money and left the next day; some hung around and wanted to be paid again. Some of them had to be taken out of the park by force. I had to take my gun out of its holster three times, but I never had to shoot. Once about two hundred or three hundred squatters surrounded us in a house wanting money. They were very angry, threatening, but we stayed in there very quietly, and after a while they went away."

A brusque, stocky man, Morales downplayed what must have been a fairly sensational period. Sergio Volio, who told me about Santa Rosa's vanishing macaws, was one of the first park guards at Corcovado. He told me Ugalde called a special meeting to ask for volunteers to go to Corcovado because of the danger. "It was like a novel by Gabriel García Márquez," Volio said. "It was a war, almost. But it gave me a heroic feeling. I had a .38 pistol with six bullets, total, and when I fired them they didn't always go. We were threatened many times with machetes.

"There was a woman, one of the biggest women I've ever seen, all muscle too. She had two husbands. And she was a witch, what people call a witch. She had one of those sugarcane cutting machetes that was shiny with use. She'd carry her two husbands across the river Sirena, you know, and everyone was scared of this woman because she was bad. Every morning, I had to sweep away stuff I found around our little house at Llorona. I used to find little plastic bags with hairs, you know, witchcraft stuff, for *me*, because I was the park guard. . . . That was the closest I've come to doing something heroic."

Juan Diego Alfaro, who was at Corcovado in 1975 with Morales and Volio, remembered that there were "very good houses at Sirena, with various houses scattered around other places. But no churches, although there were other kinds of religions. A lot of the people who weren't Communists were other kinds of Marxists, Trotskyists, so it was a kind of triangle between us, the Communists, and the Trotskyists."

"It took a year to get most of the squatters out," Roger Morales told me. "We were really happy with the success we had. There were still people there, but it was under control." It eventually cost the Costa Rican government $1.7 million to evacuate the squatters, a sum that didn't become fully available until Oduber declared the park a national emergency in July 1976. International organizations contributed $100,000 to support the park until the Costa Rican money came through.

By 1978 even the squatters' pigs and cows had been removed, or eaten by the park's jaguars (or by the park's staff or researchers, since no other source of fresh meat was available). The only squatters left in the park were some fifteen to twenty seminomadic gold prospectors or *oreros*, some of whom had been there since the 1930s gold rush. They were considered almost part of the native fauna and flora, and most of the gold-mining areas—the rivers of the south-central peninsula—were outside the original park boundary, so the oreros weren't seen as a threat to the park. If anything, they were considered a quaint historical feature (although the Park Service would have cause to regret this tolerance).

Despite the trouble Corcovado caused, and would continue to cause, I didn't encounter anybody who doubted in the least its value as a park. Janzen may have exaggerated when he called it Central America's first lowland rainforest park. Although partly logged, Tortuguero was a lowland rainforest park when it was created in 1970. As part of the huge east coast rainforest that once stretched from Colombia to Yucatán, Tortuguero actually has a greater diversity of organisms, such as birds, than Corcovado. Yet Corcovado has an extraordinarily dramatic and colorful ecosystem that strikes the observer more forcefully than the steaming greenness of the flat Caribbean coast. Corcovado seemed to me like an expanse of Sonoran Desert with a rainforest growing on it. The air has a burning clarity at the same time it is loaded with jungle smells and humidity. The thunderheads that loom out to sea every afternoon seem carved of translucent stone, and the deepest shadows under the trees have a kind of luminosity.

Corcovado wildlife sometimes seems ostentatiously showy, as though striving to come up to expectations. At Tortuguero, the iguanas and basilisk lizards were good-sized, two or three feet long, but green and hard to see among the foliage. Corcovado iguanas and basilisks were significantly larger than their Tortuguero counterparts, and they were red—not bright red all over, but with conspicuous scarlet patches on the head and back. They weren't at all retiring. Iguanas chased each other up steep river bluffs, then dove into the water with hearty splashes. Basilisks the size of small dogs eyed me from trailside, reluctant to get up on their hind legs and trot away as their lighter Caribbean cousins would have done. Even the cichlids in the little Corcovado creeks were big and reddish.

It's easy to see why the Osa Peninsula evokes thoughts of gold and precious stones. When I first arrived there the red-leaved almendro trees lining the beach were full of macaws. When I looked out the window on my first morning there I saw a half-dozen king vultures in a tree, their white plumage sparkling like enamel.

eight

Watersheds

In 1976 Daniel Oduber received the Animal Welfare Institute's Albert Schweitzer award for his role in protecting Corcovado. In his acceptance speech he said, "Our respect for our people extends to future generations, and our respect for diversity in human society includes a desire to maintain and preserve the diversity of nature. This is the reason why Costa Rica firmly and emphatically rejects the point of view that preservation of the natural environment is a preoccupation of privileged nations, and a benefit that poor nations and developing nations cannot enjoy.

"We are a developing nation, and nevertheless we consider vital the preservation and protection of the natural environment. . . . We don't need violence against the people or against nature to develop our country and escape from poverty. On the contrary, respect for nature is essential to our development policies, as it is to our philosophy of human society."

Despite his emphasis on tourism as a reason for parks, Oduber's thinking seems to have gone beyond the preservation of scenic wonders for recreation and foreign revenue. His administration saw addition to the park system not only of scenic wonders, but also of substantial tracts of land with great environmental as well as scientific significance. Oduber evidently realized, as few politicians then did (and few do now), that destruction of natural ecosystems is a real disaster, not just a nuisance or a remote pity.

"The effects of wildlife devastation," he said in an *Excelsior* article about his declaration of 1977 as a Year of Natural Resources, "are worse than those of an earthquake. Scientists estimate it takes from five to ten thousand years to completely reconstruct a virgin rainforest." That year Oduber signed decrees giving legal protection to a long list of endangered species, including macaws, quetzals, harpy eagles, great currassows, all cats, tapirs, manatees, jabiru storks, crocodiles, and caimans, and giving the park system a more independent status under a Park Service within the Agriculture Ministry, a status Boza and Ugalde had always wanted. In an October 20, 1977, *La Nación* article, Oduber said that humanity had "committed its greatest error" in hoping to improve the quality of life while "forgetting and destroying the environment which is the basis of existence."

Corcovado was not the first or the biggest park established under Oduber. On August 19, 1975, the Legislative Assembly decreed a 43,700-hectare national park around 12,500-foot Cerro Chirripó, the highest peak in southern Central America. The new park had plenty of scenery. Chirripó and other granitic peaks around it were glaciated some 25,000 years ago, so the park's upper elevations are a landscape of cirques, lakes, cols, and ice-carved, U-shaped valleys unique in Central America. The northernmost extension of the Andean association of shrubs and grasses called *paramo* grows here. In a 1965 *La Nación* article, Miguel Salguero described one of the Chirripó valleys as "perhaps the most beautiful, although silent, topographical sites in all the national territory. Rarely are so many wonderful things combined to regale man's senses."

Alvaro Ugalde told me that Chirripó wasn't a controversial park. "It was a famous landmark for hikers. A man who liked to hike there a lot proposed it in the assembly, and of course we supported it." Yet the park wasn't simply a "wilderness on the rocks." The proposal included thousands of hectares of the same high altitude oak forest that the "paper" Pan American Highway National Park had failed to protect in the 1940s and 1950s.

With over a half-dozen evergreen oak species reaching heights of over one hundred and fifty feet and diameters of over eight feet, this forest was called "truly unique" by W. R. Barbour, one of the first scientists to study it. The park proposal also contained significant areas of two other forest types, cloud forest and mid-elevation rainforest. Together, these forests (and those of the rest of the Cordillera de Talamanca stretching south from the Meseta Central into Panama) made up the biggest block of quetzal habitat in the world, and contained the biggest quetzal populations.

Putting a big chunk of the Talamancas off limits to logging set a precedent for more than quetzal preservation. "Talamanca contains the largest concentrated reservoir of water resources, in the sense of potable water and irrigation water, in Costa Rica," said Jim Barborak, an Ohioan who has been working as a conservation consultant in Central America since the 1970s. "The electricity grid that starts in dams on rivers that drain those mountains is already connected from central Panama to northern Honduras, and will soon connect into Guatemala and El Salvador, potentially into southern Mexico someday. You mess with that, and you're messing with the future of Central America. . . . Cloud forests as water factories play a role in the daily lives of everyone in the country. You can think of Talamanca rangers as sitting with the control valve to a water pipe. If they don't do their job, and the forest gets destroyed, that control valve gets shut off. Every Costa Rican, even in the most remote corner of the country, and most Central Americans, would be negatively impacted."

It's easy to get a sense of what Barborak means in the valleys surrounding the Talamancas. Slopes are dizzying, yet burned pastures and coffee plantations extend far upward from level bottomland. In daily rainy season downpours, runoff from these slopes is dark brown or orange with soil. (A vice minister of natural resources, Jorge Rodriguez, once said, "Topsoil is Costa Rica's largest export.") Only toward the heads of valleys, where forest is protected, do streams run clear. In the dry season, when valleys are parched and palled with dust, headwater forests remain surprisingly wet and green.

Talamancan headwaters reminded me of the California mountains. Alder and oak bordered streams roared over beds of clean sand and diorite boulders. (North American West Coast forests of ten million years ago probably resembled the forests of today's Central American highlands.) One day I watched a water ouzel, considered the spirit of California Sierra rivers by John Muir, searching underwater for insects in the Rio Macho watershed at the Talamancas' north end. Clay-colored robins in the alders sang just like their North American congeners. A movement upstream caught my eye, and I looked up in time to glimpse a magnificent black tayra, a tropical forest otter relative, run across the river on the stones.

In the 1960s the Costa Rican government established forest reserves to protect watersheds. Such reserves have been less successful than parks in protecting Costa Rican forest, however. As in U.S. national forests, commercial logging is allowed in forest reserves, and farmers and ranchers often follow loggers in Costa Rican forest reserves. Much forest reserve land has been converted to crops or pasture; much is in private hands. "It's a big mistake to try to manage a forest that doesn't belong to you," Mario Boza told me. "Parks have worked better than reserves because we own them, and because the Park Service has a clear mandate to protect land, while the Forest Service has a lot of other responsibilities."

Although Chirripó's creation was not controversial, the park has had its problems. Fires caused by arsonists or careless neighbors have swept large areas in drought years because access by firefighters is difficult. The fires mainly have burned the grass and shrubs of the high paramo, however, and the paramo may depend on fire for perpetuation, since forest might invade even the peaks without it. Andean plants may survive in Costa Rica because fires have kept the summits bare since the glaciers melted.

Even more environmentally important than Chirripó was another park that, like Manuel Antonio, came to be almost by accident. The Cordillera Central between the Meseta Central and the Caribbean is covered with some of the densest, wildest forest in the country, but this had been regarded more as an obstacle than an asset because it separated San José from the Atlantic seaways. An overland route to the coast was a preoccupation of Costa Rican leaders since the time of Braulio Carrillo, an 1830s strongman who did much to consolidate nationhood.

It was not until 1882 that a combined road and railroad financed by North American entrepreneur Minor Keith linked San José and the Caribbean port of Limón. The road section of this system, built for oxcarts, lasted only nine years until a completed railroad replaced it. An attempt to rebuild the road in the 1930s was a failure. Except for the railroad, the Cordillera remained virtually undisturbed, a wilderness full of jaguars and tapirs twenty miles from the booming metropolis that greater San José became after 1950. Driving to the Caribbean meant dizzying hours on bumpy roads through the populated but steep country from Cartago to Turrialba.

A modern freeway linked San José to the Pacific by the early 1970s, and pressure grew for a link to the Caribbean. In 1973 a proposal surfaced for a highway linking San José first with Guápiles to the northeast, then to Limón. The proposed road bisected the wild cordillera, cutting through a mile of its summit with a tunnel. Opposition to the proposal also surfaced. Conservationists feared a road would open the area to an Amazon-style land rush of settlers who would cut and burn the forest, destroying much of the Meseta Central's water supply in the process. Farmers on the Cordillera's west side also opposed the road because it would have required expropriation of their land.

The World Bank planned to finance the road, and hired the Tropical Science Center (TSC) to conduct an environmental impact study on it in 1975. Leslie Holdridge and Joseph Tosi found ample cause for concern. According to a *La Nación* article of August 3, 1978, the TSC study found that "the proposed road crosses zones of virgin jungle and steep, very wet terrain which, because of their natural condition, should either not be exploited, or should be managed under rigorous conservation practices, during and after construction, to prevent disastrous effects to the work itself, to the hydrological regimen of the rivers which begin in the mountains, and to the lands, economy, and people of the Atlantic plains." Holdridge and Tosi estimated the quantity of the area's 4,500-millimeter average annual precipitation that the forest transpired back into the atmosphere, then projected what that added quantity of water would do to the area's stream system if the forest were destroyed. They predicted massive floods that would, among other effects, destroy the new highway.

"The Tropical Science Center recommended that the forest along the road be protected," Alvaro Ugalde told me, "and the idea of a Cordillera Forest Reserve was born out of that concern. Then the road went ahead, and some of the conservationists' recommendations weren't being followed until a man from Heredia named Morales began to raise hell about water and watersheds."

Pedro León, the biologist who had encouraged Ugalde to take the national parks training seminar in 1969, was involved in the road debate. The son of a Cuban Protestant minister, León once told me, "If you don't have a cause, you're not an adult." By the mid-1970s he was on the University of Costa Rica faculty and active in the Colegio de Biólogos. "There was a lot of concern and organized pressure from all sorts of groups about the road," he said. "I remember writing articles with the argument that unless a park was created along the road, there wasn't going to be a road—that erosion would destroy it. There were all these discussions at the Colegio de Biólogos about whether we should just oppose the road, flat opposition, or whether there'd be something to be gained by saying, 'We won't oppose it, but we have some conditions that we want to implement.'"

"Finally," Ugalde told me, "the government began to get its act together about doing something there. Then the Park Service moved in, and we tried to declare a park not just along the road but in a big area there." President Oduber signed an executive decree establishing a Braulio Carrillo National Park in 1977. More negotiation was required before the Legislative Assembly passed a Braulio Carrillo bill the next year, but the final outcome was a 32,000-hectare park around the road. The U.S. Agency for International Developent provided a $1.2 million loan to prepare a five-year management plan for the park. "Braulio Carrillo will be the most highly used park when the road is completed," a Peace Corps advisor said in a November 1982 Tico Times article. "For this reason, we are going to build Costa Rica's main environmental education center here."

"Braulio Carrillo," Pedro León told me, "is a classic example of how you can sometimes succeed if you're willing to compromise." The August 3, 1978, La Nación article, headlined "Progress Confronts Destruction," included a similar sentiment from engineer Max Sittenfeld: "The highway and all the anxieties which construction has awakened with respect to protection of the natural watershed is the best that could have happened, because it has allowed a specific law to be sent to the Legislative Assembly and has brought an end to the creeping deforestation which, independent of the road construction, has been going on for several years." The article's author, however, was more tentative. "The engineers and ecologists have done their part," he wrote. "The one designed the future, the other expressed the means of prevention that must be taken for this future to be realized. Nevertheless, the politicians will be the ones to have the last word. In ten years, we will know the results of the most expensive road work ever done in Costa Rica." The November 1982 *Tico Times* article concluded, "If the Park Service succeeds in tightening its grip on management and development in Braulio Carrillo, residents and visitors can look forward to an unusual journey through a previously impassable wilderness treasure."

The San José–Guápiles Highway opened in 1987. I participated in one of the massive weekend traffic jams heralding the opening during my trip to Tortuguero. Traffic has thinned since then, and it takes about twenty minutes to zoom across Braulio Carrillo National Park, which, if one discounts the freeway across it, has remained breathtakingly wild. There is something eerie about the juxtaposition of a freeway and a never-logged forest extending to the horizons. One might be seeing places on distant hillsides that never have been stepped on, perhaps never will be. Only a few trails lead from the road, and they are discouragingly steep and slippery and peter out before too long.

At one trailhead, I stood on a ravine's edge with the roar of downshifting diesels in my ears and watched a lesser anteater, or *tamandua*, rip bark with its front claws and climb down a tree trunk with the bowlegged aplomb of a telephone repairman. Howler monkeys roared back at the diesels. Snowcap hummingbirds barely larger than bumblebees squeaked and squabbled over mating territory in white and yellow flowered shrubs.

"Braulio Carrillo may be one of the most interesting parks in the world," Gerardo Budowski told me, "totally unknown even though a half-hour away from a big city."

nine

The Zoo and the Sandinistas

"Fights during the Oduber administration were almost nonexistent," Alvaro Ugalde told me. "The president was supporting everything." Ugalde said that under Oduber the Park Service budget tripled; the staff increased to four hundred; and park acreage nearly doubled, with another two percent of the country added to the 2.5 percent placed in the park system under the Figueres administration.

Ugalde's open personality was suited to this rapid expansion. Some of the park people I talked to began their careers by simply walking into his office and asking for jobs. "Whatever you wanted to do, he was willing to let you try," said Jim Barborak, who was hired as a planning consultant in 1979, when "park superintendents were making more than I was as an international advisor. Those guys were bringing home about a thousand bucks a month. Nobody was drinking National Rum, it was all Johnny Walker, you know, life of Riley."

Sergio Volio, who comes from one of Costa Rica's more prominent families, found out about the national parks when he was studying meditation in an ashram in the Peruvian Andes. He saw an article on the parks on a restroom floor. "So I came back to Costa Rica and knocked on their door. Ugalde opened it himself and explained how they were making parks. I said, 'Look, I'm not even interested in pay as long as you send me where you need me,' and he said, 'Of course,' and sent me to Poás as an assistant administrator on an interim basis."

José María Rodríguez rose to the position of Park Service assistant director soon after he was hired. An architect by profession, he came to the Park Service with a little more sophistication than Vernon Cruz. "I'd been to Santa Rosa in the early 1970s," he told me. "I had a sort of an idea of national parks, and when I saw all that grass at Santa Rosa, it didn't match my idea. I'd expected to find forest. But I really knew little if anything about parks. No architect did. Then I went to work for the tourism bureau in 1976, and they asked me to coordinate with the Park Service. That's how I got to know them.

"In 1977, a number of positions were created. Actually, the Park Service staff doubled that year, and one of the positions was for an architect. I guess I was the only architect Alvaro knew, so he offered me the job. I knew little about the service, but I'd come to like it very much. I wasn't involved in nature conservation in any way before that, but I liked the way they worked. They were young and enthusiastic, and in many ways different from the bureaucracy at ICT. They were offering less pay, but I could handle that, and I wanted more satisfaction, so I made the change. I was supposed to head the planning department.

"At that time, in 1977, the Park Service was at a turning point. Resources were coming heavily, although responsibilities were also growing. The country was in a period when the economy *seemed*, at least, to be growing rapidly. We seemed richer every day, salaries were going up, opportunities were multiplying. So the Park Service had decided it was time to go beyond basic protection of the parks and go into more sophisticated management, to offer more opportunities for public use. The planning department was supposed to provide general planning for parks, but particularly for the recreational, tourist side of the parks, much in the manner of the U.S., which was the model then."

I talked to Rodríguez in the Organization of Tropical Studies office in suburban San José where he worked in 1990. During the interview, it occurred to me that we were wearing exactly the same clothes—plaid flannel shirts and corduroy Levis—an international conservationist's counterpart to the international developer's three-piece suit?

"I was supposed to work on planning with a civil engineer," Rodríguez told me, "but we just couldn't get one because they had good opportunities in other places. We also needed a surveyor, and it took us months before we could get even one of those. So there wasn't much of the work we were thinking of for the planning department.

On the other hand, Alvaro was the only person in the central office with a university degree besides me. The service had a policy that resources like trained personnel should go to the parks, not stay in San José. So Alvaro was desperately in need of technical help. I wasn't a technician, but at least I had experience in public administration, in dealing with government procedures. So I started very soon to become a sort of assistant director. There was a person before me, Luis Mendez, but he was on leave getting a master's degree."

If the shortage of experience and expertise presented exciting opportunities, it also had its dangers. One of the new responsibilities the Park Service had been handed was management of the national zoo. Located in Parque Bolívar, a leafy ravine in San José's picturesque old section, the zoo had a kind of raffish charm when I was there in 1990. One aviary had a hole in its wire, through which the resident scarlet macaws would climb to sit in the trees with flocks of wild parakeets. It was woefully obsolete, however, with rows of iron cages in one of which sat a lone, dejected chimpanzee. Hardly a month went by without a tourist writing to *The Tico Times* to complain about the zoo. The only large animal that was given much space was a lion, and that was because he had learned the trick of urinating on visitors when his cage was close to the path.

In the late 1970s the government planned to move the zoo to a much larger site in the suburbs and to turn Parque Bolívar over to the Ministry of Culture as a botanical garden. In the general enthusiasm for this excellent plan, the botanical garden was started before the zoo moved. A free-roaming white-tailed deer herd was a very popular feature at the zoo. The deer started eating the rare plants, and the Ministry of Culture told the Ministry of Agriculture to do something about their deer.

In response, Ugalde made the logical decision to capture the deer and either confine them or return them to the wild. Unfortunately, the zoo staff lacked the expertise to catch the deer, and failed to do so, Ugalde maintained, over an entire year. Attempts to subdue two deer with tranquilizer darts resulted in the deaths of both deer.

"I finally made up my mind that too much money was being involved here," Ugalde told David Carr in 1981, "and if you can't catch them alive, shoot them. It was sad. It was done in January and February of 1978, elections were February 5, and they were very vicious elections, very vicious campaigns against the government. The deer thing broke out in the press five days after the new president, Carazo, was elected, and the press was thirsty for scandal. So that added the chocolate to the ice cream. It was hell."

On February 21, 1978, *La Nación* carried an article headlined "Fourteen Deer Gunned Down in Parque Bolívar." The article reported Ugalde's explanation of the killings, but also virulent attacks on the Park Service's actions by two lawyers. "How," the lawyers demanded to know, "can the Ministry of Agriculture uphold its conservation programs if killings like this go on under our noses and with their authorization?" The next day, February 22, *La Prensa Libre* reported that some of the dead deer had been exhumed and autopsied to determine cause of death. "The mass slaughter of these innocent little animals," the article said, "has awakened a wave of protest in the whole country."

The attacks were serious. Ugalde was indicted for "destruction of government property," and his trial dragged through the courts for a year and a half. "The case was studied," he told David Carr, "to see if I could legally take the decision to destroy the deer. As a technical institution, we're supposed to be able to manage the resources we're in charge of. I could prove through witnesses that I'd tried to catch them alive for a year, and I could prove that the law itself had put me into conflict by putting two projects on the same piece of real estate, with no funds to use.

"It was an interesting case. The final hearing lasted one full day, from 8:00 to 5:00, with a lot of important witnesses. It was interesting, but it was painful, very painful, for if I had been found guilty I could have gone to jail for three or four years. I'd never cried so much in my life as I did when they said, 'Not guilty.'"

The "zoo case" was the first of many woes that would beset the Park Service in the next decade. The second was the end of the sympathetic Oduber administration in May 1978. Oduber's successor, Rodrigo Carazo, wasn't hostile to parks. He named Mario Boza, a fellow member of his Social Christian Unity Party, as an advisor on natural resources. Yet he evidently didn't share Oduber's enthusiasm for conservation. Ugalde told me Carazo spent the last months of Oduber's administration frustrating the lame duck president's attempts to create new protected areas. "I had a lot of trouble," Ugalde said, "because Oduber wanted to declare the whole Guanacaste Volcanic Range (most of eastern Guanacaste Province) a forest reserve. He wanted many other things created before he finished, and Carazo was already almost in power, opposing everything.

"Daniel actually complained to me. He said, 'I won't forgive him. He just didn't obey me for the last three months.' He wouldn't prepare decrees for me to sign." Oduber did succeed, nevertheless, in creating a Caño Island Biological Reserve on an island off Corcovado, a Palo Verde National Wildlife Refuge on important migratory waterfowl wetlands along the Tempisque River, and a Carara Biological Reserve of wet forest and river habitat for crocodiles and scarlet macaws on the central Pacific coast—all during March and April 1978.

Carazo had other things than conservation on his mind. The Sandinista revolution against the Somozas was breaking out all along Costa Rica's northern border, and most Costa Ricans enthusiastically supported the Sandinistas at that time. So the new president was not amused, during the early days of his administration, when his minister of public security received the following telegram from Park Service director Ugalde: "Your soldiers are destroying Santa Rosa National Park. The area is under the responsibility of the National Park Service and I ask you to get them out of the park."

The new security minister had established a police post at Santa Rosa to help in training and supplying the Sandinistas. "It was obviously a difficult situation because the relations between Somoza and Costa Rica were beginning to take nasty tones of confrontation," Ugalde recalled. "I disapproved of the use of the park for those activities simply because it was near the border and on government land and infrastructure. I considered it a bad precedent.

"I knew that with that telegram I was touching a very sensitive nerve in the government, but the authority of the Park Service had deteriorated to the point that even the park superintendent needed permission from the police to move around the park. They were using park fences and trees as targets for practice with heavy weapons, and there were many Sandinistas practicing with them. All my previous efforts to terminate the situation had failed, and I got the feeling we were losing the park.

"What I didn't know was that the president himself was also going to be seriously affected by my telegram and that there was going to be a Cabinet meeting that afternoon. In a matter of hours all hell broke loose. I was later informed that I was accused of being antipatriotic, or some sort of traitor, and that I should be fired from the Park Service. What saved my skin, I understand, was that my minister, the minister of agriculture, was very supportive of his staff. He told the Cabinet that even though he didn't approve of my words in the telegram—imagine using the word 'soldiers' in Costa Rica—he knew that I was only doing my job of defending the park system. Although my relations with the security minister and the president deteriorated, the police and Sandinistas left the park and never came back."

As in 1972, Ugalde decided that it was time for him to take a break. "He started looking around for something else to do," José María Rodríguez told me, "and finally got a scholarship to go back to the University of Michigan for a Ph.D. So he decided to leave me in charge of the parks. I'd been there for a little less than two years when I became acting director.

"I was afraid of the challenge. I had the support of Alvaro in Michigan, and I tried to talk to him on the phone more often than every two weeks. And I had the support of Mario Boza, who was at the parks office on quarter time as an advisor. My goal was to let things continue as though Alvaro was still there, and I think I succeeded. Of course, my style was different than his, but in terms of positions I tried to follow his line. If I wasn't sure how things were done traditionally, I'd consult elders in the service, people who'd been there longer, although usually they were younger than I was."

ten

Additions and Subtractions

Despite the misunderstanding between the parks director and the new government, the day had passed when a president could blithely ignore the park system as Don Pepe had. Parks had become potent political assets in Costa Rica, as Oduber's last-minute rush to decree as many as possible (for his successor to worry about maintaining) demonstrated. On June 12, 1978, less than a month after his inauguration, President Carazo promised in a *La Nación* article "to fight against all kinds of human destruction," adding (vaguely) that "the rights of man are constituted in all of nature."

That same month, Carazo actively acknowledged the park system's political charisma by making a well-publicized visit to the newly created (by presidential decree) Coco Island National Park. Located some three hundred miles off Costa Rica's west coast, Coco Island is a 2,400-hectare mini-Galápagos with dozens of species that have evolved in isolation, including seventy species of plants, three of birds (one of them closely related to the Galápagos' famed Darwin's finches), and two species of reptiles. There are even freshwater fish, which is odd since the island's volcanic nature suggests that, like the Galápagos, Coco Island was never connected to the mainland. Coco Island also is like the Galápagos in supporting an important seabird rookery and a very tame fauna because of a lack of native predators. Unlike the Galápagos, Coco Island gets abundant rainfall, and is covered from cliff-lined shores to its 2,000-foot summit with a lush rainforest of hardwoods and palms whose ancestors evidently drifted from the mainland as seeds.

Costa Rica laid claim to the island when its government acted to rescue a Chilean crew shipwrecked there in 1832. Such were the limitations of its maritime resources a century and a half later, however, that President Carazo and his entourage of 180 dignitaries and journalists had to hire a Panamanian ship to take them to Coco Island. The ship never materialized, so eighty of the most favored or persistent pilgrims crowded into a tuna boat and two coast guard patrol boats for the eighteen-hour voyage.

On the island, according to a *Tico Times* article, Carazo unveiled a plaque, raised the Costa Rican flag (thus emphasizing sovereignty at a time when war with Nicaragua seemed possible), heard a special mass, and was impressed by the tameness of the birds. In the introduction to *The National Parks of Costa Rica*, Boza wrote that Carazo was "the first president in the history of the country who visits the national parks to rest from his exhausting work."

Carazo's willingness to get involved in the Nicaraguan situation proved a benefit to the park system as well as a liability. The Somozas still owned another ranch north of Santa Rosa. The Park Service had been eyeing it for years with, as Boza wrote, "the objective of guaranteeing the conservation of several species that need a lot of space to maintain stable populations, such as the tapir, wild cats, mountain peccary, and some edentates."

Expropriation of the Somoza ranch, named Hacienda Murciélago (Spanish for bat) had been a popular cause since the Sandinista revolution began in 1977. The Legislative Assembly thus was generally pleased, if surprised, when Carazo signed an expropriation decree on September 13, 1978, "in order to extend the Santa Rosa National Park." "Costa Rica finds insupportable," proclaimed a September 14 *La República* editorial, "the shame of having a piece of our soil owned by a man who has shown himself capable of sending his soldiers and mercenaries to kill the Nicaraguan people." A cartoon with the editorial showed Somoza under attack by a giant bat, crying "you don't know your owner!" while Carazo holds up the expropriation decree and says, "It's because he doesn't want you for an owner anymore."

The Carazo administration didn't expropriate Hacienda Murciélago solely to please Boza and Ugalde. As Ugalde and Pedro León told me, the plans for the property went beyond conservation. "When Carazo expropriated Murciélago," Ugaldo said, "they divided it.

Most of it became part of Santa Rosa, some was distributed among poor families, and a small fraction went to the Ministry of Security as a training school."

"They trained the Sandinistas there," Pedro León said, "and when they decided they didn't like the Sandinistas, they trained the Contras there."

"Very democratic," said Ugalde.

The Carazo administration's next major conservation action was a June 13, 1980, decree designating a 9,467-hectare Palo Verde National Park next to the 9,466-hectare wildlife refuge Oduber had decreed. This area between the Gulf of Nicoya and the Guanacaste highlands had been high on the original preservation agenda compiled by Professor Rafael Rodríguez Caballero because it is part of a beautiful, unique, and threatened ecosystem. A mosaic of limestone hills and seasonal wetlands along the Tempisque River, it supports one of the highest concentrations of wintering waterfowl in Central America. Some 260 bird species live there, including 115 migrants from North America: twelve species of herons and egrets, wood storks, roseate spoonbills, and white and glossy ibis. It also has the only breeding population of the great jabiru stork in Costa Rica and the only northern Costa Rican scarlet macaw population.

A visit to Palo Verde in 1987 was surprising. The rocky pastures and dry-forested hills around it were like the rest of Guanacaste. The forest had just been burned, and the soil and trunks were charred black, but many of the trees were putting out yellow or pink flowers. Dry season is the flowering time for many trees. Troops of coatis and howler monkeys swarmed up blackened branches. The air in the leafless forest was stifling, and loud with the buzzing of insects and the moaning of doves.

We topped a little rise and suddenly descended into a green expanse of marshland stretching to the horizon. The air became fresh and breezy, with the reflective sparkle that it gets over wetlands. There weren't many birds around—except for motmots and cuckoos in a big guanacaste tree—because most of the migrants had already left to go north, but it was a beautiful place even without them.

Unfortunately for its wildlife, much of the Tempisque Basin is good for intensive cultivation of rice and other high-yield crops. According to ornithologist Gary Stiles, natural wetland in the basin declined by fifty percent from 1973 to 1983 because of agricultural expansion. So there was a good deal of political pressure not to set aside natural areas in the basin, as evidenced by the relatively late establishment of the Palo Verde units.

The Carazo administration proved vulnerable to this pressure. In a November 1979 *Tico Times* interview, an Agriculture Ministry spokesman was quoted as saying that the ministry could not declare more parks without endangering the availability of croplands. In 1981 Carazo issued a decree that withdrew or "segregated" five thousand acres of Palo Verde National Park and placed it back in the hands of a North American–owned agribusiness.

"That was a big, big bitter fight," Ugalde told me. He said the conflict dragged on into the late 1980s, when the segregated property's owner ended it by donating the land to the park system. Until then, the issue passed back and forth like a hot potato among the hands of conservationists, the Legislative Assembly, and the presidency. Mario Boza resigned his advisory position with the Carazo government because of it. ASCONA, a citizens' conservation group, took the government to court in 1981 and got the segregation invalidated. The government took it on to the Supreme Court, got the decision reversed, and reenacted the segregation.

One Liberación Party deputy, Gerardo Mora from Puriscal, became something of a specialist in park segregation. A February 3, 1984, *Tico Times* article quoted him as calling the Palo Verde issue "a choice between conservation and growth" and adding that Costa Rica couldn't "afford the luxury of passing up the revenues involved." When the reporter noticed that the deputy had on his wall a plaque from ASCONA thanking him for his work in getting other parks ratified next to a plaque from a local municipality thanking him for his work in getting parks segregated, Mora said, "That's how confused these things get."

In 1983 Gerardo Mora was instrumental in pressuring the government to segregate an already deforested part of Carara Biological Reserve. It was another confused situation, according to Alvaro Ugalde, who told me that when the Instituto de Tierras y Colonización originally donated the land for the reserve, he actually asked them *not* to donate the deforested part, but that they'd insisted. The situation at Carara was further complicated by the existence of an agricultural cooperative next to the reserve. The cooperative's access road ran through the reserve, which caused some encroachments, although Ugalde said the Park Service was consulted when the already existing road was improved.

When I visited Carara with a group from the International Union for the Conservation of Nature (IUCN) in 1988, relations between the cooperative and conservationists seemed strained. Sergio Volio led the group (he'd left the Park Service to start a tour agency), and he had made arrangements for the IUCN group to meet with cooperative representatives to discuss problems. The representatives failed to appear at a designated meeting place, however. All we encountered were some youths who had just killed a small boa constrictor with a machete. A March 21, 1989, *Tico Times* article about Carara reported that the cooperative had been "losing money steadily" and that clearing of the reserve with machetes, defoliants, and fire was continuing. Ugalde told me in 1991, however, that coop land might soon be donated to the reserve.

These subtractions from the park system generally were a part of dismal financial arithmetic in the 1980s. The Carazo administration saw rapid, drastic deterioration of the Costa Rican economy from declines in coffee prices, spiraling oil prices, a huge, growing foreign debt, and a complex of other factors. The colon had held at 8.6 to the dollar through the 1970s. By 1982, it had fallen to 65 to the dollar, inflation was at one hundred percent, and unemployment had more than doubled from 1979 figures. In 1981 Costa Rica was unable to make payments on its foreign debts.

As part of the rather top-heavy bureaucracy that had grown up in the prosperous 1960s and 70s, the Park Service was very vulnerable to the economic crisis. "We started having a really heavy downturn in late 1980," José María Rodríguez told me. "The buying power of salaries came down, and the general capacity of the government to do anything was really low. In 1980, the Park Service staff was 409. Eight years later, last year, it was 320. At the same time, the area over which the service has responsibility has increased by over 150 percent. So the staff shrank, salaries shrank, and there was always more work to do.

"It was even worse what happened to the budget for things like equipment and maintenance. I guess we lost at least eighty percent of the buying power of the rest of the budget between 1980 and 1986. After 1980, the first new car that the Park Service was able to buy was in 1989. We had them in the meantime, but they came from donations or from AID loans. There wasn't money even to keep up the old cars, and if they were running, there was no money for fuel, and if there was fuel, there was no money to pay a per diem for the driver to go anywhere. It was really hard to do anything. The Park Service went back to the policies of the first years, trying to offer basic protection to the parks.

"Some relatively sophisticated public use programs, especially at Poás Volcano, just were abandoned. There was no way the Park Service could keep the same level of attention to visitors. When the Poás Visitor Center was inaugurated in the 1970s, there were twenty-three staff people, at least. Now there are eight or nine. In the meantime— remember the 150-percent increase in parks—you had to take the staff from the old parks to the new ones. The increase in responsibility was also qualitative because under more severe economic conditions there was more pressure on the parks."

I knew what Rodríguez meant about abandoned park programs. Researching the Costa Rican parks had its archaeological side. I sometimes encountered relics of 1970s prosperity decaying in the forest like remnants of lost civilization. The Braulio Carrillo trailhead where I watched an anteater had been some kind of facility once, as concrete foundations and steps, rusted metal, and broken asphalt indicated although Alvaro Ugalde said it hadn't been a Park Service one. In 1990, Braulio Carrillo had yet to live up to its promise to introduce urban motorists to the rainforest along the Guápiles Highway. The only amenities the Park Service had been able to provide besides the poorly marked trails were a small ranger station and visitor center at a pull-off and an unpaved, unlandscaped picnic area above one dizzying gorge.

At Manuel Antonio, Under-Administrator Eduardo Rojas told me that the staff had included fifteen people in the 1970s, but had fallen to four by the time he went to work there in 1988. A former visitor center the size of a small barn sat derelict between the beach and the mangroves. Caught in a rainy season downpour, my wife, Betsy, and I took refuge in it one afternoon. In a back room we found the floor littered with the remains of nature exhibits: yellowing marine specimens and flyspecked laminated posters, beautifully drawn and hand-lettered, about sea turtles, mangrove ecology, fisheries, and local medicinal plants.

Park visitors weren't the only ones inconvenienced by decay. Part of the excitement of visiting Rincón de la Vieja National Park in 1990 had been the necessity of driving over miles of heavily eroded back roads to get there. A rattlesnake struck at one of our party when he got out to open a ranch gate, but fortunately only grazed his leg. All this enhanced the sense of discovery, but there was a less romantic side to it. The guard station at Las Pailas was squalid, its running water system broken, its trash-littered kitchen the site of an active wasp's nest, its outhouse broken in and reeking. The only interpretive signs we saw at Las Pailas were stuffed under the guard house's bare board bunk. The guardaparques we met evidently preferred staying in the woods. (Ugalde said in 1991 that this had improved.)

The Carazo administration made one more very important addition to the system before it left office in 1982, although the new park may have seemed as much a burden as a gain to the harried Park Service. Chirripó National Park had protected only about a fifth of the Cordillera de Talamanca, Costa Rica's biggest wilderness. Biologists have estimated that the Talamancas contain about sixty percent of the animal species of Costa Rica and eight of its twelve ecological life zones. Because it is so high, the region has stood above sea level longer than most of southern Central America, long enough for a number of endemic species to have evolved there.

Small groups of native tribespeople—Bri-Bris, Cabecars, Borucas, and Guaymis—live in the Talamancas, supplementing subsistence agriculture with traditional hunting and gathering. Although Indians in the area's lower valleys had been much influenced by missionaries and the cash economy by 1990, backcountry villages still practiced traditional religion and customs. Jill and Chip Isenhart, North American photographers who hiked through the Talamancas working on an exhibit for WWF, told me that "quetzal soup" is still a fairly common dish in the backcountry. Quetzals are easy to catch because they come readily to calls (the first quetzal I saw was answering a tape).

Jim Barborak, who was hired in 1979 partly to work on protecting the Talamancas, calls them "Costa Rica's Alaska . . . or Siberia." Barborak told me a park proposal for the area surfaced at the first meeting of Central American nations on cultural and natural resources in 1974, when a binational park including adjacent parts of Costa Rica and Panama was proposed. The park was to be called "La Amistad," friendship. The proposal went nowhere from 1974 to 1978, partly because the Talamancas' almost complete lack of roads, maps, and other infrastructure made it hard for planners to tackle. Chirripó National Park essentially was planned in the office by drawing lines on a map, but by the late 1970s planners saw this method had its limitations.

"Finally," Barborak said, "Rodrigo Carazo liked the idea of these border parks—he's a very peace-oriented man—and he signed a series of agreements regarding frontier cooperation with Panama. The idea was that both planning ministries of the two countries were going to put up the money to start the planning process. About that time, all those coups and changes in government began in Panama. Carazo wound up signing similar agreements with three successive governments. But finally in 1979 the planning ministry approved the money for the park planning, and we actually got rolling in 1981, right at the time of the maxi-devaluation of the colon. We got one fifth of the money we'd hoped for, but I was hired as CATIE advisor." (IICA in Turrialba had become CATIE, Centro Agronómico Tropical de Investigación y Enseñanza after disaffiliating from the OAS in 1972.) "Because we had limited resources, we got a whole team of university professors and students to do the field component of many of their basic biology courses in Amistad.

"We got interdisciplinary teams to cross with Indian guides to the heart of this area, which was almost totally unknown, and take detailed field notes, talk with the Indians and campesinos, check out the situation. The Tropical Science Center had already done a study to propose boundaries, but they had very small funds too, and they couldn't do much field reconnaissance. Right after they finished their study, we went in and found that areas where they'd said there were no people already had large squatter populations. When the government planned the Indian reserves that are adjacent to the park they made a big mistake by not talking to the non-Indians in the area too. The problem with private lands in Amistad is still being resolved today.

"We went into areas so rough that we had to use horses to help get the jeeps in. It was the only place where I've seen swamps on hillsides. We flipped one jeep, and another almost rolled into a canyon— with a girl in the back—after punching a tire on a slope like a ski jump. On one of the trips, my knees got full of water from carrying too heavy a pack or something, and I couldn't bend them. The Indians don't understand the meaning of switchbacks; they just go straight up the slopes, and they really go fast.

"So this one trip, when I couldn't bend my knees, I was in terrible shape by the last day, and another guy had advanced diarrhea, and was very weak, and we couldn't keep up. The other guys in the team were just thinking of having a beer at the next town. They were supposed to rendezvous with us, and didn't, so we fell behind. It started to rain like hell, and we had to cross the Estrella River five times in two hours, and the guy with the diarrhea couldn't swim. We'd already nearly lost him once, shimmying across a log over a river where, if you didn't drown in it, the twenty-foot waterfall a hundred feet downstream would do it.

"I was so mad when we finally got out, I left the other guy at the trailhead and said, 'You stay here awhile, I'm going to teach those guys a lesson.' So I walked into town, asked where the nearest cantina was, and there they were. I walked in, and they said, 'Hey! Everybody's happy! You made it!' I didn't say anything, just walked to the bar and ordered a beer. They said, 'Hey! ¿Qué pasa?' And I said, 'We'll start looking for Ullman's body tomorrow at dawn. He drowned in the last crossing.' I let them meditate on this for about ten minutes. Finally I said, 'He's okay, and he's a hundred yards away. But don't you *ever* do that again!'"

"I think the creation of Amistad had a lot to do with Mario Boza's being an advisor at the beginning of Carazo's administration," Alvaro Ugalde told me. "I don't know why it took us so long to create it, though—from 1974 to 1982. I guess we were just too busy with Corcovado and other things. And it's dangerous to create a park just from the desk. You really need people to go ôut there in the field. A lot of it was government land already, but there's several million dollars that we still owe for the park and the Indian reserves around it. It's pretty hard to tell, with an area that hasn't been studied, who owns it. [In 1990 the government was using debt-swap money to pay off North American owners of large parcels in the Talamancas.] Anyhow, President Carazo decided to do something for it at the end of his term."

Carazo decreed Amistad National Park in March 1982, soon after the election of the Liberación Party's Luis Monge as his successor. A March 19 *Tico Times* article on the park's inauguration quoted Murray Silberman, presidential advisor on conservation, as saying that "the precipitous, uninhabited, unclaimed area has been expropriated at no cost to Costa Ricans. . . . There are many plant and animal species in the area that have never been identified, and could well be of great use to man. Also, we may be creating a tourist draw on a par with Kenya." Gerardo Budowski recalled that the journalists at the press conference announcing the new park mainly seemed interested in the political situation with Panama, so that Carazo ended by begging them to ask him something about conservation after a half-hour of answering questions about Manuel Noriega.

Carazo then led a safari into the Talamancas similar to the one to Coco Island in 1978. This time, U.S. Army C-47 Chinook helicopters transported the hundred or so participants. John McPhaul, a young journalist with joint U.S.–Costa Rican citizenship, reported for *The*

Tico Times. "It was pretty exciting," he told me. "They piled everybody in and flew us down to Coto Brus, out in the middle of nowhere. They were flying right over the treetops, so we could see everything up close. I got so wrought up I exposed all the film in *The Tico Times* camera while I was changing the roll. They landed us in a clearing; Carazo arrived by four-wheel drive; and we had a little ceremony. There were some Guaymi Indians there, and a Cacique talked about wanting the white man to respect his land. I remember being impressed by their features, how really Indian they were."

Jim Barborak told me the administration had wanted "painted-up Indians" at the event. According to McPhaul, Barborak approached him after the La Amistad presidential press conference and asked him what he thought of the press packet that the government had given reporters about the park. McPhaul said he thought it seemed pretty good. "Well, it's all wrong," Barborak said.

La Amistad's creation virtually doubled the park system's size, but it was the end of an era. An October 15, 1982, *Tico Times* article quoted Mario Boza as saying, "We are moving out of the decade of declaration and into a period of consolidation and refined management of the parks." Jim Barborak was more pessimistic. "There are no agricultural frontiers left in Costa Rica," the article quoted him as saying. "The Costa Rican government has legislative power to reclaim lands inside parks for development. We can't be sure how the [Monge] administration's announced intent to increase production and put all unused land to work will affect the parks." The reporter, Melaney Seacat, concluded, "Essentially, Costa Rica's national parks are based on a long-range vision at a short-term cost the country can't afford. Outside support for the parks will become increasingly important."

eleven

Thinking Big

"In the Carazo years, we didn't do much, we didn't get much political support, and we had lots of trouble," Alvaro Ugalde told me. "And yet, if you look back at them from another point of view, these years were also very important landmarks. The economic crisis itself was a new lesson. The world was not stable. The ten years of 'relatively good economy' were over; the strong political support of Oduber was over. The bureaucracy was getting bigger and slower. So we realized that you couldn't trust government to be the sole doer in something like this. Neither could we trust the national economy or the financial system that we had. We hadn't done much large-scale fundraising yet."

The park system hadn't done much fundraising because it hadn't needed to. The Costa Rican government had provided most of its acquisition and operating budget. The only substantial outside funding had been an $1.8 million loan from the Central American Bank of Economic Integration to develop the visitor center at Poás, the first such loan in Latin America according to Boza in *The National Parks of Costa Rica*. Donations from international conservation groups had remained similar to the first Cabo Blanco donations in effect—enough to start parks but not enough to complete or maintain them. "I once did a very quick study of international support before 1979," José María Rodríguez told me, "and found it was about two to three percent of Costa Rican input. The international support was very important in terms of expertise and technical assistance because we needed that, but in terms of money, it was critical, but it was small."

There had been problems even with those small donations. Mario Boza tells a story about an experience he had when he was parks director, in 1972 or 1973. The World Wildlife Fund had given the parks a check for $10,000. Boza dutifully took it to the minister of Agriculture's office where they said the money would be put through channels and reissued to him as a government check the next day. He returned to the office next day (Boza mimics a trusting, optimistic smile at this point in the story), and said to the secretary, "The check?" The secretary smiled back and said, "Not yet. It will take a little longer. Tomorrow."

Boza went back the next day, smiling hopefully. "The check?" The secretary shook her head. "Tomorrow." The next day: "The check?" The secretary again shook her head. (Boza mimics the collapse of the hopeful smile.) He asked what was going on. The secretary explained that they were sorry, but the money had been used for something else. (Boza mimics astonishment.) "But it was for the parks!" The secretary shrugged. (Ugalde told me that first lady Karen Figueres convinced the agriculture minister to give the $10,000 back to the Park Service after a few days.)

Such experiences led Boza to wish that Costa Rica had a nongovernmental organization (NGO) to handle foreign donations. After leaving the government, he decided to set up a private company to handle donations and also generate other income through sales of books and other park-related items. Unfortunately, a private company would have been taxable, so that didn't work. In 1976 and 1977, however, Costa Rica passed a law exempting nonprofit corporations from taxation. After Carazo appointed him as natural resources advisor in 1979, Boza got a government lawyer to help set up a National Parks Foundation with a five-member board of directors that originally consisted of himself, Ugalde, José María Rodríguez, Pedro León, and Luis Diego Gomez, a biologist.

The foundation received its first donations in 1981, $300,000 from the Caribbean Conservation Corporation and five or six thousand from the World Wildlife Fund. Meanwhile, North American conservationists such as Spencer Beebe, then of The Nature Conservancy, were urging the Costa Ricans to use the foundation not only as a passive recipient of donations, but as an active fundraiser. Juan Carlos Crespo, a young department store executive, was becoming active with the foundation at this time. "Many friends would come and sit with us," he recalled, "and tell us, 'Hey, guys, think big.' We were thinking of getting thousands, but they were telling us to think in millions."

Another fortunate coincidence was that The Nature Conservancy had decided to begin an international program in the early 1980s. "The program had a very specific purpose," José María Rodríguez told me, "to help NGOs in Latin American countries learn how to operate and carry out the same kinds of functions the Conservancy itself was doing in the U.S. So we became sort of their pilot project. They devoted much money and expertise to helping the National Parks Foundation grow."

The help was timely. "By 1982, when the Monge administration came in," Rodríguez told me, "the crisis was hitting really hard. Our cars were still running and things were still working, although we didn't have the money to fix them anymore, but we were getting all kinds of pressure from owners of private inholdings in the parks. They all started screaming, 'We want the money! We want the money! Or we'll cut the trees in the night! We have the right! We're the legal owners!'

"Many of them started pushing very hard in different ways: going to the press, threatening to go to court to get establishment of the park on their land declared illegal. We were really afraid of the legal precedent that would set. But our lawyer, a very energetic woman named Ana Maria Tato, was very good at dissuading them from going to court, although they made her life miserable. They'd phone her at her house. She had to get her number changed. People would threaten *her* because they hadn't been paid."

Ana Maria Tato endured these trials because, like many others, Alvaro Ugalde had converted her to an almost religious faith in the Park Service's mission. "I was working in the agriculture ministry in 1977 when a job as National Park Service lawyer came up," she told me. "I thought I'd just take it for a while, until something better came along. Then I began to get involved. I saw that Alvaro was putting so much love into the parks, and I wound up getting so excited that I've been here fourteen years straight. But for all the work we do at the Park Service, there wouldn't be anything without the resources of the foundation."

In 1981 Ugalde told David Carr that land acquisition was "the worst problem we have. The government has had no doubts or qualms in establishing the present system, but it has not been able or willing to provide the funds necessary for land acquisition. That is definitely the biggest part of our, in theory, expenses. It is very easy to pass a law, to freeze the land, to say, 'That's a park,' and for us to be able to send a few rangers to take care of the land. But then what? We probably own about eighty percent of the land in the system, but around twenty percent is private property."

Aggressive fundraising through the National Parks Foundation seemed a way out of this tight spot. Alvaro Ugalde wound up doing much of the legwork to accomplish this. "Ugalde's leadership was very strong in those years," José María Rodríguez told me. "All the time I spent with the Park Service, from 1977 to 1986, there was a clear, well-defined leadership of Ugalde within the framework of Boza's ideas—even when Alvaro wasn't in the country. He had come back from Michigan in 1981, and worked on getting La Amistad decreed, but then he felt uncomfortable again with Monge's government. He felt the foundation had to think big and the country had to think big about dollars for the parks, external money. After some discussions, we all agreed with him that the main thing was buying inholdings.

"So we adopted a plan to get $5.5 million in five years," Rodríguez said, "which seemed almost unobtainable then. The Nature Conservancy was starting to train Alvaro for fundraising, and he was showing good aptitude. At first he stayed in Costa Rica for two months trying to get donations; it was an idea of the Conservancy's. But there's not much of a tradition of donating to organizations in Costa Rica, and nobody was thinking of giving money in the midst of this horrible economic crisis. Alvaro thought it would be better if he went to the U.S. to fundraise, and the Conservancy agreed to support him to go."

"It was only logical to ask our American friends for support," Ugalde told Robert Cahn in a 1983 interview in *Nature Conservancy* magazine. "Our countries have strong political ties, Costa Rican habitats are necessary for the survival of many of your migrating bird species, and Costa Rica is a training ground for many American tropical biologists. Our country, with its biological diversity and political stability, has enabled U.S. universities to establish research stations and rest assured the stations will not be affected by roads, agriculture, or commercial development. But there is an even more significant reason for fundraising in the United States: the flora and fauna that are saved in Costa Rica may play a vital role in providing the food and pharmaceutical supplies of the future—for both Costa Ricans and Americans."

An early introduction to U.S. life had equipped Ugalde for dealing with North Americans. He'd lived there for over a year in 1964, at age eighteen. "Without knowledge of English," he recalled, "I took a bus in Miami and got off in Albany, Georgia. I had a cousin at Turner Air Force Base, and I thought this was the logical place to start. My cousin picked me up and took me to an old three-story rooming house on a street with pecan trees. It was like transportation to another planet. Then I went to the employment office in Albany to look for a job. I remember my insistence on repeatedly saying, like a parrot, 'I understand, I understand. I can do anything! Washing dishes!'

"Of course, I didn't understand anything, but they sent me to a Mr. Hitchcock who might hire me to do something incomprehensible. So on my third day in the States, I got in an old truck full of machines and smells of gasoline and unknown chemistry, and went miles out of Albany to do something with chickens, I thought. To my surprise, what we did was sand and finish the kitchen, not chickens, of an old house. But I still had the job at the end of the day, and by the end of the year I was finishing whole houses by myself.

"After the first year, I decided to polish my English by taking night courses at the Albany campus of the University of Georgia. I got a new job in the shipping department of Bob's Candy Company. This was about the time antidiscrimination laws went into effect, and it worked out so that I was the first white person ever to work in the shipping department, which the blacks there saw as a weird intrusion into their territory. My arms and chest became red and sore from having candy boxes thrown at me with more force than was necessary. But that only lasted a few days. Then the whites in the office resented me for being friendly with the blacks. But at the end of five months, they all loved me, and vice versa."

Ugalde seems able to think like a gringo more than most Latin Americans. Many of the books I saw in his house were in English, including works by Ursula Le Guin, Frank Herbert, and Marge Piercy, as well as Montaigne and Kafka. He showed no hesitation or awkwardness when giving a talk to a room full of North Americans at a U.S. Citizens for Peace meeting in San José in 1990, and argued adroitly with a *Tico Times* journalist who was criticizing government forestry policies. He was also disarmingly candid. "Believe it or not," he said at the beginning of his talk, "Costa Rica is no better than other tropical countries. There's been tremendous destruction, and we're going to have to move and plan very fast to save what we have."

"I spent about three years in Washington, from 1982 to 1984," Ugalde told me. "We had this campaign to raise five million dollars in five years, and there was nobody else to do it. I spoke English and got along sort of well with North Americans and was the director of the Park Service. Geoffrey Barnard of the Conservancy convinced me to leave the parks for a while and dedicate myself to fundraising. The Nature Conservancy rented this little efficiency where I lived. I spent most of my time in hotels or airplanes, though. The Conservancy and the World Wildlife Fund helped me enormously, having receptions for me among their donors, and so on. I was doing it under the Park Service's auspices and still getting paid as director, although for a while I stopped receiving a salary from the government because it didn't sound too good to have a Costa Rican government salary paid to an official in Washington. But the Conservancy covered all my expenses, so I didn't starve.

"It was breaking new ground, you know. Nobody there knew how successful we were going to be, and nobody knew too much about the tropics. It was not a fad to donate money for conservation in those weird third world countries with unrest and corruption and whatever. Costa Rica, they didn't even know where it was. So it wasn't easy. I think we raised the funds because we could bring the donors here to show them what we were doing; because we had a good record of democracy; and because of our own dedication to the cause. It was through our efforts that articles began appearing in newspapers and magazines in the States.

"Then we got the Getty Prize in July 1983, Mario and I, and that got some attention. Maybe they gave us the prize because of that, to help us. It was a very official ceremony in which President Reagan came out to the Rose Garden, and shook hands, and said a few words to us—maybe twenty or thirty. Then he gave a speech, talking about conservation and about Mario and me, then turned the prize over to us, made a few jokes, and went back into the Oval Office. One of the jokes was that Russell Train, president of the World Wildlife Fund, knew more about Washington politics than he did."

A photo taken of Boza and Ugalde after the ceremony shows two sober-looking Latin American dignitaries in black suits and striped ties. When *The Tico Times* reported on the award, however, they ran a photo of Ugalde wearing sideburns and an embroidered vest. Evidently he'd toned down his image to hit the fundraising circuit.

"It was a nice speech," Ugalde said, "but nothing came out in the press about it because that was the day the media boycotted the White House because of something to do with the Kissinger Report on Central America. So there were no newspapers at the ceremony, no media. It was also in Watt's final days, so there was no U.S. Secretary of Interior there, either. I never had any contact with Watt, anyway. I was dealing with NGOs, not government.

"Anyway, it was much more difficult than today. You can tell even by the numbers. Trying to raise five million in five years, whereas after that Dan Janzen was able to raise much more in just a couple of years. I don't claim to parallel myself with him. It was just different times."

President Luis Monge served as chairman of the National Parks Foundation's $5.5-million campaign and gave the parks vocal support. In the January/February 1984 *Nature Conservancy* magazine, Spencer Beebe quoted him as saying, "Striving as we are toward the resolution of a severe economic crisis requiring short-term action, we run the risk of losing the long-term view of the Costa Rica we are going to bequeath to future generations. . . . This we must avoid at all costs."

It was still an uphill struggle. The January / March 1986 *Nature Conservancy* reported that the campaign had raised $3.8 million, certainly a substantial sum, but nearly two million short of the five-year goal. Yet the article reported other progress. The National Parks Foundation staff had grown from four people in 1982 to twenty-five in 1986, and 32,000 acres had been added to the park system since the foundation's beginning. Further, "the training of park employees has been greatly improved, materials and equipment have been provided, and management plans are now in place or are being formed for all parks and reserves." The $5.5 million was raised, Ugalde told me, in less than five years.

twelve

Private Partners

There was another dimension to the early 1980s push to bring outside money for national parks into Costa Rica. Two of the most important "parks" in the country were private. La Selva and Monteverde, owned by the Organization of Tropical Studies (OTS) and the Tropical Science Center, respectively, were not parks, exactly, but scientific preserves, yet both had come to serve park as well as scientific functions—protecting wilderness and giving the public (especially the foreign public) access to it. In the process of making their forests reachable and relatively comfortable for scientists and students, both private organizations had made them so (somewhat reluctantly and apprehensively) to a variety of others. As a result, by the late 1980s they were among the most heavily visited protected areas in Costa Rica.

La Selva and Monteverde also faced the same environmental pressures as the national parks. As logging and land-clearing accelerated through the 1970s, both preserves faced the prospect of becoming isolated forest patches in a countryside of croplands and pastures. Aside from aesthetic and environmental considerations, this would have reduced both areas' scientific value, since wide-ranging, rare, and otherwise vulnerable species disappear from isolated forest patches.

The situation at OTS's La Selva Biological Station was particularly critical by the early 1980s. A number of U.S. universities founded OTS in 1963 in a coordinated attempt to start tropical biology field stations in Costa Rica. Political instability and uncontrolled development had forced some of the universities to abandon attempts to start stations in other countries. In 1968 the consortium bought La Selva from Leslie Holdridge, who had been developing part of it as a cacao finca. A

1,500-hectare, still largely undisturbed rainforest tract on the Sarapi-
quí River watershed of the Caribbean coastal plain, the area was still
remote, and connected by unbroken forest to the Cordillera Central
wilderness. Located at the interface of mountain and plain, La Selva
had an extraordinary wildlife diversity—four hundred species of
birds, for example—but much of this diversity depended on connec-
tion to the much larger forest area outside the preserve. Many species
made seasonal migrations into the Cordillera to breed and feed.

La Selva's remoteness dissolved with dizzying speed through the
1970s and early 1980s, however, as roads improved, settlers moved
in, and adjacent lands were cleared. The northern Caribbean plain
was Costa Rica's main agricultural frontier, and most of its forest was
cut by 1983. Yet La Selva had a slim margin of hope in lying at the foot
of a cordillera wilderness that might be protected. In 1977 OTS member Thomas Ray had the idea of connecting La Selva to a forest reserve
in the cordillera to the south to make a transect of the forest types that
cover the mountains from three hundred feet at the coastal plain's
edge to ten thousand feet on the volcanic summits. Ray told Thomas
Lovejoy of the World Wildlife Fund about this, and Lovejoy approached the Costa Rican government with the idea.

In 1978 the creation of Braulio Carrillo National Park in the Cordillera about ten miles south of La Selva seemed an opportunity to link
the two with such a transect. The Park Service flew over and mapped
the area and drew up a plan for a forest corridor from La Selva to the
park. When David Clark was hired as La Selva's director in 1980, he
was told he'd be working in a research station adjacent to a large national park, a scientific researcher's dream. It would take a decade of
work by Clark and his wife, Deborah, before the job fit the description, however.

Unfortunately, the early 1980s' colon devaluation made it impossible for the government to buy the planned additions to Braulio Carrillo. In 1982 the government did declare the forest corridor between
the reduced park and La Selva a *zona protectora*, a designation that prohibited further forest cutting while leaving the land in private ownership. This was only a stopgap measure until the land could be
bought, however, and the estimated price of all the land parcels in the

roughly two-mile-wide, nine-mile-long corridor was $2.2 million. Costa Rica not only couldn't afford this, it couldn't afford to hire guards to patrol the Zona Protectora. OTS had to solicit emergency contributions to get the National Parks Foundation enough money to pay park personnel in the protected area (a good example of the foundation's usefulness, since such contributions might not have made it through the bureaucracy in time if they'd gone directly to the government).

Meanwhile, the Zona Protectora got publicity by some old-fashioned jungle adventure. A graduate student named Catherine Pringle took an OTS biology course that included a visit to La Selva in 1982. Hearing that the Zona Protectora's mid-elevation forests were still largely unexplored biologically, Pringle decided to do something about it. Within a year, she got an OTS grant to organize a ten-day, nine-member expedition into the Zona that would emphasize the area's scientific value.

California herpetologist Harry Greene, an expedition member, told me in 1990 that it rained for most of the ten days, but that it was an exciting experience. "We started seeing tapir and jaguar tracks everywhere," he said. "You never forget the first tapir track you see. They're three-toed, like a dinosaur track or something unimaginably archaic. Of course, everything left tracks because the ground was mud. Everything got wet and stayed wet. It hardly mattered if you were in your tent or out of it. We'd hired a couple of local teenagers as guides. The two dollars a day we paid them each was probably the most money they'd seen in their lives."

Greene, who ran a study of La Selva predators through the 1980s, thinks the area has one of the highest diversities of vertebrates, particularly of predators, in the world. The Pringle expedition didn't find any new vertebrate species, but it found lizards and birds that hadn't been seen in the province before. Members estimated the Zona provided habitat for eighty percent of Costa Rica's land bird species and forty percent of its tree species. The expedition did find twenty-eight plant species previously unknown to science.

In 1984 Murray Gell-Mann, a nuclear physicist and Nobel Prize laureate, visited La Selva with a birding tour group. The group's guide mentioned the Zona Protectora (and, no doubt, the intrepid expedition), and Gell-Mann was intrigued. He happened to be a member of the John D. and Catherine T. MacArthur Foundation's board of directors, and when he returned to the U.S. he invited The Nature Conservancy to submit a grant proposal for Zona Protectora land acquisition. The Conservancy did so promptly, and in December 1984 the MacArthur Foundation awarded them a million-dollar challenge grant. The Conservancy formed a fundraising consortium with the Costa Rican Park Service, the National Parks Foundation, OTS, and the World Wildlife Fund–U.S. to raise the million dollars in matching funds. They raised the amount within a year. In April 1986 President Monge signed a decree adding the Zona to Braulio Carrillo (it had become a tradition for Costa Rican presidents to create a new national park in the last month of their administration). Henceforth, the park would have an unusual, amoeboid shape, with the long, skinny Zona thrusting northward, pseudopod-like, from the oblong park.

La Selva director Clark didn't feel that the transect project was really finished when I talked to him in 1990, however. He wanted to see the transect widened to include more of the land in the predevaluation park plan. "It's the pre-montane zone that has the maximum plant and bird diversity," he told me, "but that's the narrowest part of the park, less than two miles wide. It's a bottleneck. Problems with neighbors will only get worse if it isn't widened. People complain about jaguars eating their livestock and peccaries eating their crops. Two years ago, a jaguar killed over twenty head of cattle, a healthy young male. Fish and Wildlife issued a permit to shoot it, and conservationists did it so as not to encourage the local people to begin jaguar hunting. That solved that problem—but it would be easy to shoot the whole jaguar population.

"Braulio Carrillo is interesting," Clark said, "because it's in this big gray area between a size of a thousand hectares and a million. With a thousand hectares, you can be sure you'll lose a lot of species as surrounding forest is cleared. With a million, you can be sure you won't lose a lot, unless something apocalyptic happens—a massive fire or hurricane. But in between, we don't know, and this is going to be typical of Central America because it has a much smaller land base than

North or South America. So we'll get to see how much biodiversity will be saved. I personally think it will be a lot, but others think less.

"Of course, we've already lost elements here at La Selva. The white-lipped peccary was hunted off in the 1960s. They're hard to conserve because they won't run from dogs and they bunch up if they're threatened. I think population sizes of most things here are big enough to persist, but nobody really knows. The jaguar and the great green macaw might not make it."

When I walked around La Selva's borders, which took less than a day, I was impressed at how much of the primary forest around it had been removed. The east and west sides were mostly pasture, with scattered trees. Even the south side, Braulio Carrillo's northern border, contained a lot of second growth. Both sides of the border were forest, but many of the plants were different. The La Selva side had a tall canopy of gavilan and other climax-stage trees and understories of palms and palmlike shrubs. Much of the Braulio Carrillo side had a relatively short overstory of balsa, cecropia, and other pioneer trees and an understory of light-loving wild ginger, heliconia, and miconia.

It was still surprising how much wildlife managed to persist in this thin strip of forest, and how well it seemed to get on with the station's fluctuating but sizable human population. I visited La Selva twice in 1990. The first time, a pair of tayras crisscrossed the residential area every morning and evening in search of fruit from old orchards, and people reported seeing ocelots, boa constrictors, and possibly tapirs on trails near the residential area. Sloths, kinkajous, and tamanduas were visible nearly every night from a bridge over the Puerto Viejo River. On the second visit, an otter seemed a little put out that I was sitting on a small footbridge it wanted to swim under, and barked at me several times before proceeding downstream.

La Selva had never had a snakebite case as of 1990, although bush-masters and fer-de-lances aren't uncommon. I went with Harry Greene to look for a large fer-de-lance female that he was radio-tracking. The snake spent all its time within a few minutes' walk of the residential area. It was curled next to a smaller male fer-de-lance (or terciepelo as it's called in Costa Rica) when we found it. Greene needed to replace the radio in the snake, and he asked a young doctor from the nearby town of Puerto Viejo to help him operate. The doctor seemed to find sewing up an eight-foot snake interesting. Involving the local community in the station was a high priority, as David Clark told me. Clark's main interest was a program to employ local people as guides for nonscientist visitors to the station.

Yet La Selva's edenic quality may be at least partly a result of a lack of wildlife habitat elsewhere in the vicinity. David Clark told me that a 1980 trip to the station had required kidney-smashing hours in four-wheel-drive vehicles. In 1990 the road was paved almost all the way, and the trip took a couple of hours from San José. We passed through very little forest on the way.

The Monteverde Cloud Forest Reserve's relationship with the Park Service has been more complicated than La Selva's. Although also founded and managed by a scientific organization, the Tropical Science Center, Monteverde is run more like a park than La Selva, where public access is strictly limited by a small number of accommodations within the reserve. Researchers must sign up months in advance to visit La Selva, and tourists can stay only in organized groups. As of 1990 only one small tourist hotel existed in the vicinity. Hotels and pensions abound at Monteverde, and, as of 1990, anybody who paid the reserve's entrance fees could walk the trails during the day.

Monteverde's similarity to Cahuita and Manuel Antonio actually has been a source of conflict between the Park Service and the Tropical Science Center. The Park Service has seen Monteverde as a logical addition to the system, but the Tropical Science Center has not. Although TSC cofounder Joseph Tosi has done much to help create parks, he is skeptical about the Park Service's land management capabilities. One Costa Rican conservationist called him "our local prophet of doom." Tall and saturnine, he did look the part when I asked to interview him in 1990. "This country is getting overrun with people studying conservation," he sighed.

"George Powell was at Monteverde studying quetzals in the early 1970s," Tosi told me, explaining the reserve's origin. "He got interested in acquiring some land to protect quetzal habitat." Monteverde lies along the crest of the Cordillera de Tilarán, the section of Costa Rica's volcanic spine running north from the Cordillera Central, and is densely covered with cloud forest and montane forest. A west-to-east walk across the reserve leads from the Pacific watershed to the Caribbean watershed. Powell put together a tract of this divide and asked OTS if they wanted to buy it, but they didn't. "So he came to us," Tosi said. "We'd already been up there five years before when Hubert Mendenhall, the leader of the Quaker settlement, asked us to look at it. He took us into the reserve, the '*bosque eterno*,' as they'd named it. We saw how beautiful it was, and recommended it be set aside for forestry and watershed."

The Tropical Science Center accepted Powell's offer and began acquiring land in the area in a series of complicated deals with Powell and other owners. "In 1975," Tosi told me, "Powell went to the World Wildlife Fund and asked for a grant for land acquisition at Monteverde. In that proposal he said that the land would eventually be turned over to the Park Service, because we would have been less likely to get the grant if we hadn't said we'd give it to the parks. But I think we've demonstrated that private reserves can manage land more effectively than public."

By the mid-1980s, the Tropical Science Center had put together a four-thousand-acre preserve with a well-maintained trail system, visitor center, and camping area. One advantage they had over the Park Service was that they could charge much higher user fees. Until 1990, national park entrance fees were twenty colones per person, appropriate for many Costa Ricans, but absurdly low for foreign tourists or affluent Costa Ricans. The Monteverde entrance fee in the late 1980s was $5 per person. With comfortable accommodations available in the surrounding cosmopolitan community of Quaker farmers and biologists, Monteverde prospered on a growing stream of birders and other ecotourists.

Deforestation was spreading rapidly up the Cordillera, however. Squatters were taking over forest reserve land in the Peñas Blancas Valley just east of Monteverde. Settlers tried to get access to the valley through the reserve. In the late 1970s the Costa Rican ministry of education built a television aerial on a peak just inside the reserve without permission from the Tropical Science Center.

Monteverde's conservationist community set up another private organization, the Monteverde Conservation League, to acquire land in the Peñas Blancas Valley and stop the reserve from becoming isolated. The League and its landholdings rapidly grew larger than the Tropical Science Center and the Monteverde Reserve. With a staff of thirty-eight by 1990, it raised several million dollars to buy out squatters, and acquired sixteen thousand acres east of the reserve. In addition, a Monteverde researcher and Bates College biology professor named Sharon Kinsman created a fundraising project with Scandinavian schools, the Children's Rainforest, which acquired another twelve thousand acres east of the League land. (According to the League's newsletter, one Swedish classroom started posting a quetzal's picture on their wall for every hectare saved, but gave up when they estimated they could paper the room four times, "a terrible waste of paper," as one student said.)

The success of these efforts led to some confusion as to who would eventually own and manage the new protected areas. Joseph Tosi told me the TSC had an agreement with the League that its land would be included in the Monteverde Reserve. The reserve's trail system already connected with the Peñas Blancas land, so this made sense. In April 1990, however, Oscar Arias maintained the tradition of outgoing presidents creating new parks by decreeing an Arenal National Park on a parcel of the Children's Rainforest.

Costa Rican governments had been trying to create a national park in the area around Arenal Volcano to the northeast of Monteverde for years. The area is the watershed of Costa Rica's largest hydroelectric project, Lake Arenal, which is threatened with siltation from deforestation. The parcel Arias decreed presumably would form the nucleus of such a park. Joseph Tosi called it "a joke," however. "Alvaro Umaña kept spouting off about starting a park there," Tosi said, "but he was blocked. So he picked up the Children's Rainforest, where nobody squawked." (In 1991, Alvaro Ugalde told me the park Arias decreed was not legal, and was no longer called a park.)

The Monteverde situation's complexity seems embodied in the person of Wilford Guindon, who arrived with the first wave of Quaker settlers in 1952. Guindon would look natural sitting on a harvester combine in Ohio, where he comes from, and calls himself "a developer at heart—basically a cheese farmer." Apparently, when Guindon asked Olof Wessberg if he could come and visit Cabo Blanco in the early 1970s, Wessberg put him off, afraid from Guindon's looks that he was up to some development scheme. Yet Guindon has become one of the main conservationists in Monteverde.

When I talked to Guindon in 1990 he was director of Forest Management and Protection for the Conservation League at the same time he was still on the TSC's payroll, although he no longer saw eye to eye with Joseph Tosi. He told me that he had helped George Powell put together his quetzal sanctuary land proposal, and then had found himself managing the thing after Powell returned to the U.S. to write his doctorate. "I puttered around at it," he told me, "and every time I thought I was backing out of it, I'd find I was backing into the middle." Eventually he became reserve coordinator, paid jointly by TSC and WWF.

"The grant said we'd turn the land over to the Park Service after three years, in 1975," Guindon said. "George would go down to San José and get Mario Boza to tell him how the laws worked. When Alvaro Ugalde became director I went to see him regularly. In 1975 Alvaro came up here with the minister of agriculture and talked to the community about a proposition to have five national park guards manage the reserve, but the TSC said, 'No, we can do better than a park.' At the time, it might have worked, because they had adequate staff, but since then we've seen the Park Service get so low that we've been glad not to get involved. They talk about megaparks now, but the Park Service has been a megaflop. But I think we will be involved in the future. I've always kept in good touch with Alvaro."

Guindon took my wife and me on a walk on Conservation League land after we talked. It was an area I hadn't seen, on the edge of a steep gorge that dropped to the Pacific plain. The transition between cloud forest and lowland dry forest was dramatic. Guindon pointed out coral bean trees, laurels, oaks, a macadamia family tree with stout, round nuts. Several emerald toucanets (small mountain toucans) hopped around with tails raised: it was April, mating season. A three-wattled bellbird, the brown and white, crow-sized cotinga that has become as much a symbol of Monteverde as the quetzal, called some-where: "Quang! Treeee. Quang! Treeee." Guindon told us he hoped the reserve might expand someday to include some of the lowlands to the west.

Later, Guindon took the bus back to San José with us because he wanted to attend the April 20 Earth Day Ceremony at the Plaza de la Democracia. (Although Arias was there, the ceremony drew a much smaller crowd than the opening of San José's first Burger King on the same day; Burger King was long the major purchaser of Costa Rican rainforest beef.) For most of the twenty or so miles from Monteverde down to the Pan American Highway, the dirt road ran through land-scape that reminded me of the California foothills—rocky grassland with scattered gnarled trees, meadowlarks and turkey vultures. "All this was forest when I first came here," Guindon said.

thirteen

Ecotourism

One of Joseph Tosi's main objections to the Park Service was that they didn't make parks accessible enough. "The attitude of the park people is that they don't want visitors in wild areas," he told me. "They want to control the parks to the extent that nothing happens. Years ago when they started developing Corcovado I suggested they franchise a rustic hotel at Sirena with a narrow gauge railway from Rincón, and then build a narrow gauge up to Llorona. They could have made a fortune, moving hundreds and hundreds of people through there at a high price with minimal impact on wildlife, but they wouldn't do it. As a result, we're getting the impact of a faulty park system that should be accommodating tourism.

"When we set up the Monteverde Reserve," Tosi said, "we figured it would be used mainly by backpackers. Now we have big tour companies bringing in busloads of seniors. There's more tourism money than there is cheese money. We're approaching twenty thousand visitors a year, and the trail system wasn't designed for it. You used to see all kinds of wildlife along the trails. Now you don't."

When I first visited Monteverde in 1987, the woods along the main trail from the visitor center to the crest were packed with birds: barbets, jays, trogons, motmots. I saw at least a half dozen quetzals feeding in a single laurel tree on the road to the reserve. The woods along the main trail were noticeably quieter in 1990, and I only glimpsed one quetzal. It may just have been a bad day, but I heard this from others too. There'd also been an ominous decline in the golden toad, an endemic species that is the reserve's main claim to scientific fame.

"The quality of the visitor to Monteverde is declining," Tosi said, "but the government and the tour companies don't want restrictions because they see dollars. We're having altercations with tour companies, so they went out and tried to get the area established as a national park. Meanwhile, our visitor center looks like the front of a movie theater, you see so many cars and vans parked there."

Wilford Guindon shared Tosi's jaundiced view of tour companies. "Sometimes I wish I'd stayed just a cheese farmer," he told me. "Then I wouldn't have any of these miserable vultures chewing on me. Overall, I have a lot of pride in what happened here. But tourism. When tour agencies come in and start selling packages, they want a national park because then their people can get in here for less, and they can make more money, which goes to San José."

Tosi's and Guindon's picture of a Park Service excluding tourists and shunting them off on private reserves seemed to go against the fundamental Costa Rican concept of the park system that Boza reiterated in remarks to *The Tico Times* after he got the Getty Award. "The appeal of Costa Rica to people seeking to learn about and experience the wilderness is extraordinary," he said. "Promoting this kind of tourism can demonstrate how, through conservation, we can put food in our mouths and make conservation a more attractive idea to politicians and people alike." Yet in October 1982 Alvaro Ugalde had taken what might be construed as an opposing stance in the same newspaper. "I will not resort to tourism as a way to maintain parks," he said. "Management of the ecosystems in parks in perpetuity is the Park Service's main goal. My personal goal is to get public and governmental recognition of the parks program, so that when the average person says 'park,' he doesn't just think recreation. The word should call to mind the complex of values associated with maintaining life support systems within the parks. What I want is for every citizen in this country to see parks on the same level as health, education, and defense."

Boza's and Ugalde's statements perhaps weren't as opposed as they seemed, however. The basic Costa Rican policy toward park tourism was always to build hotels and other tourism infrastructure not in parks but in neighboring communities, thus giving the benefits to local people instead of corporate concessionaires. The Costa Ricans had learned a lesson from the U.S. in this. Yosemite Valley's overdevelopment was universally regarded as a shocking atrocity.

Yet, not surprisingly, the basic policy proved complicated to apply. It worked pretty well in places like Cahuita and Manuel Antonio, where small parks lay near small communities, and in places like Santa Rosa, where a big park lay a half-hour's drive from a big community (Liberia, Guanacaste's capital). The basic policy did not work so well in Corcovado, whose surrounding area was sparsely populated, or in Carara, where a small, ecologically sensitive biological reserve lay a few hours' drive from San José. Big Corcovado got few tourists, while little Carara was overrun with day-trippers. The upshot of such complications was that tours billed as national park tours often wound up spending as much time in private reserves as in the parks, not only in La Selva and Monteverde, but in Marenco, Hacienda la Pacifica, Selva Verde, Rara Avis, and other small private nature resorts which grew up in the 1980s.

Despite their deliberate intention to market it, the popularity of their wilderness seemed to catch the Costa Ricans by surprise. "We spoke a lot about ecotourism in the early days of the parks," Gerardo Budowski told me, "but we never thought it would explode like this. You go to any hotel now, and it's full of ecotourists. National parks were always a romantic idea here, but in the U.S. or East Africa it's a full science and multibillion dollar business. When that kind of ecotourism got interested in Costa Rica, it caught the government and the Institute of Tourism off balance. They still are following behind what's really happened."

Budowski's daughter Tamara started a tour company, Horizontes. In an article in *Tecnitur International* magazine in 1990, she wrote that private enterprise and LACSA, the national airline, did more to get ecotourism going than the government, but that really explosive growth began after ICT began promoting it in 1985. In 1986 about seventy-five percent of respondents to an ICT questionnaire asking their reasons for visiting Costa Rica mentioned natural beauty, sixty-six percent mentioned culture and political environment, and thirty-six percent mentioned flora and fauna. "Just two years later," the article said, "one out of every two tourists interviewed during the high season indicated that they had visited natural sites . . . or national parks, biological reserves, forest, and wildlife refuges. . . . Visits to seven of the principal national parks increased by fifty percent over those two years."

Tourism generated about thirteen percent of Costa Rica's export income by 1988. Gerardo Budowski sees this as perhaps the most encouraging sign for the park system's future. "The fact that tens of thousands of Americans, Europeans, and Canadians come here to see the parks and pay a lot of money was totally unforeseen," he told me, "but it is now really big business."

The man who probably has done more than anyone to promote Costa Rican ecotourism is well aware of its problems, but makes no apologies for a business that is bringing nearly as much foreign revenue into the economy as coffee or bananas. Michael Kaye founded Costa Rica Expeditions, the biggest package tour company in the country, in the late 1970s. "What we did was pioneer lay tourism in Costa Rica," he told me in his bustling San José office. "The atmosphere that made it possible, starting way before twenty years ago, was scientific tourism. The same things that now make Costa Rica attractive for natural history enthusiasts to come here for two weeks made it attractive for people throughout the past two hundred years. There've been a lot of books about Costa Rican nature. Zane Gray wrote about Coco Island. Then scientific groups like OTS would do the occasional lay tour before I got here. Their influence and people like Kenton Miller set a proper stage to make it interesting and attractive for me to set up here.

"I actually came here in 1978 just for wild rivers, which, ironically enough, are still unprotected and to various degrees endangered in Costa Rica. In the process of doing that, I found out about the park system and the incredible diversity of wildlife, and I went to talk to Alvaro Ugalde about the possibilities."

Kaye paused at this point. "I got a lot of help from Alvaro," he continued. "It wasn't 'reluctant,' which was the first word I was going to use, but 'hesitant.' And rightfully so. He made it clear that his primary purpose was to protect the parks, and that he would help natural history tourism insofar as it complemented that purpose, and be against it insofar as it would be damaging to that purpose. One of the main reasons I was interested in doing natural history tourism here—after having been burned by a bunch of development situations in other wild areas I had explored—was that there were parks here, that there was good reason to believe that the resource would stay protected, so as to justify the investment of time and energy to get the parks known.

"So I went out and promoted Costa Rica, and the most attractive, from my point of view, destinations in Costa Rica (which are all parks and reserves with the exception of the rivers) to the major natural history tourism marketing organizations in the States, both the non-profit conservation organizations like the Sierra Club and The Nature Conservancy, and the commercial ones. I was looking for a way to make a living without as much travelling all over the place as I'd been doing. Before I was here, I lived in El Salvador, but I had no work there at all.

"So the original idea was to see if there were some commercially exploitable whitewater rivers, and there turned out to be some great ones, like the Pacuare and Reventazón. Right now there are companies making a living from whitewater rafting alone, but back then you had to have a big product mix. I realized there was a big product mix, in parks, which meant not only that it was going to be protected for a long time, but people would much prefer it to be in parks."

Jim Barborak told me that park tourism was in bad shape in Costa Rica at the time Michael Kaye arrived. "Visitation by Costa Ricans peaked around 1979," he said, "and went down in the 1980s because nobody had any money to take vacations. International visitation also went down because Nicaraguans used to be the major tourists in Costa Rican parks, and the Sandinista revolution put a stop to that."

Kaye told me that there was virtually no nature tourism in Costa Rica when he started. "What little name recognition Costa Rica had in the U.S. then was from the Robert Vesco scandal. Since then, a lot of factors have changed that. The Nicaragua situation put Central America on the map, so to speak. And then Arias's Nobel Prize helped to dispel the notion that Costa Rica must be a violent place because it's in Latin America. During the early 1980s we had people cancel a Costa Rican tour at Miami airport because they saw newspaper headlines about the Falklands Crisis down in Argentina. You never want to underestimate the geographical ignorance of the average North American. But in the last three or four years, because of this combination of positive factors, we've been getting a snowball effect, a critical mass of happy people telling their friends about the nice trip they had to Costa Rica.

"So we've finally come to the point where some parks are having visitation problems," Kaye told me. "Rightfully, pretty much everything they've done up to date has been centered on land acquisition. There's more and more acquisition stuff going on with international money. But I think at some point they're going to have to take concrete steps to deal with visitation and to learn to what extent more infrastructure is justified in order to handle visitation.

"They need to get a direct relation between visitation and income. The entrance fees are still laughably low. Indirectly, the huge rise in visitation has been a tremendous help to conservation. It's gotten big, big donations from foundations and what have you, lots of people interested, a general political constituency for protection of the wildlands on economic grounds. The big failure is that they haven't managed to create the proper relationship between visitation and management. There's not enough money, and not one dime of entrance fees stays on the ground where the visitors walk. It shouldn't all go into a general fund. They need people to develop expertise with visitation.

"They've got a tiger by the tail here, and if they don't start thinking about it and dealing with it in an effective way, it's going to be a catastrophe. The beginnings of that are clear. The place where it's most obvious is Monteverde, where you're definitely seeing some trail erosion and wildlife retirement beyond what I'd think of as acceptable levels. The biggest impact is the deterioration of the experience. People are seeing too many other people. Monteverde is no better than the Park Service. There's been no concerted attempt to distribute traffic. The only traffic distribution has been among guides talking to one another.

"There's been tremendous people pollution at Carara Biological Reserve," Kaye continued. "It's been turned into a mass place where they bring busloads of fifty people down at a time, and shore excursions off cruise ships or cheap Canadian charters. There's been incredible deterioration in the quality of the tours. There have been incidents where guides promise tourists they'll see scarlet macaws, and they take tourists to the nest and the macaws aren't visible, so the guides start throwing stones at the trees. There's no qualification of the guides, no enforcement, and there's no money to do it because they don't charge people enough money to go into the park in the first place."

I was surprised to hear what Kaye said about Carara, because the 1988 tour I'd gone on with the IUCN group had been wonderful after the no-show by the agricultural cooperative. The trail led along a river where big crocodiles slept in marshes, and birds were abundant and curiously confiding. Walking back, just at sunset, we started hearing honking sounds which rose to crescendo as a flock of scarlet macaws went over at treetop level, their plumage dark scarlet against the pink sky. The guide, Sergio Volio, had seemed genuinely and actively concerned about protecting the reserve. He'd helped to arrest crocodile poachers and had given evidence against them in court. But, like other small Costa Rican tourism entrepreneurs, Volio evidently was facing an uphill financial situation. "It's a difficult life," he told me in 1990, "because I have no money."

Michael Kaye thought the Park Service had been unrealistic about change in the parks. "If you set aside places like Cabo Blanco that are supposed to be completely unaffected by visitation," he said, "then change becomes a negative impact. If you say there'll be no such negative impact, then you perpetuate a myth that nature is this totally stable, unchanging phenomenon, the same myth that got the U.S. into trouble in Yosemite and Yellowstone. It's only artificial environments that don't change, like Central Park.

"The first thing you have to do is decide on acceptable limits of change, and then plan for that. What they're doing now is counting on the individual standards of tour operators, and Gresham's law applies there. If an operator cuts down on trail use, then people just go to another operator. You get a situation like Carara, which is supposed to be a biological reserve, not a playground, but which is getting trampled in the rush because it's conveniently accessible. In many ways, the goose has laid the golden egg, but it's not being treated right. It may keep laying something that looks like gold, but touching it may turn your hands green."

Juan Carlos Crespo, the department store executive active with the parks, worries about what will happen when Costa Rican ecotourism goes out of fashion. Crespo probably knows the parks as well as anyone, having spent most of his spare time for years visiting them and showing them to others, running what amounts to a small, nonprofit tour agency. He invited me to a weekend at Rincón de la Vieja the first time I met him, and picked me up for the trip at 7 P.M. on a Friday still wearing his jacket and tie from work. He'd invited five other people as well. He drove us all the way to the park that night, arriving at midnight, led us on a vigorous round of hikes for two days, then drove us all the way back to San José Sunday night. It evidently was just a relaxing jaunt for Crespo, who held the record for bicycling the length of the country nonstop in 1990.

"When you have more and more people, you have problems," he told me. "And that can easily happen with something the size of the Costa Rican protected areas. Conservation can be something where you can acquire power, political power, economic power, through a travel agency or ICT. It's very appealing. The last few years of the meeting they have every year for tourism wholesalers—Expo-tour—it was a nice, interesting little meeting. Now all of a sudden, you see, like, vultures circling around. It was amazing, the amount of hotels here and tourists in the country, and the amount of wholesalers coming, desperate to buy that because it's in fashion.

"I tell people: 'Tourism is an industry, like any other, like petroleum.' You can extract the petroleum in a nice way, or you can extract the petroleum destroying absolutely everything. Once the petroleum is gone . . . 'I don't care, I'm going somewhere else, I'll strike petroleum somewhere else.' Tourism is the same . . . 'Fashion, Costa Rica, nature—Okay! Let's do it!' So the energy moves to development of the parks, not so much protection. And I think that is happening faster than we thought it would. A bit too fast. I worry about that a lot because in development, once you have permitted something it's very, very hard to go back. Because all of sudden the communities depend on that decision.

"I remember a few years back Alvaro talking about the importance of trying to define things related to the concessions," Crespo said. "He was very strong on the idea of withholding them, because once you give them, it's going to snowball, and it's going to get on top of you sooner or later. There were travel agencies at that time trying to get concessions, saying, 'Hey, I'll build a nice little hotel, and a nice thing for the park people,' and it was very appealing at the time because the park people were living under terrible conditions. But then, thinking of the future, the company is going to get much more out of it than the parks. And once we've constructed that, and fashions change, people say, 'Well, I'll go somewhere else, and I don't care what happens here.' That's where we have to be very careful."

There was an interesting, perhaps significant split on the ecotourism issue between the North Americans and the Central Americans I talked to. The North Americans took it for granted that parks should have paved roads and other facilities to make visitation convenient and efficient. They took it so much for granted that they tended to perceive Ugalde's and Crespo's uneasiness about development more as a financial stance than a philosophical one and assumed that the parks weren't developed because the Park Service lacked funds and organization. There was certainly truth in this, given the Park Service's financial problems. Ranger stations at Rincón de la Vieja and Corcovado looked more like products of third world indigence than Park Service philosophy. Yet I think there was more to it than that.

Mario Boza probably is one of the more development-minded Costa Rican conservationists. Yet the main thing he stressed to me was protection. "Yes, parks are for people," he said. "We need to develop facilities. But the principal reason for parks is the need to protect nature. The real reason for parks is to protect species. I think the U.S. Park Service is more oriented toward recreation than the protection of the biological resource. They're more interested in having nice highways and picnic areas. Only recently have the U.S. parks begun to plan in a biological way, with the proposals to enlarge the Great Smokies, and the California Desert Plan, for example. [A plan to create a number of new parks and wilderness areas in the California desert that the U.S. Congress had repeatedly failed to act on as of 1991.] But the U.S. Park Service didn't approve the California Desert Plan! I was astonished by that. U.S. park policymakers aren't concerned with protecting the biological resource. The rangers and researchers are, but the policymakers aren't."

Alvaro Ugaldo told me, "The world was different when the U.S. started its park system than when we did. It's my impression that Yellowstone was created to protect the landscape and give citizens a place for recreation. We started with a system to protect biodiversity. The world was speaking more about biodiversity than recreation. We were influenced by biologists, not just a few park planners from the U.S. So recreation and scenery were secondary."

For a third world country to be more prowilderness and biocentric in conservation policy than a first world nation might seem strange to North Americans and Europeans who take for granted the priority of their nature-loving traditions at the same time they take their paved roads and picnic areas for granted. Where does the Costa Rican attitude come from, in the absence of two centuries of Costa Rican Audubons, Thoreaus, and Muirs? Is it simply a graft that has taken under favorable economic and cultural conditions? Or is there something about Costa Rican (and, by extension, Latin American) culture that might predispose at least some Costa Rican leaders to be more biocentric than North Americans?

It would take a Costa Rican to answer the questions with authority. I was struck when talking to Costa Rican conservationists, however, at the frequent use of religious terms and images in discussing conservation. Pedro León spoke of "conversion" to conservation; Ana Maria Tato described the Park Service as a "miracle" and the staff as "people of great spirit." Juan Carlos Crespo spoke often of "visions" of the park system. North American conservationists use religious terms too, but the traditions are different. Largely Protestant North America's religious tradition is a tradition of works. Churches are often seen as recreation centers just as parks are. Predominantly

Catholic Latin America's tradition is of faith: Sacred things don't necessarily have to be put to work to improve and divert the faithful. If wilderness is a chapel in the pines to North Americans, perhaps it is a cathedral in the ceibas to Latin Americans.

"The way I used to explain it," Ugalde told me, "was that the parks were part of the Costa Rican soul."

fourteen

The Desecration of Corcovado

If the park system had become an article of faith to Costa Rican con-servationists, that faith was about to be tested. By the mid-1980s, Cor-covado was widely recognized as the jewel in the crown of the system. Not only was it used for research by scientists such as Paul Ehrlich, it had become one of the most desirable ecotourist destinations after Michael Kaye began flying visitors in to the Sirena station.

Everyone who visited Corcovado during this period seemed to re-turn with fabulous stories. Jaguar sightings were frequent, and sometimes close-up. Feynner Godinez's North American wife, Deb-orah, told of feeling something warm and wet on her foot at the mo-ment she saw her first jaguar in the park. She had stepped in feces that the big cat had just deposited. In his lively book, *Corcovado: Medita-tions of a Biologist*, University of Costa Rica professor Alvaro Wille Tre-jos described a night surrounded by three roaring jaguars. "I felt a strange sensation in my stomach," he wrote. "When each roar ended, I very clearly heard purring and panting. I didn't move a finger. . . . A jaguar is incapable of attacking a tent: elementary knowledge for any zoologist. Roars are typical of jaguars in heat; I had been, simply, in the middle of a love triangle. Nevertheless, I wondered sometimes if the jaguars had read what zoologists have written about them."

"The Corcovado National Park is without a doubt the most impor-tant wilderness to be conserved of the country's national heritage," Mario Boza wrote in *The National Parks of Costa Rica* (1981). "The fact that it is one of the largest and least changed parks of the entire sys-tem, together with the extraordinary variety and richness of its spe-cies, many of which are endemic, has transformed it into one of the most important areas for scientific investigation in all of tropical America."

Boza also noted that the park had been enlarged. "On February 5, during the celebration of the tenth anniversary of the creation of the National Park Service, President Carazo signed an executive decree that extended Corcovado Park by 7,700 hectares. The objective of this extension was not only to give the park more natural new boundaries (rivers and peaks) but also to include all of the Rincón Peak area. This peak, according to Salas, has unusual scientific importance as it is the highest in the peninsula, 745 meters, and because due to the fact that it is often clouded . . . it is very rich in tree ferns, dwarf bamboos, and other epiphytic plants."

Boza apparently didn't know that the Rincón Peak area was the locus of growing gold mining activity by 1980. "At the present time," he wrote, "there are very few gold washers left working in the region and fewer still within the park. The National Park Service allows them to continue their activity on a regular basis with the condition that they not bother the wildlife, since the production of gold is considered a benefit to the country. One of the trails which is in the process of being prepared will lead precisely to one of the sites where gold is mined on the Claro River. [The Claro River is west of Rincón Peak.] The process that the visitors will see is simple but arduous. When terrain with gold is found, the washer digs out earth and sand from the river banks which he piles in a canoe or a sieve. This he carefully exposes to the current of the river. The water washes away the earth and sand and leaves the gold nuggets or other pieces."

Roger Morales, who kept in touch with the Corcovado situation after the squatters had been relocated, told me that gold mining in the park had become "a chronic problem" by the early 1980s. "At the beginning of the park, mining was not a problem," he said. "There was enough potential cash money in ranching and farming so that there weren't many people in the rivers. The problem with gold miners was that they started as farmers and then decided that wasn't enough. When the park was first established, the *oreros* were outside, but then it was enlarged, and contained the best areas for gold mining."

Massive mining and logging were in full swing on the Osa Peninsula outside the park. On July 2, 1982, *The Tico Times* quoted Alvaro Ugalde on the activities of mining companies in the Golfo Dulce Forest Reserve just north of the park. "From the reports I've received," Ugalde said, "the mining companies are using their heavy machinery to turn parts of the forest reserve into a moonscape." In November 1983 the *Times* reported on an Osa gold rush that had been well under way since 1981, driven by a complex of factors including the economic crisis, a rise in gold prices, problems in the local agricultural economy, and phony investment schemes.

Big, well-financed companies claimed most good placer deposits on the rivers outside the park. Small entrepreneurs had few opportunities. "They've had very few miners on the Osa Peninsula," a retired North American mining engineer named Vernon McClure was quoted as saying, but "they've had lots of speculators." McClure said outright crime was common, with rolling drunks a favored pursuit on the streets of Puerto Jiménez, the Osa's biggest town. He told of a miner who'd sold ninety thousand colones' worth of gold one day, and had been begging for loans on the next.

"There's one thing I've noticed with gold," McClure observed. "Even honest people steal." Thieves included con men who sold "certificates of deposit" on fraudulent gold operations to U.S. investors, and a swindler who "sold" campsites to would-be *oreros* after convincing them there was gold there and he was tired of mining it. A local doctor called miners "all migrants who carry their diseases from one place to another, affecting new populations."

This unruly situation rapidly spilled over into the park. Excluded by the big operations, individual miners went to try their luck in the one place the heavy equipment hadn't reached. Park Administrator German Haug told *The Tico Times* in 1983 that about a thousand small miners were working in the park: two hundred along the Río Madrigal and eight hundred near the headwaters of the Río Tigre. Haug said the miners worked without machinery (as Boza had described) and ate birds, iguanas, and other game to supplement their diets.

"By the Río Madrigal guard station," Haug said, "we used to count more than two hundred peccaries. Now we don't see more than forty or fifty." Once-abundant fish and freshwater shrimp had disappeared from the Río Madrigal because of siltation and pollution from mining. When the guardaparques pointed this out to miners, the miners replied that there weren't very many species of aquatic animals in the rivers in the first place, and that they could be restored anyway.

Haug said that in February and March 1983 the Rural Guard had evicted fifteen hundred miners from the park. The Guard was short-handed because of the Nicaraguan situation, however, and many of the miners had returned from detention in the city of Golfito across the Golfo Dulce to mining in the park. A syndicate of small miners was lobbying the Legislative Assembly for mining concessions in the park's Rincón area.

In response to all this, the Park Service launched a new Corcovado management plan in September 1983. To counter the impression of many local people that the park was merely "a playground for rich gringos," the service opened a public information office in Puerto Jiménez. It had moved park headquarters from Sirena, the main research and tourism site, to Cerro de Oro, a site nearer the mining that had become accessible by jeep because of a mining company road. Park guards in groups of four had begun confiscating equipment, weapons, and food from miners caught in the park.

The measures apparently were too little and too late, however. The invasion had reached critical mass and kept getting worse. Miners returned to the park in greater numbers. The Costa Rican public remained largely unaware of, or indifferent to, the park's dismantling. As late as 1985 the tourism section of the March 21 *La República* carried an article entitled "The Gold Miners: Sign of Authenticity in Puerto Jiménez." "Even today," the article enthused, "the gold miners continue to lend great attraction to the region when with their light steps they walk the riverbeds, in search of good places to start their digging for nuggets."

In 1984 upheavals in the southern Costa Rican banana industry contributed new recruits to the ranks of *oreros*. United Fruit had been wanting to terminate its banana plantations around the town of Palmar north of the Osa because it was more profitable to grow oil palms.

When a radical faction of the banana workers' union convinced its rank and file to strike for higher pay, the company pulled out, leaving many area residents unemployed. (I drove through Palmar in 1987, and it looked like a ghost town.) Without job prospects, many workers headed for Corcovado to try prospecting.

"The gold mining situation in Corcovado was another awakening for the Park Service," Alvaro Ugalde told me. "It was our biggest mistake. It was an awakening that meant, 'If you think people are going to respect the parks just because they're parks, forget it.' Gold is gold, if you get gold in this office or the church or the White House. It creates a frontier kind of culture. There's a freedom there, there's no authority. If you come and establish authority, you immediately get reactions, and especially if it's a park. If the government wants to come in and cut all the trees down, that's fine, that's production. But if the government wants to protect the trees, that's something else."

Ugalde had returned from his 1981–84 fundraising sojourn in the U.S. to "fight the Corcovado battle," as he put it. In the summer of 1985 Ugalde asked biologist Daniel Janzen to go to Corcovado and write a report on the mining for the World Wildlife Fund. Janzen, an entomologist and ecologist world famous for his research on tropical dry deciduous forest, had been associated with the park system since its beginning. "I first came to Santa Rosa in 1972," Janzen told me in 1990, sitting outside his small, cinderblock house and lab in that park, "when Ugalde was park administrator. I was busy doing biology and the park was a safe place to do it. I'd been working throughout Guanacaste on a lot of private land, and losing a lot of experiments. You set something up, and come back in six months, and the owner has changed his mind and destroyed it. I was getting tired of that, so I said to myself, 'Inside a national park, I won't have that problem.' So I just abandoned my research in the rest of Guanacaste and moved to Santa Rosa.

"I also moved for a second reason. I was on the OTS board of directors at that time, around 1970 or 1971, and when the park system became established, my gut reaction was that the long term for conservation of wild areas depended on whether they were worked in and used by people. So I said to myself, 'If I've got administrative energy and involvement, I'm going to put it in the government-supported things rather than in OTS stations.' So I deliberately stopped doing things in the OTS stations and left the OTS board, and started doing my research here. I think my instincts were in that direction because my father was director of the U.S. Fish and Wildlife Service, and I've had a long, long relationship with government and wild preserved areas. So I've long believed that, 'yes, private reserves are fine, and they have a place, but in the long run it's the government that's going to matter.'

"I got along well with Alvaro," Janzen said, "and we talked about a variety of things. But I didn't get involved in administration or conservation as we now call it. I was basically doing research, and I wasn't paying a whole lot of attention to what his problems were. As soon as Corcovado was established, in 1976, Alvaro called me up and asked me to go to Sirena and get to know it, see if I wanted to do research there. I'd never been to Corcovado before. I'd been to Rincón on the other side of the Osa, the Golfo Dulce side, a lot. But Corcovado was not part of my experience at all. So I went and got to know it, but again, I went as a biologist and got to know it as a biologist, explored it and got to understand it.

"Up until 1985 my interactions with the Park Service were just a little helping here and there, putting out a fire, loaning vehicles, very trivial kinds of interactions. Then in '85 was when the big change occurred, because that was when Alvaro asked me to go to Corcovado to do an environmental impact study on the gold miners. I invited some people to go along with me, and the Park Service came up with some people I didn't know, and a group of us went.

"Again, I went and did that as a . . . 'Okay, Alvaro's asked me to do this, so I'll go and do it' . . . kind of thing. But it became very interesting once I got there and saw what the problem was. It converted itself from a biological study to a sociological study—the sociology of the gold miners and why they were there, and what they were doing, and how to get them out of there—rather than the damage per se that they were doing. The damage per se was obvious. It didn't require great study. The challenge was in figuring out how to deal with it."

The damage was obvious because it was massive. When it came

out in July 1985, Janzen's report said that game animals had been "practically eliminated" from the affected area and that "almost all rivers" had been converted into "canals, sterile and full of sediment." The investigating team, "very experienced in field work," had found no agoutis, pacas, armadillos, tapirs, brocket deer, peccaries, monkeys, guans, curassows, or tinamous in the southern third of the park. The fruit of "cedro macho" trees, a wildlife staple, remained uneaten on branches or the ground. There was an "almost complete absence of fish, crabs, crayfish, aquatic mammals, insects, and birds in all the rivers affected. . . . Probably several centuries will pass before the communities of plants and animals that live in the rivers recover the composition and characteristics they had before mining alteration."

When Janzen talked to the miners, he found they had a saying: "If the river isn't muddy, you're not working hard enough." When one of the study team asked a working miner what a national park was, the miner replied, "A place to protect fauna and flora, and I'm careful not to do anything to the flora and fauna."

"Yes," said the researcher, "but what about the freshwater shrimp that used to live in this stream?"

After some thought the miner replied, "Well, señor, there are a lot of shrimp in the ocean."

Janzen's report estimated that there were between eight hundred and twenty-two hundred miners in the park, and gave fourteen hundred as a probable figure. Of these, about nine hundred actually were mining; the rest were hangers-on and family. Fifty of the miners were the traditional seminomadic, gold-panning type Boza described. Six hundred were full-time modern miners who worked areas intensively; two hundred and fifty were part-time intensive miners. Only about five percent of the nine hundred were professional miners; most were simply rural people who found mining life more interesting and potentially more profitable than other available employment. They came to the park because big companies owned the mining land outside. "The life of these individuals is supremely monotonous and intellectually vacuous," the report said. "All seem attracted by the possibility of making themselves rich, but each year only one to three percent make income superior to a decent living."

"When you ask many gold miners, as I did," Janzen recalled in 1990, "'Who do you know who's ever found a big nugget that made them rich for the rest of their lives?'—nobody ever knew anyone who had. There were always third- and fourth- and fifth-hand stories. But that wasn't the point, you see. If your daily salary is three hundred colones a day, and you can make five hundred colones mining gold, you don't have to find a big nugget.

"What Americans find hard to remember is that if you make $20,000 a year and somebody says: 'I'll give you $22,000 a year to move from California to New York,' you just laugh at them. If you make a thousand dollars a year and somebody says: 'I'll give you three thousand to move from California to New York,' the same two-thousand-dollar raise—you do it. In other words, if you're at the bottom of the thing, just a few pennies more make a huge difference. When you're at middle income, where most North Americans are, little gains don't mean much. You have to find the big nugget. When you aren't making much of anything, slightly better is better than nothing. Corcovado was full of people who were just making slightly better income, and they were happy to."

The 1985 report estimated that ninety percent of the Corcovado miners had other sources of income beside mining, and that thirty to fifty percent owned farmland. It predicted that most miners would leave the park without resistance, likening them to drivers parked on a city street yellow zone, who would only have to be asked by a policeman to leave. The report also predicted, however, that eviction of miners from the park would alarm the local business community, "who think the flow of gold from the park is the salvation of the area," and would also alarm the landowners outside the park, who feared the miners would then invade *their* land.

"Although there have been various minor attempts to dislodge the miners," the report said, "problems resulting from these actions reinforced the traditional idea in the nation that the Osa Peninsula is a lawless area, and led to a lack of planned activity by the Park Service. . . . . This passivity has resulted from fear, lack of administrative capacity, hope that the problem would go away by itself, a feeling of lack of support in view of other grave problems confronting government, indecisive administrators at high levels, lack of mutual understanding about the details of the problem, and a feeling, correct, that the financial and human resources of the Park Service are inadequate to the challenge.

"It's clear that in Costa Rica one encounters a curious situation. On one hand, there has been great success in attracting aid for protected natural areas, but on the other, there haven't been policies, stewardship approaches, and budgets necessary to assure protection of these areas in the face of growing social pressures. . . . Nobody in Costa Rica, from the president to the man in the street, has understood that benefits from tourism and scientific research and foundation grants depend in great part on international confidence in the stability of the government, and in its capacity to conserve and develop its enormous biological richness."

The Janzen report recommended complete removal of miners from the park as the only way to stop the damage and set the stage for future recovery of the ecosystem. It advised against directly compensating the miners as had been done with 1975 squatters, on the grounds that the miners' invasion was illegal, and that paying them would simply attract "an army of opportunists." It cited five different laws as "clear and abundant" legal precedents for removal, and suggested the Park Service seek help from the local legal establishment and Rural Guard in removing the miners.

"The Park Service in its turn should recognize that this is the most dangerous crisis it has undergone in its history, and that all human and financial resources should be directed to confront it," the report concluded. "To prevent another invasion, the service should involve itself deeply with neighboring communities and other planning agencies to show the benefits of the park. . . . It is fundamental that the service assure Corcovado be considered in the plans of other government agencies and in the minds of all Costa Ricans as a very important scientific, educational, and touristic institution contributing substantially to socioeconomic development, both regionally and nationally."

All this was, of course, easier said than done. As José María Rodríguez told me, the Park Service had little control over the situation by 1985. "The rangers would come along, and the miners would say, 'Hi,' and keep on working. The rangers would say, 'It's illegal what you're doing,' and they'd just say, 'I don't care. I'm staying.' It was like this especially *after* several evictions. First the rangers tried to evict the miners themselves, then they got help from the Rural Guard, but it was always the same thing. The Rural Guard would send a group of people for six, eight days, then leave, and the miners would go in again. So every time we had these evictions, it only meant less authority for the rangers and the park."

In a management and protection strategy he sent to World Wildlife Fund along with the Janzen Report, Ugalde wrote that the Corcovado guardaparques were patrolling in street clothes because of a government freeze on funding. Although the Park Service and National Parks Foundation had made Corcovado their top priority in 1983 and 1984 and had used most of the funds raised for the park system to buy the remaining inholdings and to clear and mark the borders, miners had lost respect for Park Service authority to the extent of threatening rangers' lives. Ugalde asked WWF for $79,100 to supplement $90,000 already appropriated by the foundation.

In August 1985 Ugalde sent a report to the government's Economic Council asking the president and virtually every government ministry to help save Corcovado. He asked President Monge to declare the Osa in a state of emergency and to publicly announce his intention to protect the park. Ugalde requested that the Ministry of Energy and Mines and the General Forestry Directorate revise their policies to benefit miners on lands outside the parks. He asked the Ministry of National Planning to increase efforts to find international aid for integrated development on the Osa, and asked the Ministry of Agriculture and the Ministry of Health and Security to intensify their services on the Osa. Ugalde asked the Ministry of Labor to participate in generating new jobs on the Osa; the Ministry of Public Works and Transportation to improve road access to the park so it would be "accessible and secure at all times"; and he asked the Institute of Tourism to consider the park a major resource. Finally, Ugalde asked the Procuraduria General to go to the judiciary and try to get offenses against the park changed from *contravenciones* to *delitos*, which is something like changing them from misdemeanors to felonies, and would allow stiffer penalties.

"In sum," Ugalde's report concluded, "the country hasn't understood the gravity of the situation, and the institutions which have charge of the problems have neither the resources nor the ability and authority necessary for solving them. . . . It's important to mention that, in the great majority, the other tropical and Latin American countries are experiencing situations as bad or worse than ours. Some of them accomplished great things, but have lost them. Mexico created a system of fifty parks. Today, only three remain. . . . What is in danger is not only Corcovado but the whole Costa Rican park system. Experience in other countries shows that, once a park is lost, the others rapidly follow."

Ugalde spent the last half of 1985 pleading for government action on Corcovado. "If we can't save Corcovado, we can forget about the national park system," he said in a July 26 *Tico Times* article by John McPhaul. He added that he was thinking of closing all the other parks to divert manpower to Corcovado. On September 6 the *Times* reported that "Ugalde believes that if the line is not drawn at Corcovado, Costa Rica's worst ecological nightmares will come true." The article quoted Daniel Janzen as saying that the miners maintained their gold was worth more to the national economy than the park (Janzen had estimated in the WWF report that Corcovado tourism brought about a million dollars into the economy a year, whereas gold mining brought about $500,000). The article also mentioned miners' rumors that park officials were plotting with big gold mining companies outside the park to exploit the Corcovado gold themselves.

The September 6 *Tico Times* article also reported the government's response to Ugalde's appeals. It had set up a commission to study the problem. Two months later, a November 22 *Times* article reported that Minister of the Presidency Danilo Jiménez had issued a "strong endorsement for Corcovado" after hearing Ugalde's proposal to declare a state of emergency in the area, but "had also stressed the need to proceed cautiously." The article alleged that a Liberación Party candidate for the Legislative Assembly was seeking votes among the miners, and telling them that the administration of his party's presidential candidate, Oscar Arias, would support them if he was elected in 1986. (Ugalde told me that people of both political parties were accused of this.)

"Alvaro Ugalde got shamefully little support from people who should have been much more vocal," said Michael Kaye about the Corcovado crisis. Kaye lost his ecotourism operation in the park because of the crisis. "We had a very portable, low-investment, low-key, de facto concession in Sirena," he told me. "We lost that when visitation at Sirena was prohibited and they needed it for park personnel, rightfully so. Wrongfully so, in that there should have been the political courage and integrity to enforce the law. Probably twenty people is the acceptable limit of impact for illegal gold panning in the park, because the amount of resources to get it down to zero would be inordinate. When it got to a hundred, they should have increased the resources and put in what they needed then to get it back down to twenty. Rather than doing that, they ended up having to spend probably twenty times as much per miner to get it down from two thousand to one hundred, and de facto raised the acceptable limit, because once you've had two thousand miners, and you get it down to a hundred, you're willing to settle."

Ugalde did more than plead for help, however. He used National Parks Foundation funds to launch a nationwide media campaign of television spots and newspaper ads that generated eight thousand "Save Corcovado" letters to President Monge. He opened negotiations with the National Mining Chamber, and began legal proceedings against one hundred miners in the most sensitive area of the park in preparation for bringing in the Civil Guard to forcibly remove them. Finally, in January 1986, the Park Service obtained a court order under the Judge of Instruction in Golfito, Licenciado Gerardo Madrigal, calling not only for the miners' eviction but also for their arrest and prosecution.

In early March hundreds of Rural and Civil Guards began sweeping the park's three main watersheds to carry out the court order. They arrested miners and ferried them to Golfito, where they were detained en masse to await trial and sentencing. Despite miners' threats of resistance, the operation was largely peaceful, although a March 9 *La Nación* article quoted miners as accusing the Rural Guard of burning their houses. "For some of them," the article said, "eviction from the park is a 'crucifixion,' because they say: 'We don't know what we'll do to feed our families.'"

The government reacted to the arrests with surprise. A March 8 *La Nación* article reported that Minister of the Presidency Jiménez had "accused the Director of the National Park Service" of having "great responsibility" for the miners' problems. "Various institutions agreed that we had to save the park," Jiménez said, "so we decided to make a complete study of the situation of the miners and who should receive state help. Nevertheless, ignoring what we'd decided, the NPS Director went to Golfito and presented the *denuncia* to start the evictions at a time when the government was unprepared." In a *La República* article two days later, Minister Jiménez maintained that Ugalde had "acted in a precipitate manner, disconnected from the presidential mandate. . . . The act of the Park Director is going to trigger a tense situation for which we don't have real solutions to offer." Ugalde had "forced the government's hand."

When I talked to him in 1990, Ugalde had no doubts about the rightness of his 1986 actions. "I had no confusion about the responsibility I had and the power I had to do it," he said. "Jiménez was not my minister. The law gives responsibility to the rangers and the Park Service. The political structure, of course, sometimes doesn't help. But there was no doubt in my mind that if we didn't go ahead and do it—he wouldn't have allowed it. If we'd asked for permission, we wouldn't have gotten it. So I did it, deliberately, of course.

"We didn't want a confrontation, but we couldn't wait until this guy decided—which was going to be after elections—*if* he decided. And so we had to do what the law told us to do, and take them to court. Taking somebody to court if they're breaking the law, you don't ask somebody's permission for that. It's your duty, and we've always done it, without permission, of course, with hunters, whatever."

As in the past, Ugalde got after-the-fact support from the Agriculture Ministry. (He told me he didn't remember if he'd asked the Agriculture minister's permission to file the Golfito denuncia.) Rodolfo Navas of the Agriculture Ministry said that the national interest should prevail over the private interests of miners, and asked the Ministry of Energy and Mines to locate places where they could be moved. The March 8 *La Nación* article that aired Jiménez's complaints about Ugalde also quoted Navas as saying, "I respect the opinion of Jiménez, but I think the responsibility goes higher than that which the Director of National Parks could have."

The San José papers buzzed with Corcovado for a few weeks. As well as Jiménez's and Navas's charges and countercharges, the March 8 *La Nación* reported a miners' protest march against the evictions in Golfito (illustrated with photos of Rural Guards unloading surprised-looking miners on the Golfito docks), and a promise by judicial sources to release from detention miners who promised not to return to the park. The March 10 *La Nación* carried an article about a lawyer who planned to accuse the Rural Guard of damages to miners, and a National Parks Foundation ad asking readers to sign petitions in support of the park. "We Need Corcovado" the ad proclaimed, over a scarlet macaw's picture. It asked President Monge and President-elect Arias to "give highest priority to consolidation of the park as an area of biological richness and tourism, and to immediately stop all mining in the park" (which was redundant, since this already had been done).

The March 11 *La Nación* featured a Rural Guard repudiation of charges of damages to a miner's home, and a letter to the editor from Mario Boza headlined "Damage in Corcovado" and illustrated with a photo of miners digging a deep, muddy hole. "We are concerned," the letter said, "that in the case of the evictions from Corcovado National Park attention has been centered entirely on the plight of the miners. There has been no mention of the damage they have done in the protected zone, in violation of the laws safeguarding our national heritage, in spite of the measures which have been placed before the government with sufficient foresight to prevent just such a situation as now presents itself."

The March 12 *La Nación* reported that the Guard would conclude its evictions within twenty-four hours and that Guard Colonel Luis Orozco had "highlighted the collaboration of the miners with the police." The paper also reported that the miners were preparing their own petitions to the president, and it printed an appeal for volunteers to work in other national parks now that most Park Service personnel had gone to Corcovado to deal with the miners.

By March 14 most of the Guard had left the park, and Ugalde declared it "free of miners for the first time in ten years." He told *The Tico Times* that the National Gold Miners' Union had acknowledged damaging the park, and would accept relocation of the Corcovado miners. He added that the miners' trials would continue, but predicted that the sentences would be light. Ugalde also said that the government had committed itself to help the miners relocate, and to provide them with low interest loans over a five-year grace period.

A March 21 *La Nación* article reported that the Rural Guard had declared the case closed, but planned to leave forty-five police in Corcovado to prevent further invasions. The article quoted Park Service Subdirector José María Rodríguez as confirming the conclusion of the evictions. Rodríguez added that people had been detained for mining in the park at night during the past few days, however, and that miners might still be hiding in the forest.

Despite Rodríguez's caveat, media and public turned their attention away from Corcovado after March. "This system is very crisis-oriented," Daniel Janzen told me. "It responds very strongly to crises by mobilizing energy toward the crisis. As soon as the crisis is over, the same energy and effort is diverted to some other crisis instead of staying on the crisis situation and then flipping into the second mode of more long-term planning, of saying: 'We've got the fire out, now let's set up a fire control program so we don't have another fire.' Instead, what happens is you put the fire out, and you run to another fire, and next year the same set of processes that generated the first fire will just generate another one. Corcovado is a very good example of this. As soon as the gold miners were out, the immediate pressure was off, and people then responded to whatever their concept of the next crisis was."

The gold miners didn't forget the Corcovado crisis, however. In April 1987, after a year of waiting for government aid in makeshift shelters in Golfito and Puerto Jiménez, hundreds of miners marched the 226 kilometers to San José and camped in downtown parks. I rode past these camps during my bus ride to Tortuguero. The miners and their families seemed underdressed for the breezy and foggy San José climate.

The miners picketed the Legislative Assembly (located near the parks they camped in), and seventy miners went on a hunger strike to pressure the government to do something. The government responded by agreeing to indemnify 294 of them, and to consider the cases of another two hundred. The miners left San José in May, but in October they were back. The government then arranged a 45-million-colones loan to "end the problem" as *The Tico Times* reported.

José María Rodríguez served as executive secretary of an institutional commission on the miners. "In 1986 I worked almost full-time on the problem," he told me. "There was a lot of inter-institutional coordination for attempts to do it so that different agencies would give the miners what they were supposed to—so they could make a new living, a legal one. But it was really complicated. It was easy to think of giving them land to plant, but the majority of them weren't farmers. The government was willing to help them mine legally outside the park, but only if they got organized. Our mining laws give very little room for individuals mining. So we asked them to form cooperatives so the government could help them.

"But these people are very individualistic. It's not by chance that they became gold miners in the Osa. There's something in them that makes them choose that, although many were there from desperation. So it was difficult. Very few were organized. All that year, only one cooperative really went along the steps to become legally established with a concession right outside the park. They soon started making good money. Then other groups tried to make cooperatives, but most couldn't get along. Very complicated people to deal with.

"Their representatives weren't good. Very often large groups were completely opposed to what their committees were saying to the government. So sometimes an agreement with the committees wouldn't work. The thing the government least wanted to do was give them a cash compensation, because it was thought that they'd spend the money and there'd be no real solution to the problem. After they were compensated, we tried to establish a monitoring program to see what would happen later, but we can't really say now what became of those who received the compensation."

Mining remained a problem in Corcovado. Rodríguez told me in 1990 that one hundred to two hundred were still sneaking into the park for short periods. In 1988, when the Minister of Natural Resources, Energy, and Mines, Alvaro Umaña, flew over the Osa Peninsula with Project Lighthawk, he saw both miners and loggers operating illegally, although Ugalde said they were outside the park. Over eighty miners were arrested in Corcovado that year. In September 1989 *The Tico Times* reported that fifty miners had held two park guards hostage overnight when the guards had surprised them digging illegally near Cerro Oro. Four of the miners were arrested.

Tourism and research in Corcovado recovered slowly from the 1985 crisis. In 1990 visitors had to charter a plane, hire a boat, or walk across the Osa Peninsula from Puerto Jimenez to reach the park. Ugalde told me that Michael Kaye resumed operations in the park in 1991, however, and that tourism was "slowly but surely picking up."

fifteen

Branching Out

The Corcovado evictions were as traumatic for the Park Service as they were for the gold miners. The crisis brought to the surface problems that had been developing for years. "The gold mining situation was kind of the last gasp of the old Park Service mystique," Michael Kaye told me, "from the days when they were swinging machetes shoulder to shoulder at Santa Rosa, living in primitive conditions, eating simple food, and being away from their families for long periods because they were building this park system. That just doesn't exist anymore, and that isn't a criticism, because by its very nature that kind of mystique is of limited duration.

"I think the mystique had gotten very sick around 1981 or 1982," Kaye said, "when Alvaro had left the Park Service and gone into funding and the Parks Foundation. Then Alvaro came back in 1985 and brought it back. I don't know if he alone could have brought it back, but he had this situation where he became the man alone against all of Costa Rica, staking his prestige, publicly defying the Minister of the Presidency who was clearly speaking for the president . . . .Alvaro really burnt himself out and made a lot of enemies forcing the government to either show themselves as charlatans or enforce the law in Corcovado. Very acrimonious situations. It took a real emotional toll."

Ugalde resigned from the Park Service in April 1986, right after the evictions. "I was burnt up . . . 'burnt out' I think is the way you say it, from that crisis," he told me, "and the new administration kept Danilo Jiménez, the former Minister of the Presidency, not as a minister, but as an adviser with ministerial rank, so to me that was a big blow. It was pretty obvious to me that in the cabinet—as was proven later—he'd do nothing but badmouth me. Throughout all the discussions about Corcovado, he blamed me constantly.

"But it was different to blame a guy who was now a civilian than to blame the Park Service director. He could complain about me, but who was I? Nobody. The Park Service was clean from that hatred of his. And I didn't want to deal with a whole new set of politicians. I was tired, and I needed a break from twelve years of being the director of the Park Service, and I think the institution needed a break from me."

The Arias administration appointed Luis Mendez as park director in Ugalde's place. Mendez had been sharing the subdirectorship with José María Rodríguez since the 1970s and had acted as director in 1984 when Ugalde and Rodríguez had both been away, Rodríguez studying in Michigan and Ugalde fundraising. A January 1984 *Tico Times* article described Mendez as "a biologist with a reputation for being an efficient, hard worker." It quoted Mendez as saying that his main goal was to "technically define" Park Service policies on inholdings and to facilitate expropriation of them. "All that's needed," he said (apropos the Palo Verde National Park segregation issue), "is a little communication with the congressmen and recognition of the interests of the country."

The Arias administration provided the Park Service not only with a new director but with a new ministry. It moved the Service and other conservation agencies into what had been the Ministry of Energy and Mines and renamed it the Ministry of Natural Resources, Energy, and Mines (MIRENEM). Arias appointed Alvaro Umaña, a brilliant young environmental engineer and economist, to head the new ministry. Luis Mendez told *The Tico Times* he was pleased with the move. "The Minister of Agriculture has his hands full coordinating the nation's production of foodstuffs," he commented, and "he seldom has time for other problems." *The Times* added that Mendez had "timidly requested" an additional eighty rangers in addition to the existing "ill-equipped" 250 to provide "minimal protection" to the parks.

Conservationists generally applauded moving the Park Service out of the Agriculture Ministry. "It was absolutely necessary to separate natural resources from agriculture," Mario Boza commented in a

February 1989 *Tico Times* article. "A minister like Umaña can spend his time on conservation. I think he has exceeded our expectations; he has done more than we thought he'd do." The new ministry didn't mean a greatly increased budget for parks, however. Director Mendez was still complaining about an inadequate staff in 1989. A *Tico Times* article that year quoted him as saying he'd have to double his ranger staff to maximize protection for the parks.

Yet even a doubling of rangers wouldn't really have maximized protection, except in the limited sense of reducing fires, poaching and other manageable, if grave, problems. For some years, conservationists' worst nightmares had been shifting away from what happened in parks to what was happening around them. By the mid-1980s, after forty years of a deforestation rate of about one percent of national territory a year, the end of Costa Rica's unprotected primary forest was in sight.

During the International Union for the Conservation of Nature's 17th General Assembly in San José in 1988, Costa Rica revealed that it had even less loggable primary forest than it had thought. Aerial photos had seemed to show about eight or nine percent of the country outside parks and reserves as primary hardwood forest. New satellite photos showed, however, that much of that was palm forest, useless for timber production. It appeared that Costa Rica's logging industry had about five percent of the national territory to operate on, less than a decade's worth at most. This was considered very bad news for protected forests, forest reserves, and national parks. Not only would parks be increasingly threatened by illegal logging and political land grabs, but their isolation in a deforested country would increase every other outside pressure.

Isolation was already a reality for most Costa Rican parks by the late 1980s. When I toured the parks in 1987, farmland extended to almost every park border I saw. Sometimes it was inconspicuous, as at Tortuguero and Corcovado, where the fruit trees and second growth of low-intensity traditional farming softened the contrast. Sometimes the contrast was blatant, as at Palo Verde, where a line of dry forest trees newly bulldozed by a government agricultural project marked the border.

Corcovado wasn't the only protected area to be invaded because the people living around it were insufficiently convinced of its value to them as a nature preserve (although Alvaro Ugalde says it was the only national park). In 1990 I heard from several sources that over a thousand families were living in the large Barra Colorado Wildlife Refuge north of Tortuguero on the Nicaraguan border. John Mc-Phaul, who began writing about Costa Rican park issues in 1981, told me: "When I first came here, I was surprised by people squatting in reserves. I couldn't understand why they just didn't arrest them. After being here awhile I could see people go into the reserves not from malice but from poverty. Costa Ricans aren't as authoritarian in treatment of this kind of problem as the States." McPhaul nevertheless thought the conservation system was threatened. "It's reaching the critical stage where deforestation is reaching park boundaries," he said, "and it's pretty obvious that once those forests are gone, people will start looking at the parks for a wood supply unless reforestation and education take hold."

The parks' growing isolation and vulnerability may have been a factor in the shift away from the old mystique that Michael Kaye talked about. Joaquin Gamboa, a long-time parks worker who was Santa Rosa's chief of operations when I talked to him in 1990, had experiences that seemed typical. "I started with the Park Service when I was nineteen, in 1972," he told me. "I was studying to be a mechanic when a friend suggested we go to work for the parks. I didn't know what they were, but when we went to the parks office, the salary seemed attractive compared to what I'd get as a mechanic. I started as a workman at Santa Rosa. We were like a family then, eight of us in the park. If I didn't have enough money, my compañero gave it to me.

"In those days there were lots of jobs everywhere, so only the really dedicated worked in the parks. There was no need to be cold and hungry in Santa Rosa. People didn't work for a salary, but for adventure, chasing hunters. I thought of myself as a policeman, and of the national park as a kind of zoo that I had to protect from the local people, the people living around the park. We didn't feel we needed those people. The important thing then was for the parks to get as much land as possible and protect it. And that worked. We would have lost all the woods if it hadn't been for the parks. Our forests now correspond to the parks.

"But little by little, a series of internal changes have occurred to this idea of protection. In 1978 and 1979, we began to realize that we wouldn't be able to protect the parks in the long run if we were alone, if it was just us in the park against the world outside. We used to want to please ourselves, but we've had to learn to please others. We realized that we should be promoting the park to the local people, acting as guides as well as rangers. We started having groups of schoolchildren in, doing environmental education. We began to see local people had things to offer us.

"When I worked in Tortuguero," Gamboa told me, "it was strange at first because the language and mentality of the people there is different. At first, we were just concerned with saving the turtles, doing what outside experts said. Then Archie Carr told us, 'Why don't you share with the local people more?' We needed to try to learn their culture, learn that they're Costa Ricans too. So we started asking the local people about how to save the turtles, and things began to change. They had needs that we could help them with as well as helping us protect the turtles."

The old mystique was largely masculine, if not macho. This also began to change as the police mentality shifted to a guide mentality. Gladys de Marco, environmental education coordinator in San José in 1990, went to work for the Park Service in 1978. "I started as a guide," she told me. "Before, the only women in the parks were cooks. I felt a little odd. The men were *machistos* and I couldn't cut wood or climb mountains. I was the only woman in a house with fifteen men. I worked as subdirector at several parks; then, during the mining situation, I worked doing public relations at Corcovado. We had to present ourselves to the Osa community, which was against us. We gave talks, showed films, made a theatrical group. It was a very fruitful experience, the first time I went out and presented myself to the community. The experience was valuable in other work. We have to understand what's going on in the community. In turn, the parks can act as guides to help communities make their own solutions to conservation problems."

Gladys de Marco told me that about fifteen percent of Park Service staff exclusive of cooks were women in 1990. When I talked to her, she was working in the same office as her husband, Juan Diego Alfaro. The couple hadn't always been able to live and work in the same place, however, and family life continues to be a particular problem of Park Service personnel.

"I've been with the parks fifteen years," Guanacaste park administrator Sigifredo Marín told me. "When I was single I didn't mind living with a bunch of guardaparques. But when I got married, I wanted to live in San José." Marín had moved his family to Santa Rosa National Park, however, unlike many employees who left theirs in Meseta Central towns and visited them on leave. "Park people should live in the region where they work, not start thinking about leaving as soon as they arrive. If people who have their families and friends in the region work for the parks, the parks become less celestial, more down-to-earth. The work can't end at the park boundaries. We should give more to the professionals who work in the field so they don't have to ask San José for everything." Marín's decision had not been an easy one, however. "Some people think I'm crazy," he said. "My kid has to get up at 4:30 to take the bus to Liberia and go to school."

Mario Boza stated the park system's dilemma with his usual discernment in his Getty Award acceptance speech in 1983. "Creating a park on paper is easy. . . . Preserving it is another story. We have to teach the people what conservation is. That more than simply protecting animals and plants, conservation is a tool of development. Without the support of the people, though, we go nowhere." Yet it was one thing for individuals to perceive that "no park is an island" and quite another to develop policies that would transform parks from increasingly isolated enclaves to integrated elements of regional economies and cultures.

At this point, after a hiatus of some years, Costa Rica's scientific community again assumed a leadership role in parks. Instrumental in getting the park system launched, the University of Costa Rica Biology Department and the Colegio de Biólogos had been less active in the late 1970s and early 1980s, perhaps because the numbers of professional conservationists had increased. Pedro León, possibly the most active university professor in parks work from the time he encouraged Ugalde in 1969, told me he spent most of his spare time in the early and mid-1980s involved in the peace movement. After Corcovado nearly collapsed, León became active in parks again, and helped to bring in another figure who would become very influential.

Rodrigo Gámez had just been named head of the brand-new Costa Rican Institute of Biodiversity when I talked to him in 1990. Created with a $5 million endowment from a debt-for-nature swap, the Institute was so new that the cabdriver who'd brought me from downtown San José to the suburb of Santo Domingo de Heredia was not sure how to find it. A white building behind high iron gates, it looked from the outside more like a small, high-technology factory than a place for cataloguing tropical organisms, and this reflected the pragmatic orientation that Gámez had given to Costa Rican conservation since 1986. Inside, the Institute looked more biological, with large arums, palms, and Monsteras in pots and pictures of terns and spoonbills on the walls, but there was so much shouting and bustling from the sizable staff that Gámez and I had to retire to the air-conditioned herbarium to talk. It was an unusually hot day for the Meseta Central, so that was no hardship.

"This Institute is devoted to getting use out of protected areas," Gámez told me. "We need to change people's attitudes to nature toward a greater level of complexity. To change attitudes, we need to know what we have, because one doesn't value what one doesn't know, and the tragedy of tropical forests has been that they have had no value more than the wood in them and the land they grew on. The North American forest disappeared because what was valued was land and wood. The rest had no value. We want the tropical forests not to disappear because they have many other valuable things, but to value them, one must know them. Yet the truth is that we hardly know them. That's why we say, 'Let's make an inventory of all we have, where it is, and what it's good for.' In other words, let's prove that we should conserve the biodiversity of the country because we know it and use it."

Gámez's new job of putting the forest to work represented a career shift for him as well as the forest. "I worked in scientific research all my life," he told me, "first on basic information for agriculture, not just agricultural production but the basics of botany, entomology, soils, and climatology. Agriculture interests me because of the perspectives it gives on social problems and the relationship between the human being and nature—all the historical aspects of agriculture. Then I gradually got interested in other things, the problems of viruses, viruses of plants and insects, and the molecular aspects. We created a center for research in cellular biology and a course in electron microscopy.

"I was working with Pedro León on this, and he was the first to get me to look at conservation problems in Costa Rica, mainly in the national parks. I've been a nature aficionado since I was a kid. My father encouraged me, and I was a Boy Scout for twelve, fifteen years. Pedro and I have always been professional and personal friends. We've published a lot together. So I got acquainted with Alvaro Ugalde, Mario Boza, Luis Diego Gomez and others of what might be called the 'conservation cartel.' At first I acted as an advisor to the National Parks Foundation; later they asked me to join the board of directors, a position I accepted very enthusiastically. I worked on fundraising, taking visitors to the parks, and got to know the people and problems from the perspective of someone coming from outside.

"I was very impressed with what had been created there, by Mario as initiator and Alvaro as consolidator," Gámez said. "I did feel, as a scientist accustomed to working in teams, for research or organization, that the Foundation never really functioned as a team. The parks were in a very serious crisis—a crisis of organization and of human and economic resources. The parks had been increasing gradually in area while the infrastructure and resources of the Service had been shrinking. Alvaro was mainly working at fundraising, and there was a great emphasis on money and methodologies of fundraising. But we weren't talking much about basic concepts. They were taken for granted. But, I asked myself, 'Why do we want parks? What do we want to do with them, really? Make them part of Costa Rican society? Are parks really part of us, or a luxury, something for the few?'

"It seemed to me that we'd made in Costa Rica a copy of the national parks in the United States, based on the idea that nature should simply be left alone to take care of itself. The only thing required was to protect nature from threats, which of course were threats from humans. Maintaining humans at a distance, outside, would solve the problem, so the thing needed was guardaparques. The Park Service had a very pyramidal structure. Everything was in San José, and parks were out there on very tenuous lines of communication. There was a whole constellation of ideas, practices, and traditions of park management which didn't make much sense or have much practical function.

"For example, guardaparques had to be from somewhere else than the park, usually San José. Local people couldn't work in parks because they were the hunters, the ones who'd damage the parks. The Park Service was like an army, invading these strange countries, living on very low salaries under very poor conditions, but supported by a mystical sense of purpose—as long as they had a strong leader like Alvaro Ugalde. But without a strong leader, when Alvaro had to go and spend his time fundraising, the pyramid began to collapse.

"Alvaro and I talked about this at a conference he invited me to co-author a paper for. It was the first chance I'd had to speak seriously on the subject. Alvaro at first didn't agree with my ideas. But I felt it was essential to see things in the whole socioeconomic context. The problem of the parks wasn't biological, it was social, political, and economic, and if we didn't pay attention to that, the parks wouldn't have any future. From there, we began to talk a lot about the need to create another organization than the National Parks Foundation. That was in 1984 and 1985."

A need had become evident for an organization that would deal with the relationship between parks and surrounding areas, as the National Parks Organization was dealing with the relationship between parks, government, and conservation organizations. Discussions such as Gámez's and Ugalde's resulted in the creation of Fundación Neotrópica in 1985. The new foundation didn't seem to be the immediate answer to problems like the Corcovado invasion, however. Operating out of the same building and with the same staff as the Parks Foundation, in its early years Neotrópica remained something of an appendage of the older foundation, according to Vera Varela, Neotrópica's new director in 1990.

"Neotrópica wasn't carrying out its intended task of working on buffer zones for the parks," Varela told me. "Instead it was basically serving as a bank for debt swaps and other national park funding ventures." When I talked to her, Varela and Neotrópica had just acquired an office and staff all their own. "When separation came," she said, "it was decided that the National Parks Foundation would continue to act as a bank, while Neotrópica would work on buffer zones. We feel like a new organization, although we're going to have to seek funds aggressively to reach our objectives."

With the nongovernmental organization segment of the conservation community proving slow to respond to problems Gámez perceived, his actions eventually took the form of more direct involvement with the park system itself. "We'd never heard of the phrase 'sustainable development' then," Gámez told me, referring to the popular late 1980s catchword for third world conservation. "It didn't exist in 1985. But I'm a generalist. I know the practical problems of food production in marginal areas, which is where most of the parks are. It's not possible for a population to have a sufficient level of development, a satisfaction of basic needs, working under such poor conditions. I could see that if we didn't pay attention to that, we'd be like Africa in a few years, with impoverished people pressing on the parks from all sides. The campesinos living near the parks, trying to make a subsistence living—all they'd hear from the parks was, 'No, you can't go in there. No you can't hunt there. No, no, no.'

"The funds that had been raised had all been for protection and land acquisition—nothing for socioeconomic planning, nothing for management, nothing for research. And the parks were being managed without any knowledge of biology. I was amazed at meetings about park matters where there was no discussion of biology. I'd read a little ecology and conservation biology, and it was very obvious that, proud as we were to have put a quarter of our land in some kind of conservation unit, there was a problem with viability of wildlife populations. Populations were shrinking, but nobody was focusing on the problem. Biological researchers were seen almost as undesirables, like the *crudo* Daniel Janzen who dared to criticize management at Santa Rosa. He was a nuisance, although to be tolerated because, after all, he really liked the park.

"I'd met Janzen at the conference where Alvaro and I gave the paper. He was one of the first to come up to talk afterwards, and we wound up saying, 'We have to work together on this. Let's see if we can find a strategy for how to instigate a process of change.' I say 'process' because we were barely beginning to understand the problem. We didn't have any solution to how to make development, as we now say, sustainable in marginal areas.

"At this point came a very important decision," Gámez said. "Alvaro Ugalde and I participated in a campaign commission of the Liberación Party on the quality of life. It wasn't strictly on the parks, but it was very interesting because it put environmental problems in a social and economic context. Another commission came to the conclusion that there should be a Ministry of Natural Resources, which we supported completely. Here appeared a figure who was totally unknown to us named Alvaro Umaña, who of course became the Minister. We put together a group of conservationists who supported the idea, including Janzen, Boza, Ugalde, and Pedro León.

"Then Umaña asked me to be his vice minister for natural resources. I didn't want to get involved in a government job, but I talked the idea over in a meeting with the group to see what would be of most benefit to the parks. My position, which finally had the support of the whole group, was that I was more interested in being an advisor, but with a certain degree of authority, which would allow me to push forward the process of change which we'd been discussing.

"It happened that President Arias was an old friend of mine, not for political reasons, but because we came from the same town, Heredia. My father had been involved in politics in many ways, and during the Figueres administration he'd been Minister of Education when Arias was Minister of Planning. So there was an old familial, political, and local relationship in practical terms. I didn't want to go through the minister, but to have a direct relationship with the president. This opened many doors, always remembering that the president never said to us, 'How much do you need for the parks? Lots of millions, right?' The president said, 'Forget it. It's not viable politically to commit so many millions to the parks because parks don't have any function, they're a luxury. Costa Ricans are very proud of their parks, but it's pride in an adornment.' That perception was evident in politicians. 'You need money? You don't say? What do you need money for?' And a lot of money had been spent on parks.

"So we started this new movement of reexamining the subject," Gámez told me, "because if we didn't put the parks in the socioeconomic context of the whole country, we wouldn't receive the resources we needed. It was getting harder and harder to get funds simply for the parks' scenery and wildlife. Janzen had been working on the idea of a national park in Guanacaste Province which would put into practice important ecological considerations. It would mean a radical change in management, a change totally inimical to Park Service people, who saw Daniel as an invader. Daniel is a tremendous critic, and he's usually right, but nobody likes to be told they're ugly.

"Now, examining objectively Janzen's point of view, it wasn't difficult for Umaña and me and others in the scientific and academic community to see that the idea had merit. So we got to work and really supported the changes that would help Guanacaste to develop. Using Guanacaste as a pilot project, we put together a commission of representatives from key institutions—Boza from the foundations, Luis Mendez from the parks, Alberto Vargas from the Forestry Directorate—and tried to discuss how to put ideas into action that could be carried forward."

sixteen

Boosting the GNP

Daniel Janzen outlined his idea for a new park that would consolidate the existing Santa Rosa and Murciélago areas with additional land in a little book entitled *Guanacaste National Park: Tropical Ecological and Cultural Restoration*, published in 1986. "When the Spaniards arrived," he wrote, "there were 550,000 square kilometers of dry forest on the Pacific side of lowland tropical Mesoamerica. . . . This dry forest occupied as much or more of the Mesoamerican lowlands as did rainforest. Today less than two percent of this dry forest exists as relatively undisturbed wildlands, and only .08 percent of it lies within national parks or other kinds of protected areas. . . . To save what dry forest we have, we are going to have to give some land back to it. Habitat restoration is essential before natural and anthropogenic fluctuations and perturbations extinguish many of the small populations and habitat remnants that have survived to this date.

"Likewise, when the Spaniards arrived," Janzen wrote, "the dry forest was occupied by peoples with intimate, if pragmatic, factual knowledge and cultural understanding of the dry forest. Today, virtually all of the present-day occupants of the western Mesoamerican pastures, fields, and degraded forests are deaf, blind, and mute to the fragments of the rich biological and cultural heritage that still occupies the shelves of the unused and unappreciated library in which they reside. The schoolchildren of a Mesoamerican town have neither their predecessors' contact with the natural world, nor the human cultural offerings of the large cities that are supported by their parents' agricultural activities. What gives a greater return—build a cultural center in the fields cut from the forest or lead the audience to the cultural center that already exists in the forest? We must lead the audience to the forest, or all the well-meaning conservation efforts in the tropical world will disappear down humanity's throat."

Janzen outlined three overall functions for the new park: to "use existing dry forest fragments as seed to restore about 700 square kilometers of topographically diverse land to a dry forest that is sufficiently large and diverse to maintain in perpetuity all animal and plant species, and their habitats, known to originally inhabit the site"; to "restore and maintain a tropical wildland so as to offer a menu of material goods such as plant and animal gene banks and stocking material, reforestation examples with native trees, watershed protection, manipulation of vegetation by livestock, recreation sites, tourism profits, wildlife management examples, agroforestry research data, educational programs (from elementary levels to international symposia), and basic wildland biology data"; and, finally, to "use a tropical wildland as the stimulus and factual base for a reawakening to the intellectual and cultural offerings of the natural world."

The area Janzen proposed for the park stretched from the Pacific to the volcanoes of the Cordillera de Guanacaste, and included fifteen habitats, not only dry forest and the evergreen riparian forest, live oak woodland, and savanna-grassland interspersed with it, but also four kinds of semi-evergreen or wet forest growing on the hills and peaks east of the plains. Janzen wanted to include the highlands because he'd discovered that many species he was studying in dry forest depended on wet forest for part of their livelihood.

"It is commonplace to think of the Pacific Mesoamerican dry forests as ecologically distinct from the rainforests and upper elevation forests of central and Atlantic Mesoamerica," he wrote. "However, recent studies of flying animals in Santa Rosa and other parts of Guanacaste Province's dry forest make it abundantly clear that many 'rainforest' insects and some birds spend the rainy season in the dry forest and the dry season in the rainforest or in nearby moist forest refugia. Obliteration of either wet or dry forest will obliterate the animals. One cannot view Costa Rica's national park system as a series of islands, but rather as a network partly connected by migrants."

Janzen projected an $11.8 million "startup and endowment" cost for the Guanacaste National Park Project (GNP, also GNPP), "the cost of one medium-sized new building in a U.S. university campus." The projected acquisitions included about a dozen sizable haciendas and a number of smaller squatter parcels being carved out of the unregulated Orosi Forest Reserve on the volcano slopes. He also projected a five-year "window of opportunity" to accomplish the project. "Within the next five to ten years the wildland component of Costa Rican society will be forever fixed in place," he wrote. "What Costa Rican habitat is not in preserves will be dead, and the next stage (which we have already entered) is that of improving the quality of both wildland preserves and agriculture in the ecosystem. The preserves that do not become adequately integrated into Costa Rican society will die as well. Small parts of the GNP plan are of crisis urgency, and if the entire plan is not in place and functioning by 1990, there will be no choice but to retreat to the 108 square kilometers of Santa Rosa National Park and apply the GNP plan on a scale that is biologically and socially much inferior."

When I talked to him in 1990, Janzen told me that the GNP idea had been partly a result of sociological implications from the Corcovado miners study. "I finished that in July or August of 1985," he told me, "and gave it to Alvaro and went away, back to my own things. But, simultaneously in August of that year, Winnie Hallwachs and I went to Australia at the request of the Australian government to take a look at their tropical dry forest—its biology, administration, and future, and what do you do with it—all those kinds of questions. So we spent a month looking at a lot of dry forest and trying to figure out what would you do with it if you had it to use and manage. And we also were very impressed with the damage that had been done by fifty thousand years of continuous burning. [Australian dry forest was long burned by Aborigines for hunting, then later by whites for ranching.]

"We came back here with a couple of major questions in our heads," Janzen said. "One was asking the same questions about this dry forest as we'd been asking about the Australian one. And we came back here with the Corcovado experience in our minds, asking what should have been done to prevent the gold miners from invading Corcovado. Finally, we came back here with the observation that if fires kept on in Guanacaste as they had in Australia, there wasn't going to be any forest to try to conserve anyway. So, those three things: how do you avoid invasions in the first place; how do you use land so that people feel it's being used valuably; and how do you stop the fires?

"September or October of 1985 was when the idea of the project jelled. At the time, Mario Boza said, 'I'll get the description of the project published,' which he did with the book by Universidad Estatal a Distancia [UNED] in 1986. Mario was a professor at UNED. So I had Mario helping to get the plan published and helping to find the project a home at the foundations. He was very much in favor of the project at the time; he thought it was a great idea. When I went to Alvaro with the project, he was very against it, basically because it allowed some expansion of the system when it was already overextended. He thought they didn't have the administrative abilities, people, or budget to handle a big thing like that.

"I said, 'Yeah, but part of my job on this is to raise the money. I'm not saying you guys should go out to find the money.' Then in August of 1986, after Alvaro had been on some kind of vacation, he came back, and we were talking on the telephone, and I mentioned that I was going to Volcán Cacao, part of the eastern half of the project, which Alvaro had never been on. So I said, 'Why don't you come along?' Because that was when we were still kind of planning and thinking. So he did, and in the process of that trip he changed his mind about whether the project could work. And I think in his mind the basic things that brought it into reality were, first, that the wet forests of the volcanos are a critical part of where those dry forest organisms migrate; second, that Santa Rosa is too small to sustain serious use by people and still save what's there. So if you're going to save this piece of dry forest and have people use it for recreation and research and all these things, you've got to enlarge it substantially.

"Alvaro Ugalde has been sort of a solid point out there all the way through," Janzen told me. "Someone we knew who understood what this was all about, the basic framework and the little details, although we weren't necessarily in agreement on every particular detail. Mario also has been a strong supporter on part of it. It's just that as we got closer to 1986 and the elections came up, Mario was involved with one party while many other people were involved with a different party. Mario distanced himself from the project because it was involved with the Liberación government. It wasn't easy politically for him to participate that much, although we've both been on the five-member commission for developing this thing over the past four years. We talk a lot about a lot of things, and Mario supports these activities strongly, although again we may not agree on details.

"In November of 1985, after we got the idea of GNP, Rodrigo Gámez took us to see Arias. This was before he was elected. My friend Winnie Hallwachs and I sat there in the living room and described the thing pretty much as you see it today. And Arias and his wife, Margarita, said: 'Sounds fine, but don't count on us for a penny.' And we said: 'That's fine.' We weren't looking for money, we were looking for approval. None of this could have occurred without the political approval of the Arias government, any more than it could have occurred without Boza's and Ugalde's support."

As it happened, political support was all that GNP needed from the government to take off. The project soon began to generate funding beyond conservationists' dreams. "Daniel Janzen has an extraordinary capacity to raise funds and develop grant proposals," Rodrigo Gámez told me. Following Ugalde's example, Janzen hit the circuit of charitable foundations and other sources in the U.S. He had amassed considerable scientific prestige over the years, for example, by winning the Swedish Academy of Science's Craaford Prize, called "the Nobel of ecological science." (Janzen used the money to bring electricity to the Santa Rosa administrative area.) Janzen also has a colorful, original personality: he's been said to have referred to himself as "an archetypal spoiled brat." These qualities combined to make him a darling of U.S. media for several years, with articles in *Time* and other mainstream publications and a PBS television documentary about GNP.

Janzen apparently disliked his temporary celebrity. "There's a very, very, *very* negative behavior on the part of the U.S. gossip scene to want to lionize individuals," he told me in 1990. "Bullshit. A particular need or challenge occurs. Somebody puts his hand up first and says, 'Okay, I'll do that job.' So he does it, and we look at the job and say, 'That was important.' But if he hadn't done it, somebody else would have." Janzen put his celebrity to good use, in any case. With the help of the National Parks and Neotrópica foundations, The Nature Conservancy, the World Wildlife Fund, and others, he managed to raise three million of the estimated $11.8 million needed for GNP by 1987.

The GNP also came at the right time. The northern Guanacaste Province cattle industry was in decline, and the Nicaraguan situation had discouraged speculation in other kinds of investment, so many of the haciendas needed for the project were willing to sell. Janzen convinced owners whose land he was not yet able to buy to take it off the market for a year in expectation of purchase by the project.

The Guanacaste National Park Project quickly began using applied sociology. A potential problem was that squatters and small landowners who had sold land to the project might be tempted to move back into the area once the money from the sale was gone. Sudden large amounts of cash injected into the rural community might also cause crime and other disruptive effects. To mitigate this, GNP arranged with the bank that was handling land payments to open accounts for land sellers as soon as it paid them.

In July 1987 Alvaro Umaña informed Janzen that the Costa Rican government would be able to greatly magnify the GNP fund through the newly invented debt-for-nature swap process. "After we adopted GNP as our pilot project," Rodrigo Gámez told me, "we started to work with the president of the Banco Central, Eduardo Lizano, the president's economic advisor, Carlos Espinach, and natural resources Minister Umaña. Thomas Lovejoy of the World Wildlife Fund had talked of exchanging external debt for nature conservation, and we tried to develop a mechanism for doing it here. Eduardo Lizano is very intelligent, with good political insight in the best sense of the word, and we were friends because we had been members of the National Council of Scientific Investigations. We took the idea to President Arias, and he liked it a lot."

The debt exchange mechanism Costa Rica developed was basically simple. As Pedro León and Vera Varela explained it to me, money donated to the National Parks Foundation was used to buy title to Costa Rican government debts held by U.S. banks, at a fraction of their original value. The Foundation then turned the debt titles over to the Costa Rican Banco Central in exchange for credits in the form of low-interest bonds that effectively doubled or tripled the buying power of the original donations to the Foundation. The U.S. banks got some money in exchange for their overoptimistic investments of the 1970s, the Costa Rican government got some of its burdensome external debt retired, and the park system got money for land acquisition and management. In practice, each swap had its own complexities, because each was negotiated under different financial conditions, but the basic mechanism was the same for each.

Costa Rica approved its first debt swap in November 1987, and announced it at the IUCN's February 1988 General Assembly in San José. The swap produced $5.4 million worth of credits, not only for Guanacaste, but for Corcovado, Braulio Carrillo, and La Amistad. By mid-1988 Janzen was able to report that fifty-eight percent of the GNP project had been purchased, and thirteen percent was pending. One landowner donated an 18,000-acre ranch adjacent to Santa Rosa that would be operated commercially to help fund the park's endowment.

"We began by needing about $12 million for the GNPP," Janzen wrote in a letter to supporters. "Three million is now needed to finish all land purchase, establish all physical infrastructure, and establish all of the management endowment into perpetuity." A several-million-dollar endowment fund was a key feature. As Mario Boza said, "Without that, in the end, we would inherit a big problem— how to protect and maintain that large area without the proper personnel, equipment, facilities, and procedures."

The remaining twenty percent of the project's proposed land acquisitions brought up a new problem, however. It was a heavily burnt and eroded, but ecologically fascinating, piece of real estate named Hacienda Santa Elena between Murciélago and Santa Rosa. Like them, Santa Elena was a legacy of Costa Rica's sometimes stormy relations with northern neighbors. Unlike them, it belonged not to a

Nicaraguan dictator but to some rather shadowy North American businessmen. It would prove even harder to acquire for the park system than Somoza's ranches.

The Park Service had been trying to acquire Santa Elena almost from the beginning. Not only does it contain remnants of dry forest, it is otherwise extremely interesting botanically and geologically. It apparently has stood above the ocean longer than any other part of Central America, and its bedrock is peridotite, a rock from deep in the earth's crust that has unusual effects on vegetation. A savanna of native grasses and small, gnarled nancite and *Curatella* trees covers most of Santa Elena, a habitat more typical of central Venezuela than Costa Rica. It seemed to me that this savanna might be a relict of drier prehistory, when savannas extended farther into Mesoamerica. The area is still unstudied botanically, however, so nobody is sure. (I got the impression Janzen thought it was all dry forest before the Spanish conquest, and that I was being a romanticist with my peridotite savanna.)

The government had been unable to come to terms with Santa Elena's owner of record, a U.S. businessman and Costa Rican resident named Joseph Hamilton. Hamilton evidently had other plans for it. In early 1985, according to *The Tico Times,* a company called Udall Research approached the Civil Guard in Liberia to oversee a tourism project in Santa Elena. Thereafter, Civil Guards and North American engineers were seen shuttling heavy equipment back and forth through Santa Rosa and rebuilding an airport in Santa Elena's Potrero Grande Valley near the coast. According to a September 6, 1986, *Tico Times* article, civil guardsmen detained a Costa Rican who at one point had wandered into Santa Elena from Santa Rosa overnight. The guardsmen told the detainee that the North Americans had been dining on sea turtle eggs and venison while they rebuilt the airport and constructed barracks (Santa Rosa has one of the largest Kemp's ridley sea turtle nesting beaches in the world).

In May 1986 the Civil Guard withdrew from Santa Elena, but large planes continued to come and go from the rebuilt airport. In July the nearby municipality of La Cruz asked the Civil Guard to investigate the flights after numerous complaints from local residents about the noise. In September the Civil Guard reoccupied the property and the flights stopped. Shortly thereafter, the mysterious situation made international headlines.

Tico Times reporter John McPhaul was one of a small group of local journalists who broke the Santa Elena airstrip story. "We heard stories about huge airplanes flying into northern Guanacaste, and we figured the best way to find out about it was to ask the park people," he told me. "We asked one guy about it, and he said, 'Well, it's about time somebody heard about it.' He told us where the place was, that it had been busted by the Civil Guard three weeks before, who'd been seen bringing out trucks full of fuel drums. The park people were outraged because they'd been taking heavy equipment through the park without permission.

"A bunch of us hired a plane and overflew the area," McPhaul said. "Then we went and talked to the Minister of Public Security. It became the smoking gun of arming Contras by the U.S. government." Santa Elena was the famous secret airstrip which Eugene Hasenfus confessed flying from while bringing Contra arms to Nicaragua, and which Manuel Noriega allegedly contracted to furnish for Oliver North in return for funds from arms sales to Iran. In January 1987 ex-president Monge admitted that he'd agreed to allow the airstrip's rebuilding and use "in case Nicaragua invaded Costa Rica because the U.S. had invaded Nicaragua from Honduras."

On July 3, 1987, President Arias announced the Costa Rican government's intention to expropriate Santa Elena and annex it to Guanacaste National Park. Arias formally declared the annexation at a ceremony at the Santa Rosa Casona on July 25, the anniversary of Costa Rica's annexation of Guanacaste. "Highly placed Costa Rican officials," *The Tico Times* reported, called the park annexation "a statement to the international community that Costa Rica is concerned about the conservation of its natural resources, firmly in charge of its internal affairs, and committed to a policy of neutrality." The officials also said that the government would open negotiations with "U.S. textile manufacturer" Joseph Hamilton to buy the land.

The World Wildlife Fund had already contributed $100,000 for Santa Elena's purchase. In October 1987 three eminent U.S. scientists, Edward O. Wilson, Peter Raven, and Thomas Eisner, wrote a letter to the editor of the *New York Times* urging readers to contribute another $158,000. "The Santa Elena tract has great biological value of its own," they wrote, "a diversity of animals and plants known only from the site. . . . At the price of $4 an acre, the venture may well be the conservation bargain of the century." In April 1988 Janzen reported that the World Wildlife Fund money had been used to buy $625,000 of Costa Rican debt.

The Santa Elena owners remained unwilling to sell, however, and took the Costa Rican government to court to fight the expropriation. The government also apparently had trouble figuring out whom to negotiate with for the property. In 1990 John McPhaul told me that the last time he'd talked with Alvaro Umaña, the MIRENEM Minister had still been trying to discover whether Hamilton, somebody named Haskell, or others were the real owners. When I went to Guanacaste in June 1990 I saw the remains of a large fire that Janzen said had been started just inside Santa Elena's border. The fire had burned into Santa Rosa, burning many young trees in the old cattle pastures that Janzen was trying to restore to forest and blackening groves of older trees. Judging from the heavy equipment tracks around it, the fire had cost the government some money to put out.

Janzen told me in June 1990 that the government had reached the negotiation stage with the Santa Elena owners, but that the attempted purchase could go back into the courts if negotiations broke down. He seemed confident that the planned acquisitions would be completed, though. "There's still land purchase going on," he said. "[There are] arguments over the value of this or that, but that's just bureaucratic chug-along. I don't know if we have enough money or not, because we haven't signed all the contracts. In general, the attitude is that we've raised it, and it's probably true, but we might end up a few thousand dollars short or something. But basically it's done, unless the colone devalues terribly on us or something.

"We calculated what this area was generating from agriculture before 1987," Janzen said, "and it came to about $180,000 a year. The management budget for this park alone is $800,000 a year. That's $800,000 a year for the community. That says nothing about research

and all this other stuff that's going on. Anybody who was just thinking economics—nothing about culture or anything else—would say
that Guanacaste National Park is by far the most economically viable
use of this particular piece of land. That's not saying I'd ever dream of
saying the whole province of Guanacaste should be turned into a national park—just this particular piece right here, which is sort of a
combination of Alaska and a dust bowl, not what you'd call prime real
estate. That's why there's still forest here to look at."

In 1988 Janzen wrote, "By the time GNPP is fully financed, the
Costa Rican government will have contributed more than three times
the funds that have been raised internationally. That is to say, the
Costa Rican economic, financial, and banking community has em-
braced the conservation of wildlands as an integral and socially important portion of her public health—up there with roads, electricity,
hospitals, schools, foreign trade, etc."

Janzen's main concern when I talked to him in 1990 seemed to be
the transition between managing the park in the old, mainly protec-
tive way, and managing it in the new, socially oriented way. "What
the park represents," he said, "is a nucleus of administratively com-
petent people with good educations who understand bigger, more
global pictures. And so their job, in the ideal world, is to occupy themselves with helping the community solve whatever its problems are.
That makes the community think well about the park, which means
the community is less likely to mine gold or cut its trees down or whatever. What I'm describing is time-consuming, it's expensive, and it in-
volves a *lot* of emotional work by high-quality people, who normally
don't like to spend their lives out in the rural boondocks. They want
to go to San José, so we're talking about good salaries to bring them
out here and other kinds of conditions like that.

"If you manage a park with reference to activities of that nature,
you're not worrying about how many trees there are on that hillside,
or how pretty the birds are, or any of that kind of stuff. What I'm describing is the transition that there was a lot of fighting over in the last
two or three years—that is, getting the Park Service to shift from
being a janitorial, custodial service to aggressive community relations—which was strongly resisted, and still is being resisted by

many Park Service people for a whole lot of reasons. It gets you into this ironic situation where a proper park budget probably spends three-quarters of its money outside the park.

"Many parks still have some land acquisition problems," Janzen said, "and land acquisition's always expensive, so it needs a big chunk of the budget. So it seems to be a very important thing. But as soon as these parks get themselves paid for, which is the case now for many Costa Rican parks, then the much more difficult thing of community relations and relations with neighbors comes up. And many of the people who were hired to be park directors or guardaparques don't have that ability, so that leaves you with yet one more big expense, that of retooling and retraining these people, or else of going through the social disruptions of getting rid of them and getting new people. Either way, it costs you time and energy, lots of it, like the course I'm teaching up at Volcán Cacao right now, retraining fifteen park guards to be biodiversity managers and parataxonomists."

It's generally easier for outside observers to see the theory behind the kind of sweeping reforms Janzen and Gámez were talking about than the results. I did see noticeable changes at GNP in the three short visits I made there between 1987 and 1990. In 1987, when I visited Santa Rosa for a day, it seemed like any other national park, with a few rangers and workmen in a sleepy administrative area. (Actually, Santa Rosa reminded me more of a regional park agency I'd worked for in Ohio than a U.S. national park because of its landscape of old pastures and forest fragments.) Our guide pointed to some young people walking into a tin-roofed, cinder-block shed (Janzen's house, I later found) and said, "Those are Janzen's research assistants. He keeps them pretty busy."

In 1988 Janzen was encouraging North Americans to come to GNP as informal volunteers as part of his fundraising drive, so I spent three weeks there as volunteer and journalist. The administrative area had gotten a lot busier. Being there was like participating in a visionary social experiment with vaguely bohemian overtones. I slept in the library until a park guard and his family moved in, then in a bunkhouse with other volunteers as well as tarantulas, scorpions, whip scorpions, bats, and several species of treefrog (which occupied toilets, sinks, and showers). We couldn't complain that Janzen didn't live like his troops, however. He shared his house with a pair of small and inoffensive but wild and free skunks.

I spent my first day at GNP driving across the project with a member of the Swedish parliament. She thought her government had been neglecting Costa Rica unfairly in favor of Nicaragua, and the poverty of some of the squatters' shacks we saw at the fringes of the project tended to support that. I spent my second week living with a dairy farmer family on Volcán Cacao near the project's east edge. The family had sold their backwoods farm to the project, but instead of moving them out, Janzen hired them to build and maintain a biological station. This they had done, cutting already downed trees from their pastures into boards with a chain saw to build a bunkhouse and lab. A party of aquatic biologists and potential donors from Philadelphia arrived when I was there, looking for a place to start yet another biological station. I sat around the forest with them while they collected moths and creek organisms.

Back at headquarters, I collected seeds with two of Janzen's assistants, a fisherman's sons from a nearby town; fought a small fire and helped manage a controlled burn; and walked into Santa Elena to look at the peridotite savanna. Then I went to Cerro El Hacha, a large hill between the dry-forested plain and the wet-forested volcanoes, where Janzen had hired a farm family to maintain another nascent biological station. There I stayed in a former squatter's shack and lumber shed on a hillside with dish-sized cockroaches, six-inch scorpions, and a young North American aquatic biologist who was having trouble adjusting. He told me he'd been ill his first night there ("the worst night of my life—worse than Africa") and had heaved up all his beans and rice outside the shed door. The next morning it was gone. The ant column that seemed to operate permanently along the edge of a nearby ravine had gathered it all up, bit by bit.

It seemed in 1988 as though various groups were arriving or departing from various places continually, sometimes late into the night: groups of park guards and biological station custodians to whom Janzen gave talks or tours of his lab; groups of North American and Costa Rican students who were shown around or put to work;

groups of biologists, aviators, financiers, politicians, journalists, filmmakers. Britain's Prince Philip put in an appearance as part of the IUCN meeting in San José.

In 1990, when I visited the Santa Rosa headquarters again for a few days to interview Janzen, GNP had become more sober. Fundraising completed, the park had turned off the tap on the stream of North American visitors and volunteers in the interest of building the professional Costa Rican staff. The main administrative building, which had been empty except for a lone counter in 1988, was now full of office cubicles with bright-looking young people working at computer terminals. Only in Janzen's house, where the strata of people, pets, papers, publications, and specimens surpassed even my memory of 1988 levels, did eccentricity prevail.

seventeen

In the Land of URCs

The GNP project, like all visionary schemes, didn't lack for critics. Even when I was there in 1988, I heard grumbling among Costa Rican taxonomists whom Janzen had hired to collect specimens for a lepidoptera inventory. They felt they should have been collecting in the Caribbean rainforests because there is more biodiversity there. That GNP was using resources needed in other parks, or throughout the park system, was a complaint I heard from other field workers as well, regardless of the fact that GNP was itself generating the resources it used.

One of GNP's critics was Gordon Frankie, a North American entomologist and ecologist involved in dry forest conservation in Guanacaste Province. Frankie began studying Costa Rican dry forest in 1968, when OTS established a biological station at Palo Verde, then owned by a wealthy ranching family, the Stewarts. Frankie got interested in Lomas Barbudal, a small part of the Steward hacienda just north of the present Palo Verde wildlife refuge. A range of steep limestone hills, Lomas Barbudal got its name ("bearded hills") from the unusually diverse and mature dry and riparian forest that continued to cover it long after neighboring flatlands had been cleared for crops. It contained healthy populations of the tropical bees and wasps Frankie was studying, and some rare plants and animals such as the cannonball tree, a member of the Brazil nut family seldom found in Costa Rica, and scarlet macaws.

When the government bought the area and transferred it to the Costa Rican Institute of Agricultural Development in the late 1970s, Frankie wrote a proposal for establishing Lomas Barbudal as a wild bee reserve and showed it to the National Parks Foundation, which liked the idea and developed it into a proposal for a new biological reserve. With support form Mario Boza, Rita Alfaro, and Luis Diego Gomez, Lomas Barbudal became a six-thousand-acre national biological reserve in 1986. The Park Service lacked the manpower to manage it, however, so Frankie and others formed a group called Friends of Lomas Barbudal which managed the reserve for the next four years.

With help from the World Wildlife Fund, the local municipality, and other sources, the group established a fire control program (fires had scorched eighty percent of the reserve in 1986), built a visitor center, hired resident managers, and ran volunteer programs. The Friends also set out to involve the local community in the reserve by offering educational programs and other services, and by asking their help in protecting and improving it. Frankie told me that their relations with their neighbors were "quite good," citing an occasion when nine local people came and did some repair work on the reserve unasked at a time when Frankie and his wife, Jutta, were away. (Like Janzen, Frankie spent part of every year at a university teaching post in the U.S.)

When I talked to Frankie about the Costa Rican parks in 1987, he expressed a lot of reservations about the GNP project's future. He feared that northern Guanacaste Province would come under renewed pressure for agricultural development after the Nicaraguan situation quieted down, and that GNP's ambitious scale would make it very hard to consolidate and administer. He also echoed the complaint that other parks were going begging while GNP absorbed millions.

Frankie seemed more positive about GNP's prospects when I talked to him again in 1990, although he still feared future agricultural pressure. His main concern seemed to be that the benefits of GNP should reach other parks. "What they're doing at Guanacaste is really innovative," he said, "like the way they're retraining guardaparques to be parataxonomists, giving them a reason to be in the park instead of just hanging around the guard stations. If things like that get spread through the Park Service, it will be really positive.

"They have to motivate those people who've been sitting in little cabins in La Amistad and Corcovado for the past ten years to become public relations experts. They need to provide staff with decent homes in parks, instead of this commuting thing they have now, where personnel work in the park for a couple of weeks, then go back to San José. This way, when the park director goes home, nobody does anything while he's gone. They need to hire more local people. The people around Lomas Barbudal don't want all the park personnel to be from San José. We've had people tell us they won't work with the Park Service because they're all Joséfinos. They want some Guanacastecos working in the park too. The parks need to have really high quality people as directors. With the $23 million they've raised, GNP should be able to accomplish all this. But if it just happens there," Frankie said, "we've got a problem."

GNP's critics generally seemed to object not to what was being done there, but to what wasn't being done elsewhere. The Arias administration's response to the problem of promoting GNP-type activities in other parks—decentralization, community involvement, creative fundraising—was to organize a system of regional conservation units (Unidades Regionales de Conservación, or URCs) which, like GNP, could be funded semi-independently of the Park Service. GNP itself and Rincón de la Vieja would form a Guanacaste URC; Lomas Barbudal, Palo Verde, and Barra Honda would form a Bajo Tempisque URC; La Amistad, Chirripó, and Hitoy-Cerere (a rugged rainforest biological reserve midway betwen coast and cordillera) would form a La Amistad URC, and so forth.

The URCs would include forest reserves, wildlife refuges, watershed reserves, and indigenous reserves as well as Park Service-administered parks and biological reserves. They would be run through a combination of governmental and nongovernmental organizations. "The NGO manages the money," Daniel Janzen told me. "What you need is high-quality financial management for the funds available; and you need a strong philosophical framework for managing the land itself. That framework is based on a combination of government and NGO input, and local business leaders, and other kinds of prominent community figures. That's what the structure is for the URCs.

"An NGO runs the finances of each of the URCs," Janzen explained. "The finances of the Guanacaste URC are all handled by the National Parks Foundation, for example. The decisions about the detailed annual operations here are approved by a regional committee which is made up of local businessmen, some people from the private community, and some people from rural government. That then has to be approved by the Park Service at a higher level in the MIRENEM office as well. So the approval is coming at the governmental level, it's coming at the regional level, and of course it originates—ideas of what to do to what—from the staff inside the URC. They're paid by the foundation, but their operating philosophy is that of a proper, government-run park service. In other words, the traditions and philosophies they follow are those established by government laws, and by a very thick document called a 'management strategy.' The National Parks Foundation in no way determines what happens here. It manages the money so that there's a maximum amount available, like the business office at a university."

When he explained the URCs to me in June 1990, Janzen seemed surprised at how little I knew about them. His explanation was the most thorough I'd heard, however. I'd heard nothing about URCs in 1988. In 1990 people I interviewed referred to them fairly often in passing, but when they were talking of specific problems and solutions in the park system, the URCs drifted aside. People then talked about individual parks or about the system as a whole. They apparently found it harder to think in terms of the URC system's groups of parks.

People generally thought of the URCs as a step in the right direction. "The parks were like building blocks lying around," said Juan Carlos Crespo, who became president of Fundación Neotrópica in 1990. "Most of the big parks were created in the mid-eighties. So then there was a bunch of areas that were protected very haphazardly. 'What's there?' 'Let's protect it.' 'What's the ideal size?' 'I don't know, let's protect it!'

"Now Mario's talking about the ideal size of a park," Crespo said, "but nothing of that was taken into consideration before—it was mostly forest cover and special ecosystems that determined park boundaries. And then all of a sudden the megapark idea began to come around a few years back, with the Guanacaste project, talking about bigger areas. And then URCs were the next step, which cover protected areas plus the area of influence around them. And that's where I think a lot of visionary planning has crystallized. What had been done at the beginning, without knowing it, became building blocks for what's happening right now."

Crespo's favorite area, the Talamancas, exemplified some of the URC concept's most workable qualities because it was a real cultural and natural unit to begin with. In 1982 most of the area was designated a La Amistad Biosphere Reserve by UNESCO. The reserve consisted of two parks, two biological reserves, a wildlife refuge, a zona protectora, three forest reserves, and four indigenous reserves. So the government had been trying to coordinate administration of these diverse components for nearly a decade by the time the URC system arose. When I talked to Mario Rojas, coordinator for Park Service activities for the La Amistad Biosphere Reserve and URC, he said they were in the process of finishing a management plan to be presented to local communities for discussion and input. He added that they still didn't have enough money to endow the La Amistad URC, however, and that 15 percent of land acquisition wasn't completed.

Crespo, who'd backpacked often in the Talamancas, saw promise in cooperation between the Park Service and the area's indigenous population. "They're a very attractive group to get involved with and get to know," he told me, "for many reasons. They live in the forest, and there is a lot to learn from them in that sense. If we're able to support the Indian reserves and the Ley Indigena, then we have very good buffers for the parks. If we make the reserves effective, we can take our guardaparques and put them somewhere else. I definitely think that if we're able to support the traditional culture of the indigenous peoples, it's good for the parks. We can use Indian reserves not only as the protection of a culture but also for protection of the forest. There are still some nice patches outside the parks, and if we don't do something different than parks, we won't be able to save them. The reserves are a nice alternative, and there are many others— community-owned forest, or watershed reserves.

"The Indians have been divided between traditional and development factions, but both factions have found the park system as something of benefit to them. For instance, on the Atlantic side of the Talamancas there are a couple of sacred sites, and they were saying, 'Let's make sure these sites are *inside* the park, because then we know they'll be protected. If they're in the reserve, we don't have the support, so they could be destroyed.' They know that in Costa Rica the national parks have been respected. I can take you to any of the areas on the maps, and you can see the park—they're not paper parks. In Costa Rica, we have developed—without knowing it, really—a respect for the protected areas, in general. There are a lot of times when it's not true, but generally people have an idea of parks, and respect it, and the Indians know that."

Chip and Jill Isenhart, the photographers who explored the Talamancas, told an interesting story about attitudes to the parks. When they first arrived in the lowland parts of the Talamancan Indian reserves, they were shunned, particularly by the powerful Catholic missionary. Apparently the missionary and the reserves' development faction thought they were anthropologists who had come to ally themselves with the reserves' traditionalist faction higher in the mountains. When it was discovered that they had come to photograph the park, attitudes changed completely. The missionary offered to fly them in his plane. (When the Isenharts entered traditionalist territory they tended to be politely avoided because the small backcountry villages distrusted all strangers.)

"The only real conflict between the parks and the Indians may be hunting," Juan Carlos Crespo told me. "If they deplete the game on the reserves, there could be pressure to go into the parks. But their hunting is subsistence, not commercial or sport, so if we can help them to get protein, then the hunting will go down, and that is happening. The Indians now eat a lot of chicken, and they always have pigs around. But hunting is part of their cultural roots, so there's always going to be a little bit of conflict. But there's much more conflict with hunting in some of the communities outside the Indian reserves, where people travel from all around the country and go with dogs. The Indians don't have a bunch of specialized hunting dogs. I worry more, in terms of protecting the parks, about the areas of colonization by the dominant culture, the white culture."

White colonization is also a problem on Indian reserves, however. While the Ley Indígena passed in 1977 prohibited non-Indians from owning land in reserves, it didn't provide funds to buy existing white inholdings, and illegal encroachments of various kinds continued. On April 1, 1990, two white poachers murdered a sixty-seven-year old Cabecar Indian named Antonio Zuñiga with machetes. Zuñiga was trying to defend his son, who had stopped the men from hunting illegally on his property. The reserve where this occurred, east of the town of Buenos Aires on the Talamancas' Pacific side, has suffered terrible deforestation.

I visited an adjacent reserve of the Bri-Bri tribe a few weeks before Zuñiga's murder. I saw no untouched forest for miles, just scrub, thin teak plantations, and charred places where huge stumps protruded from soil so sterilized by perennial burning that it would support little except bracken fern (which is poisonous to livestock and also may be a cause of high stomach cancer rates in Costa Rica because of toxic residues in milk). Juan Carlos Crespo, who was there, told me the stumps probably had been living forest until the mid-1970s. A dark line of big trees on the crest of a ridge miles to the east perhaps marked the border of La Amistad National Park.

We visited the Bri-Bri Reserve, Salitre, to attend a meeting at its Casa de Cultura, a communal structure that the community recently had built as a traditionalist gesture. Casas de cultura on the Talamancas' still-forested Caribbean side are thatched with palm leaves, but this one had a tin roof because there wasn't enough thatch palm left in the vicinity. It was a pleasant building anyway, spacious and cool in a landscape unshaded by big trees. Butterflies fluttered and lizards darted through the open sides during the meeting.

A Bri-Bri activist named Doris Ortiz, wearing a University of Nevada football jersey, talked for an hour about encroachments on Bri-Bri land, beginning with the Spaniards "who killed hundreds of women and children with a sword in one hand and a cross in the other," and ending with modern Costa Rica, which is forcing the Bri-

Bri farther and farther into the mountains if they want to hunt and gather plants for food and medicine. "For us," Ortiz said, "development isn't roads and bridges. It's being able to hunt a guan for dinner. If we don't have living land, we have nothing." A reserve headman spoke after her, partly in Spanish and partly in Bri-Bri. He and the other Bri-Bri people there lit up when he spoke in Bri-Bri—evidently he was being witty. The Bri-Bri were short, but big-boned, and they revealed a lot of energy when they laughed at the headman's witticisms.

A reserve guard got up and made a vehement speech in Spanish about protecting the land. He criticized anthropologists and other visitors for always taking information away with them from the reserve, but never bringing any back. Then our hosts gave us a lunch of rice, beans, canned tuna, and soda crackers. "Indian food," Doris Ortiz said, smiling.

Several other URCs seemed very promising from the park system's viewpoint in 1990, although Guanacaste was the only one fully functioning, and the legal basis for the system had yet to be passed by the legislature. Cordillera Volcánica Central URC, made up of Volcán Poás, Braulio Carrillo and Volcán Irazú national parks and adjacent reserves, was a UNESCO Biosphere Reserve and a natural montane unit like La Amistad. In 1989 the U.S. Agency for International Development announced a $22.5 million program called Foresta to endow the URC. (According to Alvaro Ugalde, financial technicalities resulted in Foresta funds being reduced by about $5 million.) Another natural unit that seemed virtually unassailable was the Parques Marinos URC, made up of Coco and Caño islands.

Lowland, mainland URCs faced more problems, since these were the areas of heaviest development pressure, but several were the locus of nongovernmental organization (NGO) fundraising and activity. Gordon Frankie told me he thought the Bajo Tempisque URC would be good for Lomas Barbudal, despite problems with URC administration and personnel, and although a three-kilometer corridor of swamp forest that had connected Lomas Barbudal to the Palo Verde wildlife refuge had been recently cleared for farming. Frankie hoped the URC would be able to add another fifteen thousand acres to the fifty thousand already protected in the region. (Unfortunately Lomas Barbudal suffered another major fire in 1991.)

Nongovernmental organizations were well established in Costa Rica's two main rainforest wilderness URCs—Península de Osa and Llanuras de Tortuguero. On the Osa, a WWF- and U.S. AID-funded project called Boscosa was working under Fundación Neotrópica to provide economic alternatives to deforestation, which URC Director Edwin Cyrus characterized as much more of a problem "in terms of destruction of resources and biodiversity" than mining. Boscosa Coordinator Richard Donovan said their goal was to conserve forest by producing "cold, hard cash for the campesino" through agroforestry. In Llanuras de Tortuguero, the Caribbean Conservation Corporation (CCC) continued to serve as a conduit between North American and European financial support and Tortuguero area land management and acquisition. In 1989 U.S. AID made a $675,000 grant to the CCC for planning, guides, compatible development, and land acquisition to connect the park with the Barra Colorado Wildlife Refuge to the north. When I talked to him in April 1990 (see below), Jim Barborak was working full-time on Tortuguero funding.

One heard little or nothing, however, about other URCs. The Pacifico Central URC contained only a scattering of small park units such as Manuel Antonio and Carara. The Arenal URC contained no park units until Arias made his farewell gesture of decreeing one in the Children's Rainforest east of Monteverde. To me, at least, it seemed doubtful whether the small, threatened, or embryonic park units in these URCs would serve as the nucleus for sustainable regional conservation and development that Gámez and Janzen envisioned. This raised the specter that the integration of parks with poorly protected forest reserves and struggling local economies might drag parks down instead of helping support all three.

Jim Barborak, one of the park system's most persistent friendly critics (to the extent, he told me, that he almost got kicked out at one point), expressed such a fear when I talked to him. "My personal concern with the URC ideal—although what they're trying to do is theoretically sound, the biosphere reserve concept—is that they're going to draw down something they've done well to try to bring up something that's incapable of being brought up to snuff. So, do you want the parks to go downhill in a general trend of everything going downhill? Or do you at least keep your islands of green?

"It'll probably be a matter of decades to bring buffer zone management up to snuff," Barborak said. "I believe strongly in the concept of buffer zone management, but I worry about the way they're talking about administering it, which is to expand the scope of the Park Service to be like something they've never managed to accomplish in the United States—to combine the Park Service, Forest Service, and Bureau of Land Management in one bureaucracy. That to me is the most troublesome point of everything that's going on right now. Everyone has caught on to sustainable development—it's the buzzword of the moment—but I'd like to see the cores assured."

Another critic of the URCs was Mario Boza. In a March 2, 1990, *Tico Times* article, reporter David Dudenhoeffer quoted Boza as calling the URCs "a mess." Earlier in the year, Boza had complained to Dudenhoeffer of the lack of "vertical organization" within the URC system, and had said, "I spoke to the director of one of the units, and he told me he didn't even know who his boss was." In a later interview, Boza told Dudenhoeffer that he agreed with the URC system's basic goals, but that the URCs needed "some big changes." "For one thing," Boza said, "they now cover half the country. That's just ridiculous." Boza was a very important critic in March 1990, because the Social Christian Unity Party had just won the presidential election, and he was likely to have a major role in the new administration's conservation policies.

eighteen

The Two Students Return

It was inevitable that divisions should multiply within Costa Rica's conservation community as conservation moved toward the center of national politics, toward becoming "as important to Costa Ricans as health and education," as Arias's MIRENEM Minister Alvaro Umaña put it. Umaña himself was something new to Costa Rican conservation, a member of the intellectual elite with a doctorate from Stanford University and polished political skills. It was interesting to watch the difference in style between Umaña and the conservation old guard at meetings. Boza and Ugalde would stand and chat in their sports clothes; Umaña in his tailored suit would work the room, circling to shake hands.

Everbody I talked to praised Umaña for helping to bring major new financial support for conservation. As Rodrigo Gámez told me, "When we started, there was a little more than a million in capital for parks in Costa Rica. Three years later, we're managing more than eighty million dollars in equivalent bonds." Alvaro Ugalde told me he thought Umaña and Gámez were responsible for holding the park system together through the late eighties. "If it hadn't been for them," he said, "I don't think there'd be anything left by now. Umaña was very smart, an excellent speaker, especially at international forums. He supported keeping the miners out of Corcovado; he lobbied hard for debt swaps; and he promoted a good international image for Costa Rica."

A major division developed, however, over administration of the Park Service. Some members of the old conservation "cartel" gave the Arias administration poor marks for its management of the Park Service. José María Rodríguez, who left the Park Service in 1986, was outspoken. "The Arias administration has been very good at getting congratulations, especially internationally," he told me, "but in my opinion, they have done a poor job. They destroyed the Park Service in the name of the new administration they were going to create, but they created very little. They got lots of money. The money was coming anyway, but they were good at getting even more. They have done good things too, but regarding wildlands administration, park administration, I think it's terrible. The Park Service is a mess."

Despite his praise for Umaña, Ugalde also felt that the Arias administration had let the Park Service slip. "The Service in general lost leadership," he told me. "There was no internal leadership nor national leadership. The power within the Park Service all split into little groups here and there. There was no institutional consensus of what to do, where to go. With the government being broke, Luis Mendez didn't have the political leverage to keep the budgets up or get government support, so it was an economic debacle, losing positions, losing all kinds of support. It was very bad to watch the internal fighting. It was a kind of lost institution.

"So the power rested in the minister and his advisors, not in the Park Service. Policy was made without consulting the Park Service. And despite Umaña's achievements, I never saw him with any kind of leadership internally here. He took good ideas and pushed them, but he was never able to work as a team with anyone here. He was never a true administrator, so to speak. When the Park Service director wasn't responding to expectation, he didn't dare to remove him until almost at the end of the administration, and only because disaster was coming."

In 1988, *The Tico Times* quoted Park Service Director Mendez as saying that "within a few years, the Park Service will gradually find itself in a position to do something other than hang on for dear life." In 1989 Umaña replaced Mendez with Alonso Matamoros, an official in the Forestry Directorate. José María Rodríguez told me that Ugalde had wanted Matamoros to succeed him as director in 1986, but that the Park Service staff had preferred that the new director be someone already in the Park Service.

The Park Service evidently had evaded disaster when I visited in

1990. Staffs and budgets were up slightly from 1988. Guard stations and visitor centers were always manned, although with varying degrees of enthusiasm. At Manuel Antonio's single entrance, guards stood in the booth all day, giving tourists directions and taking the hundred-colones entrance fee (newly raised from twenty). At Cahuita's north entrance, several miles from the administration center, guards lounged in the sand before a closed booth and seemed reluctant to take the entrance fee, much less answer questions. I recognized one guard from Santa Rosa in 1988, where he'd been equally lackadaisical.

There were some clouds on the horizon. Parks were closed for several days in April 1990 because employees went on strike. Park Service members of a professionals' union had been on strike at the San José headquarters for weeks, and field workers joined them for a few days to show solidarity. The San José workers were still on the Agriculture Ministry's payroll, demonstrating that—as I'd been told—the new MIRENEM ministry still wasn't altogether established.

There were other divisions, for example, between the Park Service and the foundations. "The friction started very soon, when the foundations were very small," José María Rodríguez told me. "I remember hearing somebody in the Park Service complain that someone in the foundations was buying rugs for the office. That was viewed as an inappropriate luxury. The foundation staff was more worried about their organization than the Park Service staff because, as government employees, the Park Service staff was hired for their lifetimes if they wanted, but a job with the foundations was fragile. One could easily get fired, or the foundations simply could fall apart. In the beginning at least, the foundations barely had administration money for more than a year ahead. So the staff really felt strongly about how they should be run, because their jobs were at stake.

"As long as Alvaro Ugalde was head of the Service and the foundations," Rodríguez said, "conflict tended not to result except in secondary matters, because Alvaro would take a position on issues and then assign complementary roles to the Service and foundations. I think Alvaro thought he could manage the Service through the foundations after he resigned as director in 1986. They were starting to have more money than the Service, and the money was more manageable, so it seemed that it would be easier to take positions and implement them.

"But somehow, Alvaro didn't fit comfortably with the foundations. He started to go less and less to the foundation office. He'd have a driver bring him papers to sign at his house. I don't know exactly what happened, but perhaps the staff had ideas of their own about how the foundations should be run. When Alvaro started taking a strong position, they might have said, 'No, we can't do that. We don't have the budget for that.' "

Rodrigo Gámez saw these divisions philosophically, as part of the process of integrating the parks into society. "The new ideas have been partially absorbed by the Park Service," he told me. "These changes happen very slowly, especially in a bureaucracy. The reason we've been able to advance as quickly as we have in the Guanacaste project is that employees are paid by the foundations. Not all the regions have the resources to advance as quickly. We still lack people capable of putting together projects on that scale, capable of getting major donations from the government of Sweden or the U.S. as Janzen has done at Guanacaste.

"On the other hand," Gámez continued, "local communities need to be prepared to handle the authority and responsibility of taking a part in managing wildlands. We have to educate people. It's a process of change that will take several years."

Gámez and Janzen both thought that Boza and Ugalde had been influenced by the new ideas of decentralization and regional integration of the park system. "Alvaro is totally permeated with this philosophy, and is converting himself into the new leader of this process of change," Gámez said. "Mario Boza is more of a hard-core conservationist. He still has doubts about whether local communities are ready to have influence over the parks. But the differences between us are not about final objectives, but how to get there."

"The last four years have represented a fairly major change in attitude and structure of operating the parks," Janzen told me in June 1990. "And Mario, sort of being on one side during these changes, his reaction was to go back to the system he knew well, which was, let's say more conventionally protectionist than very involved with people and management. But he's had an awful lot of people talking with him over the past few months, and he's come to see that the old-style park as just a big pretty area managed by putting a fence around it isn't viable. I think what happened was that during the last couple of years of the Umaña administration he'd become isolated from this general process that was going on—not so much because of philosophical disagreement, but because of not being involved in the details and seeing how it was growing. He saw it as something of the other political party. He's gradually come back to being more 'enterado' [informed], as we say."

In 1987 Boza left the directorship of the School of Environmental Education he'd founded ten years earlier at the Universidad Estatal a Distancia to become salaried director of the National Parks and Neotrópica foundations. He'd been president since 1980. Under his leadership, the foundations had become information and environmental education sources as well as park funding mechanisms. With grants from the Tinker Foundation in the U.S., they had begun by putting out pamphlets, then had moved on to publishing books and a variety of other materials, including an international newsletter.

Foundation publications also included a series of posters on Costa Rican forest types and other natural features that became enormously popular. One couldn't go into a Costa Rican hotel or a U.S. biology department in the late 1980s without seeing the puma padding through the Bosque Tropical Seco poster, the ocelot crouching in the Bosque Tropical Nuboso poster, or the jaguar lurking in the Bosque Tropical Humedo poster. In 1990, Fundación Neotrópica Director Vera Varela told me, foundation publishing had fifty million colones in assets, and had grossed nearly 2.5 million in the first four months of the year.

Ugalde spent much of the 1986–1990 period as a kind of roving conservationist. "In the first year after I resigned from the Service," he told me, "I was appointed a senior fellow by the Conservation Foundation in Washington, D.C. I told them I was going to look for a job teaching, or whatever. They said, 'We want you to be a senior fellow, but to continue in San José, not teaching, but helping the foundations—full-time in conservation.' The second year, The Nature Conservancy appointed me something they called a conservation associate, and sent me to Paraguay to advise the Park Service there and help create a strong NGO, and sort of train this young guy who's now a conservation leader there.

"Then, as part of The Nature Conservancy position, I came back to Costa Rica in 1987 and 1988, and helped in designing the Foresta Project, the AID grant for the Central Volcanic Range—a project which is now beginning to see the light. The third year, 1988 to 1989, I was pretty much on my own. I worked as a tourist guide for Costa Rica Expeditions from December to March. I took groups to the parks and made sure they didn't break their legs. I enjoyed it. . . not a whole lot, although it gave me an opportunity to see the parks as a visitor rather than a manager, which was interesting.

"Then I had some short consultancies. I worked with MIRENEM for a month or two designing the regional conservation units, or conservation areas as Mario now calls them. I went to Guatemala for a couple of months to consult with their protected areas system. They had a grant from WWF. I was hired to help in drafting the Tropical Forestry Action Plan, in the ecosystem chapter, and I did a short consultancy on an environmental impact statement for a tourist hotel at Monteverde.

"Then in November of 1989, Mario asked me not to make any commitments because he felt his party was going to win the elections. So when his party actually won the elections, Mario immediately got some funds from The Nature Conservancy. The foundations gave him a salary and an office to begin preparing his position, and I began working with him February 15, two weeks after the elections."

I interviewed Boza and Ugalde in late May and early June 1990, when they were newly ensconced on the eighth floor of the MIRENEM building, a smallish, concrete highrise on a hill overlooking the massive limestone edifices of the government judicial bureaucracy. The floor reception area contained two secretaries, one aged electric typewriter, and a bench filled with people waiting to see Boza and Ugalde. The walls, cracked by San José's frequent earthquakes, were decorated with a picture of a quetzal, a picture of a scarlet macaw, an oropendula nest, a gaily painted oxcart wheel, and a large photo mural of

New England fall foliage (a popular decoration in Costa Rica). On her desk one of the secretaries had a goldfish bowl of tropical fish: neon tetras from the Amazon and zebra danios from India.

Boza had been appointed vice-minister for Natural Resources under the new MIRENEM Minister, Hernan Bravo, a former beverage company executive. Ugalde had been appointed to a new position, director of Wildlands and Wildlife, while Alonso Matamoros had been kept on as Park Service director, an arrangement which frustrated Ugalde somewhat. "Mario didn't let me go back to the Park Service, which was where I wanted to go," he told me, "because he feels I can do more from this position, where I don't have to deal with the day-to-day business of the Park Service. I took it on condition that the Park Service is clearly out from under the dark ages. If that doesn't happen, I'd rather not be here. So, in a way, to leverage more political support for the Park Service is why I'm up here on the eighth floor— in spite of the earthquakes—although I'd prefer to be down there getting my hands dirty with the parks." (In March 1991 Ugalde became director of the Park Service again.)

Ugalde's new position seemed typical of the approach Boza was taking toward the government conservation system, of an emphasis on reforming and strengthening administration. From what Boza told me, I did get the impression that Gámez's and Janzen's ideas had influenced him. "We don't see parks as isolated as we did in the past," he said. "We want to learn about minimum critical size to preserve viable populations of large animals in an area. The fact is that Corcovado's forty-one thousand hectares isn't big enough to protect big cats or harpy eagles. I think Corcovado should have a hundred thousand hectares of suitable habitat. One way to do that is to increase the park, another is to increase the effective area for doing that by other designations. Different areas have to be managed differently. We need to think in terms of the very distant future, of how to build endowments for the parks, how to plan enlargement of them."

Yet Boza's approach also seemed different than Gámez's and Janzen's (although not necessarily in a way that would conflict with theirs). He spoke more of improving park administration than of integrating the parks into society. As vice-minister responsible for all conservation agencies, Boza had to approach the Park Service's problems as part of the whole natural resources system.

In my talks with Gámez and Janzen, they didn't dwell much on agencies other than the Park Service. (Of course, I was interviewing them about the national parks.) When I talked to him in 1988, Janzen said he thought most of the forest reserves would be taken over for agriculture, an expectation that seemed realistic considering the substantial ongoing deforestation rate. On the other hand, about a third of the Renewable Resources Action Plan that Boza prepared for the Calderón administration in December 1989 consisted of measures for reforming the national forestry system, with the ultimate goal of maintaining twenty-five percent of the country as forests *outside* the park system. Along with major judicial, legislative, and financial changes to encourage reforestation, the plan proposed replacing the forest reserve system with a national forest system like the United States' in which forest lands, "where industry can't manage," as Boza told me, would be nationally owned and managed by a forest service.

Boza planned to simplify the entire renewable resource conservation system. "Look at this," he told me, waving at a map of the system. "We have a Palo Verde National Park right next to a Palo Verde National Wildlife Refuge, and a Chirripó National Park right next to a La Amistad National Park." He shook his head. The Action Plan proposed reducing the system's units to national parks and biological reserves, national forests, and national watersheds (areas of critical hydrological concern that would be kept in forest and managed by the Forest Service). Wildlife Refuges would be integrated into the park system, which was one reason Boza wanted Ugalde in the new Wildlands and Wildlife directorship.

"In Latin America," Ugalde told me, "Fish and Wildlife is perceived as a little bureaucratic office with no political support, no support of any kind. That's been the case in Costa Rica. It used to be the Fish and Wildlife Service—'Fish' meaning basically fishing, and 'Wildlife' meaning basically white-tailed deer research, and hunting permits and seasons. Very symbolic activities. Well, I think it's reached the lowest. What I've been finding out in the past three weeks is that there's really nothing left. The Fish part of it is in Agriculture, and it's still fishing, nothing to do with ecological management, and the Wildlife part has been relegated to twelve people within this Ministry to take care of the whole country.

"The new administration feels that wildlife should be given a bit more importance," Ugalde said, "and rather than leaving it as a little entity within the Forest Service, they want to bring it up and try to see how we can improve its efficiency—take the pressure off wildlands by creating things like the green iguana and tepiscuintle projects to use wildlife without endangering it—look into the situation with species of high commercial value. That's sort of the new thrust that we want to give to the whole thing. But don't ask me what I'm going to do about it, because right now I'm just trying to understand what it is, and get it clearly under my jurisdiction. It's still not under my jurisdiction."

Within the park system itself, Boza planned to "divide the national parks and equivalent reserves into two large groups: (1) areas that can be expanded and that possess great biological diversity, and (2) areas of small size that can't be expanded and that will protect a limited number of species." The Action Plan cited seven areas in the first group: "Santa Rosa, Tempisque (including Palo Verde and Lomas Barbudal), Corcovado, Monteverde (proposed new park), Los Volcánes (including Poás, Irazú, and Braulio Carrillo), Talamanca (including Chirripó and La Amistad), and Tortuguero." The plan also proposed to study the feasibility of creating four new parks: one in the Monteverde–Arenal area; one at Playa Grande, a turtle beach on the northwest coast; and one each at Tenorio and Miravalles volcanoes, the Cordillera de Guanacaste peaks that Oduber had tried to designate in 1978. Parks would be administered through a system of regional offices and in coordination with those areas "under responsibility of different entities of the ministry."

The Action Plan characterized the Park Service as "in very bad condition. . . . Personnel for protection and visitor service is very scarce, no general plans for management exist, almost no installations for public use, and the problems of forest fires and poaching have become very serious." It proposed to assign "public funds and donations to develop installations for protection and public use such as trails, overlooks, visitor centers, camping areas, housing for personnel, and others." To increase protection from fire, poaching, squatters, and illegal collecting, the plan proposed to "restore to the Park Service the positions which have been eliminated, [to] develop education and information programs for the communities neighboring the parks, [and to] improve the living conditions of the employees in these areas, allowing them to live with their families, offering them job training and career planning." Boza proposed to use international aid to "establish endowments for each of the 'areas silvestres,' to construct installations and develop research and interpretation programs."

The plan proposed what seemed to be a modification of the URC system: "pilot projects" for environmental management in "seven of the zones that have suffered major environmental degradation. . . . The Osa Peninsula, the Salitrales–La Cangreja Zone, the Tortuguero–Barra Colorado Zone, the south part of Lake Arenal, the Cahuita-Gandoca-Manzanillo area, the Pacific slope of the Talamancas, and the south part of the Nicoya Peninsula." "In these zones," the plan said, "we will establish what have been termed internationally 'conservation areas' consisting of a conjunction of absolute protection areas—national parks or nature reserves, of buffer areas for research, teaching, tourism and other controlled uses, of areas in rehabilitation or soil recovery through reforestation, and of areas of traditional land use—farming or ranching, but using soil and water conservation techniques." (Ugalde informed me in 1991 that the URC designation had been changed to "conservation area.")

Boza's plan also contained substantial sections on ecotourism and environmental education. It proposed that "areas silvestres y diversidad biologica" become the main focus of national tourism promotion; that ICT, the tourism institute, should "dedicate an important part of its resources to planning, development, and protection of natural areas"; and that the Ministry of Public Works and Transportation should improve or build park access roads. The plan proposed a National Endowment Education Program jointly administered by MIRENEM and a variety of environmental and educational institutions, and creation of several new educational facilities—environmental education centers, a national natural history museum, a new zoological garden, and a national aquarium.

Another thing Boza wanted to do, he told me, was to increase the private sector's participation in park administration. "The basic idea of the foundations was to use the private sector to have an easy way to receive and use international funds," he said. "To take this one step further, we might get the legislature to sign agreements with NGOs to administer national parks. The public sector finds it difficult to do things that are easy for the private sector. For example, it's almost impossible to fire a government employee who's lazy or irresponsible. Running some parks along the lines of Monteverde would greatly increase efficiency and productivity.

"It's not only that we're interested in this," he added. "It's growing spontaneously. There's a foundation in Guanacaste that's interested in managing the Santa Cruz watershed. It's something we'd like to try in the next four years, if we can get legislative approval.

"I think parks and adjacent conservation areas and buffer zones should cover twenty to twenty-five percent of the country as the ultimate goal," Boza told me. "When we include the other twenty-five percent of land occupied by national forests and commercial forestry plantations, that will mean about half of Costa Rica will be under forest cover of some kind." He went to the map and made a sweeping gesture across it. "Eventually, we hope the system will form a corridor of wildlands throughout Costa Rica that will link up with the Panamanian La Amistad Park and a San Juan River watershed park in Nicaragua to form a biological migration corridor throughout Mesoamerica."

Alvaro Ugalde seemed more comfortable talking about short-term tactics than long-term strategy and goals, but he echoed the new vice-minister's vision of the future with enthusiasm when we talked a week or so after the Boza interview. "The ultimate goal is to maintain Central America as an ecological bridge," he said. "That of course is a very difficult dream to achieve because it doesn't depend on us, it depends on every little country in this region. But yes, on a national basis, that is the ultimate dream. How do we keep genes flowing north and south, and evolving? I know it's farfetched. Not only that, but to try to save every single species in the country, which is also a far-fetched vision.

"But my feeling," Ugalde continued, "is that if you don't go for the highest, then how will you decide where to go? So we have to go for big, big visions. And it probably means getting to manage twenty-five percent of this country, maybe more, because if we have twenty-five percent now in these conservation areas, or regional units, and we haven't even been making concrete steps to make this ecological bridge along the country—some of the major units are still isolated, such as the central volcanic range—well, if we're really going to maintain a bridge, we need to work very strongly with the populations between the areas. So, ultimately, we may be talking about managing very strongly about twenty-five percent of the country, and then on a more loose basis another ten or fifteen percent. It's quite a task, and of course it'll take decades to accomplish, but it's what we hope."

Reactions to Boza's Renewable Resources Action Plan were varied. The commonest seemed to be that the plans would be wonderful if they could be accomplished. As Gordon Frankie said in October 1990, "The plans are good, the theory is good, the concept is good. Very good guidelines and policies have been laid down, and indications are that the government wants to promote conservation. But these are very ambitious goals, easier to set than to realize. It's going to take some time. The Action Plan basically says Costa Rica is very committed to develop conservation, but a lot of the plan may be overly ambitious. It may be unrealistic to think Costa Rica can do it by itself. They may not have taken into account the limits of their own resources in the country."

José María Rodríguez said, "We have somehow to resurrect the Park Service. That was really a great agency. It really did a good job, and if Boza and Ugalde can work together as they used to, I think it's promising. I think they're working in the same direction. Most of the Park Service is very happy that Alvaro is coming back. I think it's a job for a superman. Alvaro has been one, under very different circumstances, and I hope he proves to be one now. If it happens, we will have an incredible park system for the year 2000."

Daniel Janzen was cautious, "through painful experience," about criticizing the new administration's plans. "The traditional way here of establishing a policy," he told me, "is to propose it and look at reactions to it, and then modify it accordingly. The format in which the reaction comes has a strong influence on who you regard as your friends and enemies."

Janzen did express doubts about nongovernmental organizations administering parks. "What happens here in Guanacaste is in no way determined by the National Parks Foundation," he said. "The decisions about what to do, where and why and how, are the Park Service staff's under a set of plans approved by a regional committee and MIRENEM. I don't trust an NGO to run a major responsibility like a park system. They're very useful, they have their place and function within the system, but in no way can you absolve government from taking a continuous and major role in policy and structure of how conserved areas are managed."

Janzen also had doubts about ecotourism's potential as a conservation mainstay: "Farming ecotourists is an art that can be done, and generates lots of income and is quite compatible with parks. But there's a big capital investment, and somebody's got to put that money in, and that money is probably not going to be Costa Rican. It's going to be a foreigner's money, and he's going to want a return.

"Someone with the drive and initiative to make that kind of thing take place is very likely to be someone with a strong profit motive, not a civil servant or equivalent thereof taking care of a park. The money won't go into the park budget. Even if it did . . . okay, say you bust your ass, and you do this, and after you take your costs away, you end up making $50,000 a year on it. That amount of money put into writing grant proposals and developing international agencies could end up bringing in a lot more than $50,000 a year. Or it might produce a lot more for the country to take the energy required to run that ecotourism operation and use it in a school program."

Costa Rica's new president, Rafael A. Calderón, did seem prepared to support an increased emphasis on conservation. In his inaugural speech, Calderón said not only that Costa Rica "must preserve" its "untold ecological riches," but that it should "expand the conservation revolution beyond our borders . . . by advancing a series of initiatives rallying all governments to protect the greatest legacy a people can bestow on humanity, a new ecological order."

Reactions to Calderón's speech also varied. A May 11, 1990, *Tico Times* editorial called Calderón's remarks "a gratifying surprise,'" adding that he had "indicated no special concern for the environment" previously. "Calderón's idea is a logical and timely sequel to the Central American Peace Plan of his predecessor, former President Oscar Arias," the editorial continued. "Costa Rica is the obvious country to assume the role which Calderón has envisioned. The country has unquestioned moral authority as well as practical experience in the form of protected parklands, debt-for-nature swaps, and a growing conservation ethic."

A May 15 *La Nación* editorial by Otto Fonseca was more hard-nosed. It acknowledged the president's good intentions, but complained that Calderón "spoke only of conserving and protecting the environment, applauded the traditional work of the national parks. . . . A country's development can't be held back by a sentimental protectionist commitment." The editorial called for "the application of the modern concept of sustainable development, which allows an adequate and reasoned exploitation in keeping with natural regeneration, without obstructing economic and social advantages."

Yet for all the divisions about conservation in Costa Rica, I was impressed by the amount of communication maintained among the various factions, a quality that seemed characteristic of the country in general. I'm not sure why this is so. Of course, it's such a small country that rivals and enemies have trouble avoiding one another even if they try, but rivals and enemies in neighboring small countries sometimes communicate only with guns. The quality may go back to colonial times, when various groups were thrown together without much access to the outside world and had to get along as best they could. Anyway, Costa Ricans do seem unusually reluctant to exclude or isolate others. The thing that struck me most on returning to the U.S. in June 1990 was the tent city of homeless people in Civic Center Plaza in

San Francisco. I'd barely noticed it when I'd left, but when I came back the spectacle of several hundred desperate people being publicly ignored for month after month seemed strange. It probably would have been an immediate national scandal in Costa Rica, as when the Corcovado miners camped in the San José parks.

Costa Ricans' unusual gregariousness helps explain their historical friendliness to foreigners, another unusual quality for which Daniel Janzen coined the term "xenophilia." When I talked to Rodrigo Gámez, he showed me a book written in the 1920s on the influence of foreigners on Costa Rican science. "There have always been people like Daniel Janzen and Leslie Holdridge here," he said.

One of the most interesting events I attended in San José was a meeting of one of the committees I'd been reading and hearing about that had steered the park system since the 1970s. The meeting probably included as many foreigners as Costa Ricans, which might have suggested imperialism writ large except that each foreigner represented a flow of wealth into the country instead of out. It gave a new twist of the concept of empire, and recalled Umaña's talk of biological superpowerdom.

The meeting was at the Tropical Science Center in March 1990, with Boza and Ugalde presiding. Boza began by saying that he wanted the committee to develop clear concepts that could lead to political action. Now was the time to plan for the minimum critical size of the seven big parks, so they wouldn't end up like Cabo Blanco, without tapirs or ocelots. How to increase Corcovado to one hundred thousand hectares? The park was meant to protect the ecosystem of the Osa Peninsula, not just the land within its boundaries. Should private lands play a role in increasing the park's influence?

José María Rodríguez said that conservation biology should be applied to determining the minimum critical size of parks. One should have a clear idea of what one was trying to protect. Was this the present level of diversity in the park, or some past level of diversity that one wanted to restore?

Daniel Janzen expressed doubt about minimal critical size as a guideline for managing conservation areas. What you did with land was more important than how much you had. The best way to succeed with conservation areas was not through counting the species saved, but by integrating the areas with society. Areas should be considered individually, not according to some textbook criterion, and the people working in the areas should be the ones to consider them.

Joseph Tosi said he agreed with Janzen, but with a slightly different concept. He thought the national park system was big enough, but that the country needed small natural areas that the Park Service was not in a position to manage. There were an impressive number of such areas, little studied, but very important for species preservation and education. The government needed to figure out a way to help them, a national trust, for example.

Jim Barborak brought up the opportunity Costa Rica had to enlarge its effective wildlife habitat with international parks on the Nicaraguan and Panamanian borders. He added that Central America had a certain advantage over some much larger regions, such as Amazonia, in protecting biodiversity, because Central America contains more altitudinal relief in relation to size, and diversity is concentrated into small areas. Because of this, ideas of minimum critical size developed through Thomas Lovejoy's experiments with various sizes of forest plots in the Amazon had limited significance for Costa Rica.

Pedro León brought up the issue of population growth. He asked whether the present park system would be enough for projected population levels. He said it was an issue conservationists needed to pay a lot more attention to.

Mario Boza agreed with Joseph Tosi that there was a need for more small preserves and privately owned protected areas.

José María Rodríguez said the concept of the keystone species could be useful in determining how much to protect—for example, the scarlet macaw in Corcovado. Protecting the habitat of the quetzal, a "tourist species," had helped conserve many other less glamorous species.

Daniel Janzen thought it was a mistake to orient protection programs toward single species. A keystone species was any species that you knew well enough to perceive its ecological importance. You had to balance the economic value of saving macaws at a place like Carara against other economic factors. The tourist value of species like macaws and quetzals was ephemeral.

Joseph Tosi said it was not only a problem of protecting species, but habitats.

Mario Boza said that this pointed back to the meeting's opening theme: what to do about the neighbors of the protected areas? He said he liked Janzen's idea of a committee of biologists and others who were working in each park to consider the problem.

Daniel Janzen said that one person should have the responsibility of running the discussion at meetings. He added that people needed confidence that this wasn't "just another exercise."

Jim Barborak referred back to Pedro León's remarks about the effects of population growth on protected areas. He agreed it was an overwhelming problem, but added that conservationists shouldn't be paralyzed by it. Even if Costa Rica ended up with a population of eight million, and if global warming inundated all the coastal parks, it wouldn't be the end of the world from a conservation standpoint.

On that hopeful note, the next meeting date was set, and the committee adjourned. The "conservation cartel" had reaffirmed its intention to keep the park system growing in *some* direction—geographical and/or cultural. The prospects for such growth perhaps seemed "farfetched," as Ugalde said, considering the other processes that were growing around the parks: deforestation, population, urbanization, pollution. Yet these influences had been growing even faster in 1970, and the park system's growth had seemed even more "farfetched" then.

"If you can blame the park system for any one mistake," Jim Barborak told me, "it's lack of foresight on the lands issue. In Corcovado, parcels have been paid for two or three times. A lot of the problem isn't the park system's per se, but one thing Costa Rica has done a miserable job on has been the totally unnecessary expenditure of reincorporating what was until recently public land *back* into the public domain. With the money they've spent on land, they could have endowed the park systems of Central America. Nicaragua, for example, is going to be able to set up a five-hundred-thousand-hectare wilderness in southeast Nicaragua without spending a penny on land, whereas on the Costa Rican side, to acquire just about seventy-five thousand hectares they're going to have to spend probably four to five million dollars.

"Having said that, then why do people give so much money to Costa Rica? First of all, that xenophilic attitude. Ticos really like foreigners. Second, people trust the Ticos because of their government system, proven stability, and leadership, particularly in people like Boza, Gámez, Ugalde, Janzen, Rodríguez, and the people in the universities. Third, Costa Rica has all these international organizations like OTS, TSC, and CATIE headquartered here, so it's had easier access to the resources than other countries. Fourth, they've created a generation of park users. They've created constituencies locally, because they have so many biology and geology students using the parks, but more important, because the majority of visitors to Costa Rican parks are Costa Ricans. Ten to twenty percent of Ticos go to at least one national park a year. Fifth, they've managed to put conservation on the political agenda. Going back to Figueres's administration, they've managed to win and maintain friends in high places, and take advantage of political opportunities.

"When I go to other countries, Honduras or Guatemala, and they say—extremely jealously, because Central Americans are very proud of the Costa Ricans, of their success and system of government, but also consider them big egotists like the Mexicans or Argentineans— 'What is it with these guys? Why do they get all the breaks?' . . . that's what I tell them."

nineteen

Cabo Blanco

I didn't actually get to meet Karen Wessberg until near the end of my 1990 stay in Costa Rica. The town of Montezuma is easier to reach now than it was in 1955, but it still required a long day of traveling from San José—by bus to Puntarenas, by launch to the Nicoya side, by bus again to the town of Cóbano, then by four-wheel-drive taxi to Montezuma. Peninsula roads were unpaved.

The sun was setting during the bus ride to Cóbano, and the landscape looked bucolic, not a conventional picture of deforested devastation. Valleys dotted with trees and marshy swales and with Brahma steers and cattle egrets, stretched toward steep hills that were at least partly wooded. The deforestation had happened fifty years ago, but the pastures didn't look good. They were full of the spiky weeds that thrive in Costa Rican lowland pastures.

I thought of something Jim Barborak had said to me. "Granted that the trend for at least the next decade will be continual degradation before they turn it around. But people lack a sense of history about tropical deforestation. Although in places like the Amazon it's appropriate to say that once you cut the forest down you may never get it back, that's obviously not the case with the fertile volcanic soils in most of Costa Rica. The process of degradation to cattle pastures is now at its worst point. There's already calculations that five percent of the country or more is now in abandoned cattle pasture.

"It won't take even one generation of farmers in areas like Talamanca and the swamps around Tortuguero to totally trash those areas. The future for most of those people is not living in isolated farms with nasty soils, five meters of rain a year, and far from schools and markets. This country's becoming urban, and, particularly in areas of soils not suited to permanent agriculture, you're starting to see abandonment already. Ten years from now, an awful lot of Costa Rica's going to be in second growth. Places like the Nicoya Peninsula. A lot of former cattle pastures are going to be forest plantations."

It was dark when we arrived at Montezuma. Karen's guest house was a small wooden structure, the first building past the turnoff. It looked dark inside, and I felt some apprehension. From what I'd heard about her independence and austerity, I was expecting a somewhat forbidding personality, someone Nordic and aquiline. "The world has much to learn from the way they live together," Alvaro Ugalde wrote of the Wessbergs, "and from Karen on her own today. Their home is the most humble place. There is not one single item of the few one can find that is not absolutely necessary."

A small, pretty woman in white answered the door. With a round face, graying blonde bangs, and plastic glasses, she looked not at all forbidding. When she smiled after my wife, Betsy, and I identified ourselves, Karen seemed the kind of person who is as much amused by life as worried by it, who would invite you into a house full of knick-knacks and comfy chairs and give you a nice cup of tea.

The guest house was as austere as Ugalde had described. The rooms were tiny, the furniture made from bare boards, and the water cold, but Karen's personality made it seem as hospitable as if it had been full of comfortable chairs, perhaps more so. There was no sense of intruding on her possessions. And she did give us tea.

Montezuma was much changed from the pioneer farming town the Wessbergs had found in 1955. Its warehouses and stores long vanished, it had become a sleepy hamlet and low-key resort for the more adventurous sort of tourist and expatriate—young Germans in Guatemalan clothes, new age entrepreneurs on early retirement. A young North American had started a health food restaurant next door to Karen's guest house, and had branched out into showing VCR movies on weekends. *When Harry Met Sally* was playing as Karen gave us tea, and erotic cinematic noises punctuated our conversation. Even this didn't disturb the comfortable atmosphere, although Karen was obviously a little disturbed at finding Hollywood six feet from her back porch.

We slept very well, after the movie ended, and woke to the calls of roosters, donkeys, and howler monkeys. The monkeys sounded close, but weren't visible. A handsome variegated squirrel with gray, black, white, and chestnut fur scolded Karen's cat from a backyard tree. Karen gave us coffee, then we went and collected mangoes from a big tree beside the town church a block away. We took these and a bag of vegetables out to Karen's farm, a mile's walk from town along the beach. The vegetables were for a Los Angeles woman who was vacationing in the farm's guest house.

The shore was rocky, with wooded bluffs rising to the north. Big, red-barked Indio desnudo trees and spiny-barked pochote trees grew right down to the beach, their pale green leaves just starting to unfold after the season's first rains the previous week. It looked fairly wild, although plastic bottles and old shoes littered the beach. Karen said pumas could still be seen occasionally. "The last one I saw was three years ago," she told us. "It walked under the farm window in the moonlight."

Mixed with the pochotes and Indio desnudos were some even larger trees with green bark, a species of ceiba. "I think these trees were sacred to the indigenes," Karen said. "We heard that people came down in canoes from as far as Nicaragua to bury their dead here." She showed us some piles of rocks in the forest back from the beach; they didn't look as though they'd gotten there naturally. "A woman who was visiting here told some boys that if they dug around those rocks, they might find gold. That night, she had dreams of Indian faces scowling at her all night, very frightening. So the next day, she told the boys, 'Look here, don't dig in those rocks!' "

The Wessberg farm was set on a hill above the beach, from which one could see parts of gray wooden buildings. It looked more like a natural forest glade than a clearing; the fruit orchards had become overgrown after Olof's death. The farm buildings were even more austere than the town house, with bare wooden tables, benches, and beds (with foam mattresses), a cold shower, and an outhouse. The kitchen consisted of a sink and a gas hotplate on the back porch. The weathered boards, salvaged from older buildings, had none of the luxuriousness that one associates with tropical hardwood.

Yet the farm had the same comfortable atmosphere as the town house, and there was a secluded spaciousness about it that was not only comfortable, but somehow palatial. Huge windows on three sides of the house opened right on the forest. These were un-screened—to my surprise, there were no biting insects (not at that season, anyway)—and we could leave the shutters open all night. When the moon rose and threw tree shadows across the bed, it was as though the forest had moved right in with us.

Karen took us to Cabo Blanco the next day, along with her guest, Rita, and Sergio León, who was the director of Manuel Antonio whom we'd missed on our visit there the week before. He was on leave, thinking about where he wanted his career with the parks to go next. The Manuel Antonio staff had told us that León was largely re-sponsible for the good shape in which we'd found the park. He was responsible for implementing the camping ban and cleaning up the damage. The giant spider web full of litter also had been his idea.

"I like to make big statements like that," León said about the web as we sat in Karen's town house before leaving for the reserve. "You need to get people's attention about things like littering, pollution, protecting the parks. It's easy to ignore little signs saying 'no litter-ing.' People get so much information through television and adver-tising that their attention threshold is very high."

León said Eduardo Rojas, his sub-administrator at Manuel Anto-nio, had been embarrassed by the spider web, and that Gladys de Marco, the environmental education specialist in San José, didn't like his ideas of "big promotion." Another thing he did at Manuel Antonio was put up huge antilittering banners across the trails so low that people had to duck to get past them. "I've always felt of myself as kind of a wild horse," he said, "a romantic. I was born in San José, in San Pedro, but I fell in love with the Indians and the rural areas. I didn't like being confined."

León worked as a rural teacher for ten years, from age eighteen, at various Indian reserves in Talamanca, and at Caño Negro near the Nicaraguan border. He also worked as a hotel manager in San José (which he disliked) and worked for Oscar Arias when he was minister of Development and Planning. One day he heard that the Park Service was having trouble with land acquisition in an area he was familiar with, so he went to speak to Ugalde about it. That was on a Friday; the following Monday Ugalde hired him.

That was seventeen years ago, and León had been with the Park Service ever since. Like most Service staff, he'd worked all over the country. At one time he was administrator of both Cabo Blanco and Rincón de la Vieja, which are at least two days' hard traveling apart. Now León was thinking he'd like to work in San José a while. "It's hard to have influence on Park Service policy if you're working in the parks, unfortunately," he said.

A bearded young man drove up in a jeep, and we climbed in for the roughly ten-kilometer drive to Cabo Blanco. Again the road led through heavily grazed bottomland pastures edged by steep, partly wooded hills. It was hard to believe it had been forest wilderness within the century; it looked like someplace in India. A native strangler fig beside the road had developed so many trunks it looked like some ancient village banyan. We passed a number of houses and cottages, some of which belonged to squatters, Karen said. She added that more and more of the land was going into the hands of rich people, many of them foreigners.

A large woman passed us on one of the balloon-tired, giant tricycle off-road vehicles the Japanese make. Karen said she was one of the new owners, an Italian. "She goes riding up and down here every day, looking for more land to buy," Karen said, shaking her head. "She keeps making more pasture for her cows. She doesn't reforest it."

Karen pointed to a scrubby patch of leafless trees on a hillside. "The owners logged the native trees on that, then replanted it with teak using 'reforestation' grants from Holland and Denmark," she said. "That's what they're calling 'sustainable development' now. But the trouble with teak is that it exhausts the soil."

We approached the Italian woman again, standing in the road beside her tricycle. She had run out of gas and flagged us down to borrow some from our driver. After she refueled, she remounted and said, "Death is the only certain thing in life, so better not worry about it," then lurched away. This seemed a non sequitur. Maybe our driver had said something to her about the dangers of riding giant tricycles (recently banned in the U.S.). Karen sighed and said, "People like that have so much energy." (Ugalde later told me the woman's husband, Albert Jugulls, was a donor of land and cash to Cabo Blanco.)

We came to a fairly wide river, which our driver gingerly crossed, the water coming up to the chassis. It seemed a lot of water considering that it was the end of the dry season. When I was at Santa Rosa a few weeks later, the rivers were still dry. "We're trying to buy more land so we can extend the reserve north to the river," said Karen, "so the animals will have water in the dry season. But land has become so expensive because the rich people have bought up the whole coast and paid whatever they were asked for it. Now even the people inland feel they can get much more than they could before." Karen had set up a fund for the reserve, and had a reliable source of donors among the visitors at her guest house, who must have had plenty of money left over after paying the rates she charged.

When we reached Cabo Blanco, the glare and dust of the grazing land gave way to a green shade that was as impressive as the river's flow in persisting after five dry months. Transitional between the rainforest to the south and the dry deciduous forest to the north, the Cabo Blanco forest is largely evergreen, although without the rainforest's effulgence of epiphytes and lianas. With its hilly terrain and sunny leafiness, it reminded me of the Appalachians in summer. As at Karen's farm, it was without biting insects that day, in great contrast to the Manuel Antonio forest a week before, where some kind of no-see-um had made exposed skin itch unbearably.

Reserve headquarters was beautifully maintained, with a young sub-director on duty. "It's a shame the director, Joaquín Alvardo, isn't here," Karen said. "He's so active, always making things better. When ITCO [the Institute of Lands and Colonization] ran the reserve, they'd get a donation for Cabo Blanco and use it for something else. But now the money gets used here." Karen said that a group of young European architects and carpenters were planning to come to Cabo Blanco and build a new visitor center as a donation. "But look here," she said, pointing to the plans for the new center, "the windows they made are much too small for this climate. They'll have to make them bigger."

I saw a sign on the headquarters building that said snorkeling gear was prohibited in the waters off the reserve. (The shore of the Gulf of Nicoya was visible from headquarters.) I wasn't sure I'd read the Spanish right, so I asked the sub-director if the sign meant ordinary snorkeling masks and flippers as well as scuba gear. He said it did: this was a *reserva absoluta* and the habitat came before the visitor. It was also hard to distinguish between snorkelers with spear guns and those without.

We started up the trail that led across the reserve to the cape's Pacific side. A beautiful green and buff snake had draped itself on vines beside the trail. When Karen saw it, she pointed at a small lump on her neck. "That's a lora, a parrot snake, the kind that bit me while I was working in the orchard," she said. "It struck so quickly that I hardly felt it, but then the bite got inflamed." Disturbed by our presence, the snake crawled away, making a strange, watery undulating movement as it climbed the vines.

"Look at that," said Sergio León. "It may do that to confuse predators."

It was late morning, and the forest was quiet in the heat. Yet it was clearly full of the small birds that give neotropical forest the greatest avian diversity on the planet—wrens, antwrens, antshrikes, woodcreepers, warblers, tanagers, flycatchers, vireos. We heard them all around us, inconspicuously busy in the underbrush and canopy. Occasionally we passed a larger bird, a red- or yellow-breasted trogon, a green-and-blue motmot, or a black guan. Some of the trees on the slopes were enormous—panamas, espavels, and ceibas.

It was a steep climb, and we stopped to rest at a little creek shaded by big trees. Rita produced a bottle of Sprite, and offered it to us, saying she just wanted it for the container. Like many visitors to Montezuma, Rita was a health food enthusiast. She'd recovered from cancer, and didn't consume soda pop. Betsy and I had no such scruples, and drank it.

"You can probably drink this water," Rita said. The creek looked clean, and had a good flow, but we demurred.

Karen was looking at a big espavel beside the creek. Espavels are related to cashews, and their plump fruits are very important wildlife foods. "One of the wardens sold a tree like this on the reserve to local people so they could make a boat out of it," she said. "That man. He never did any work. So finally I complained to the Park Service, and they said I could fire him if I wanted. So I called him in, and he started trembling and crying, saying: 'Señora, what will my wife and children do? I'm supposed to retire in six months, and I need my pension.' So I didn't fire him. That was years ago, and the last I heard, he's still working for the Park Service, the liar."

Karen asked Sergio if he knew the man. León said he did. The man was working at such and such a park. "What's he doing there?" Karen asked.

Sergio León laughed. "Nothing."

I asked Sergio what he thought about the future of the parks. He said he thought they needed to do more research, not only on park resources, but on how to make the parks benefit the poorer people who live around them. "Take Manuel Antonio, for example," he said. "It's very important, for such a small area. Two hundred thousand visitors a year. But the local people don't understand why the government protects it, because it produces nothing for them. It's a very dangerous situation. In twenty or thirty years, I don't know if the local fishermen and campesinos will support the park if it's only producing for hotel owners who come from other places."

León was hopeful about Boza and Ugalde taking over the park system again. "I think Mario still has the spirit of the vision that led him to start the park system," he said, "and now he has the experience at the political and international level of how to manage the system. And after four years of being outside the parks and working internationally, I think Alvaro has a more dynamic vision of the parks. He can see them from inside and outside.

"Now, with that experience, and with political power, I think they can accomplish what they weren't able to before, because they didn't have the power. I think Boza and Ugalde will be an excellent combination to give Costa Rica the protection it needs. Alvaro has a spiritual vision, and Mario has a vision of economic development. I think combining these will be very important for the parks."

After some more climbing we reached the crest of the ridge separating the gulf and the Pacific Ocean, of which we could catch glimpses through the trees. The forest on the crest was younger and thinner than at lower elevations, evidently having been cut and burned. Patches of second growth continued as we descended the ridge's west side. Coastal settlement in Costa Rica generally has moved from the shore inland, since boat travel was easier than forest travel.

When we got to the beach, on a crescent-shaped bay under cliffs of sand and cobbles, we saw the first man-made structure we'd encountered since leaving reserve headquarters, a small corral made of cliff cobbles. "This might have been for pigs," Karen said. "They'd bring them here to fatten in the forest, and keep them in these corrals before they shipped them to market."

Many brown pelicans flew or floated just beyond the surf. Brown boobies and frigate birds soared farther offshore. Cabo Blanco is an important seabird refuge. An island two kilometers offshore is a rookery for thousands of pelicans, boobies, and frigates.

"The last time I came here," Karen said, "it was with a Danish television crew that was filming a program about the reserve. There were even more pelicans than there are today. They covered the water. There was a bunch of boobies on the beach, too. The television crew wanted me to walk up the beach past them. Then they wanted me to raise my arms, so all the birds would fly away at once. It would look good on television. But I didn't want to do that."

We ate lunch, drank from a spring labeled *agua potable* that flowed from the cliff, and sat around awhile. When we started back it was late afternoon. The forest was awakening from its midday nap. As we got into the bigger trees east of the crest, we began hearing loud, melodious whistles that sounded like "To-le-do." Rasping, Bronx cheer-like noises often followed the whistles, as though some less musical bird was responding to the whistlers. The same birds were making both calls, however. They were long-tailed manakins, a common species of northwest Costa Rican forests that makes up for its insignificant size (about like a chickadee's) with remarkable plumage and behavior.

Male long-tailed manakins are blue-black, with azure backs and scarlet crowns and legs. Two slender plumes fork out from their tails, often growing longer than the birds themselves. Females are greenish, with short tails. The species lives mainly on fruit, a resource so abundant and reliable in tropical forests that manakins have had the leisure to evolve elaborate and idiosyncratic mating behavior.

A male manakin forms a partnership not with a female, but with another male. This odd couple spends most of the time singing and dancing with each other. This was what we were hearing along the trail—male manakin duets. The dancing that goes with the singing includes a "cartwheel dance" in which, as Gary Stiles describes in *A Guide to the Birds of Costa Rica*, "each male in turn flutters up and backward to descend to the spot from which his dance partner has meanwhile shuffled forward." Strange popping noises accompany the dancing. Occasionally the act attracts a female. The dominant male of the couple mates with her, then returns to his dancing partner. The female goes off to raise the young manakins on her own.

I'd never seen so many long-tailed manakins singing and dancing as at Cabo Blanco that afternoon. A pair of males seemed to be carrying on every few yards along the trail. Tapes I recorded of Sergio and Karen were almost drowned out by "To-le-dos" and Bronx cheers when I played them back later.

Howler monkeys also grew noisy as the sunlight reddened. We'd seen some capuchins in the morning, but as we neared reserve headquarters we still hadn't seen any howlers. Betsy hadn't seen howlers in the wild yet, and she had to go back to the U.S. in a few days. I was walking down the last stretch of trail, with the headquarters in sight, when I happened to look up. A large troop of howlers sat quietly about a dozen feet overhead, feeding on the new leaves of a vine. Most were young, which suggested that the reserve's population was growing.

The howlers regarded us with the profound calm that seems characteristic of the species. I had wondered to Karen if this calm disposition had something to do with the howlers' diet. They eat mainly leaves, unlike the more aggressive and excitable capuchins and spider monkeys, which eat more fruit and animal foods. Many leaves contain alkaloids, which can be narcotic. Karen told me she'd tried living on leaves for a while herself, and that she'd felt very good while doing so. Pochote leaves were the best.

Back at headquarters, the sub-director gave us a drink of an amber liquid which Karen said was guayabo—guava. It was cool from the refrigerator, and deliciously sweet. "That's right from the tree," Karen said.

"It's not sweetened at all?"

"No, no, it's that way naturally."

I thought of a story Karen had told us earlier, about when she and Olof had been living in the town of Esmeralda in Ecuador after fleeing from the Swedish Simon Legree. "We were staying at a hotel," she said, "and we got very sick, to our stomachs, you know. And we just kept getting sicker and sicker. We got so weak, we could hardly move. We didn't know what to do. Then one night, I dreamt we were eating potatoes. It felt so good, in the dream, that the next morning, I went out and bought some potatoes, and we ate them. Right away, we got better.

"You can make things happen," Karen said, "if you envision them."

Bibliography

Allen, William H. "Biocultural Restoration of a Tropical Forest." *Bioscience* 38, no. 3 (March 1988): 156–161.

Barnard, Geoffrey S. "Costa Rica: Model for Conservation in Latin America." *Nature Conservancy News* 32, no. 4 (July–August 1982): 6–12.

Beebe, Spencer. "A Model for Conservation." *Nature Conservancy News* 34, no. 1 (Jan.–Feb. 1984): 4–8.

Boza, Mario. "Costa Rica: Un Ejemplo del Estratagia para Establecer Parques Nacionales en un País en Desarrollo." In *Segunda Conferencia Mundial sobre Parques Nacionales*, edited by H. Elliot. Morges, Switzerland: IUCN, 1974.

———. *Costa Rican National Parks*. San José, Costa Rica: Fundación de Parques Nacionales, 1986.

———. *Una Década de Desarrollo*. San José, Costa Rica: Universidad Estatal a Distancia, Programa de Educación Ambiental, 1981.

Boza, Mario, and A. Bonilla. *The National Parks of Costa Rica*. Madrid: IN-CAFO, 1981.

Cahn, Robert. "An Interview with Alvaro Ugalde." *Nature Conservancy News* 34, no. 1 (Jan.–Feb. 1984): 8–18.

Cahn, Robert, and Patricia Cahn. "Treasure of Parks for a Little Country that Cares." *Smithsonian* 10, no. 6 (Sept. 1979): 64–75.

Clark, David B. "The Search for Solutions: Research and Education at the La Selva Station and Their Relation to Ecodevelopment." In *Tropical Rainforest: Diversity and Conservation*, edited by Frank Alameda and Catherine Pringle. San Francisco: California Academy of Sciences, 1988: 209–224.

Edelman, Marc, and Joanne Kenen. *The Costa Rican Reader*. New York: Grove Weidenfeld, 1988.

Edgar, Blake. "Seeds of Change in the Dry Forest." *Pacific Discovery* 42, no. 4 (Fall 1989): 22–37.

Fournier, Luis A. "Development and Perspectives of the Costa Rican Conservation Movement." Unpublished ms., 1988.

Gámez, Rodrigo, and Alvaro Ugalde. "Costa Rica's National Park System and the Preservation of Biological Diversity: Linking Conservation with Socio-Economic Development." In *Tropical Rainforest: Diversity and Conservation* (op. cit.), 131–142.

Greene, Harry. "Species Richness in Tropical Predators." In *Tropical Rainforest: Diversity and Conservation* (op. cit.), 259–280.

Hecht, Susanna, and Alexander Cockburn. *The Fate of the Forest: Developers, Defenders, and Destroyers of the Amazon.* New York: Verso, 1989.

Holden, Constance. "Regrowing a Tropical Forest." *Science* 234 (Nov. 1986): 809–810.

Janzen, Daniel. "Complexity Is in the Eye of the Beholder." In *Tropical Rainforest: Diversity and Conservation* (op. cit.), 29–51.

———. ed. *Costa Rican Natural History.* Chicago: University of Chicago Press, 1983.

———. "Costa Rican Parks: A Researcher's View." *Nature Conservancy News* 34, no. 1 (Jan.–Feb. 1984): 22–23.

———. *Guanacaste National Park: Tropical Ecological and Cultural Restoration.* San José, Costa Rica: Editorial Universidad Estatal a Distancia, 1986.

Janzen, Daniel, and Winnie Hallwachs. "Ethical Aspects of the Impact of Humans on Biodiversity." *Pontificae Academiae Scientiarium Scripta Varia,* May 1990.

MacFarland, Craig, Roger Morales, and James R. Barborak. *Establishment, Planning, and Implementation of a National Wildlands System in Costa Rica: A Case Study.* Turrialba, Costa Rica: Centro Agronomico Tropical de Investigación y Enseñaz, 1982.

McLarney, William O. "Guanacaste: The Dawn of a Park." *Nature Conservancy News* 38, no. 1 (Jan.–Feb. 1988): 11–16.

Margolis, Kenneth. "La Zona Protectora." *Nature Conservancy News* 36, no. 1 (Jan.–March 1986): 22–23.

Maslow, Jonathan E. "A Dream of Trees." *Philadelphia Magazine* (Nov. 1987): 198–285.

Murphy, Jamie, and Andrea Dorfman. "Growing a Forest from Scratch." *Time* (Dec. 29, 1986): 65.

Palmer, Paula. *What Happen: A Folk History of Costa Rica's Talamanca Coast.* San José, Costa Rica: Ecodesarrollo, 1977.

Pringle, Catherine M. "The History of Conservation Efforts and Initial Exploration of the Lower Extension of Parque Nacional Braulio Carrillo, Costa Rica." In *Tropical Rainforest: Diversity and Conservation* (op. cit.), 225–241.

Raven, Peter. "Braulio Carrillo and the Future: Its Importance to the World." In *Tropical Rainforest: Diversity and Conservation* (op. cit.), 297–306.

Stiles, F. Gary, and Deborah Clark. "Conservation of Tropical Rain Forest

Birds: A Case Study from Costa Rica." *American Birds* 1, no. 3 (Fall 1989): 420–427.

Stiles, F. Gary, and Alexander Skutch. *A Guide to the Birds of Costa Rica.* Ithaca, N.Y.: Cornell University Press, 1989.

Sun, Marjorie. "Costa Rica's Campaign for Conservation." *Science* 239 (March 18, 1988): 1366–1369.

Trejos, Alvaro Wille. *Corcovado: Meditaciones de un Biólogo.* San José, Costa Rica: Editorial Universidad Estatal a Distancia, 1983.

Ugalde, Alvaro. "Park Service Stories." Unpublished ms., 1990.

Wallace, David R. "Communing in Costa Rica." *Wilderness* 51, no. 181 (Summer 1988): 52–54.

———. "Preserving Forested Riches of Costa Rica." *San Francisco Examiner* (July 5, 1987): 5–7.

Index